FRUIT AND VEGGIES 101 - CONTAINER & RAISED BEDS VEGETABLE GARDEN

GARDENING GUIDE ON HOW TO GROW VEGETABLES USING ORGANIC STRATEGIES FOR CONTAINERS & RAISED BEDS GARDENS

GREEN ROOTS

Fruit and Veggies 101

CONTAINER & RAISED BED VEGETABLE GARDENING

GARDENING GUIDE ON HOW TO GROW VEGETABLES USING ORGANIC STRATEGIES FOR CONTAINERS & RAISED BEDS GARDENS

(Perfect For Beginners)

GREEN ROOTS

CONTENTS

A SPECIAL GIFT TO OUR READERS

Included with your purchase of this book is our list of "27 horticulture Myths Debunked"

This list will provide and aid you as a new (or soon-to-be) gardener by actively informing you of the myths and irrelevant practices to avoid during your gardening journey.

Visit the link below to let us know which email address to deliver to

www.gardengreenroots.com

INTRODUCTION

AN INTRODUCTION TO CONTAINER AND RAISED BED VEGETABLE GARDENING

Welcome to the captivating world of vegetable container and raised beds gardening. These gardening methods are not only a delightful hobby, but also a practical way to grow fresh, organic produce right at home. Whether you live in an apartment with limited outdoor space or a house with a spacious yard, container and raised beds gardening can transform your living space into a thriving green oasis.

Vegetable container gardening refers to the practice of growing vegetables in containers instead of planting them directly in the ground. These containers can be pots, buckets, planters, or any other vessel that can hold soil and plants. The beauty of this approach is its versatility and convenience. You can move your containers around to maximize sunlight exposure, protect them from harsh weather conditions, or even bring them indoors during winter.

Raised bed gardening, on the other hand, is a method where vegetables are planted in elevated plots filled with high-quality soil. The raised beds, typically made from wood, stone, or metal, serve as a barrier to pests like slugs and snails, and they help improve soil drainage, ensuring your plants get the right amount of water they need. They also make it easier to manage weeds and can alleviate the strain of bending over when tending to your plants.

Throughout this guide, we'll delve deeper into the benefits of these gardening methods, discuss how to choose the right containers and materials for your raised beds, provide tips on selecting and caring for various types of vegetables, and share insights on how to troubleshoot common gardening challenges.

By the end of this journey, you'll be equipped with the knowledge and skills necessary to start your own vegetable container and raised bed garden. So let's roll up our sleeves and get started on this exciting adventure of growing our own food, nurturing our health, and cultivating a deeper appreciation for nature.

What Is Container & Raised Bed Vegetable Gardening?

Vegetable container and raised bed gardening are two popular methods of growing vegetables that offer many advantages over traditional in-ground gardening. Container gardening involves growing plants, particularly vegetables, in various types of containers such as pots, tubs, or barrels, rather than directly in the ground. Raised bed gardening, on the other hand, refers to the practice of growing plants in large, soil-filled boxes that are elevated above the ground level.

Understanding the concept of vegetable container and raised bed gardening is incredibly important for several reasons.

Firstly, these methods are ideal for those with limited space. Urban residents or people with small yards can still enjoy the pleasure of growing their own produce with these techniques. Containers can be placed on balconies, patios, or rooftops, and raised beds can be built to fit any available space. They offer a wonderful opportunity to grow a variety of vegetables in areas that would otherwise remain unused. By understanding how to utilize containers and raised beds effectively, one can maximize their growing potential regardless of space constraints.

Secondly, vegetable container and raised bed gardening allow for better control over the soil environment. You can choose the right soil mix for their plants, which could lead to healthier, more productive growth. This method of gardening also offers an effective solution to dealing with poor native soil conditions, as one can fill their containers or raised beds with high-quality soil that provides the right nutrients and drainage for their plants.

Moreover, these gardening practices are more ergonomic than traditional gardening. The elevated nature of containers and raised beds reduces the need for bending and kneeling, making it easier on the back and knees. This accessibility makes gardening an enjoyable hobby for people of all ages and abilities.

Container and raised bed gardening can add an aesthetic appeal to your outdoor spaces. Containers come in a variety of shapes, sizes, and materials, allowing for creative expression. Raised beds, too, can be designed in unique layouts, adding structure and interest to your garden.

Understanding the concepts of vegetable container and raised bed gardening is crucial for anyone looking to make the most out of their gardening efforts. These methods not only make gardening more accessible and manageable but also allow for creativity and personal expression, enhancing the overall joy of growing your own food.

The Science Behind Why Vegetable Container & Raised Beds Vegetable Gardening Works

Vegetable container and raised bed gardening are not only practical methods for growing plants, but they also have a solid scientific basis behind their effectiveness.

The first principle is related to the control over soil conditions. In traditional in-ground gardening, gardeners must work with the soil they have, which may not always have ideal characteristics for plant growth. However, with container and raised bed gardening, gardeners can fill their containers or beds with the optimal soil mix for their specific plants. This allows for better control over the soil's physical properties (such as texture and drainage), chemical properties (like pH and nutrient content), and biological properties (including beneficial organisms).

In addition, the elevated nature of container and raised bed gardening provides improved drainage. Excess water can easily drain out of the bottom of containers or raised beds, preventing saturated soil conditions that can be detrimental to many plants. At the same time, these methods allow for more efficient water and nutrient uptake. The loose, well-aerated soil in containers and raised beds facilitates root expansion, enabling plants to access water and nutrients more effectively.

Temperature regulation is another scientific factor at play. Soil in containers and raised beds tends to warm up more quickly than ground soil in the spring. This can give plants a head start on the growing season, leading to earlier harvests. Conversely, during hot weather, containers can be moved into shade to protect plants from overheating.

Furthermore, the spatial arrangement in raised bed gardening can lead to higher yields. Raised beds are typically planted in a grid pattern, rather than traditional rows. This method, known as square foot gardening, maximizes space by reducing the amount of room wasted on pathways. As a result, you can grow more plants in the same amount of space, increasing your overall yield.

Finally, container and raised bed gardening can reduce pest and disease issues. By raising the growing area above the ground, it becomes more difficult for pests to reach the plants. Similarly, many soil-borne diseases can be avoided by using clean, fresh soil in the containers or raised beds.

The science behind vegetable container and raised bed gardening involves a combination of factors including improved control over soil conditions, enhanced drainage, efficient temperature regulation, maximized space utilization, and reduced pest and disease problems. Understanding these principles can help gardeners make the most of these methods and grow healthy, productive plants.

CHAPTER 1
CONTAINER & RAISED BED VEGETABLE GARDENING (TECHNIQUES)

BENEFITS & DISADVANTAGES OF VEGETABLE CONTAINER GARDENING

Considering the benefits and disadvantages of vegetable container gardening is crucial for several reasons. Firstly, it allows you to assess whether this method aligns with your lifestyle and available resources. For instance, while container gardening offers flexibility in terms of location and plant variety, it also requires consistent care, particularly in watering and nutrient management. Understanding these aspects can help you prepare for and address the demands of this gardening method, thereby increasing your chances of success.

Secondly, it enables you to make cost-effective decisions. Container gardening can involve considerable initial investment in containers, potting soil, and other materials. By weighing these costs against the potential benefits, you can determine if this method provides good value for your money.

Lastly, considering the advantages and disadvantages can guide you in selecting suitable plants for container cultivation. Not all vegetables thrive in containers due to space limitations. There-fore, understanding this constraint can inform your plant selec-tion, ensuring that your garden is not only productive but also enjoyable to maintain.

Vegetable container gardening has become increasingly popular, especially for those living in urban areas or homes without ample garden space. This method of gardening has numerous benefits and a few disadvantages worth considering.

Benefits Of Vegetable Container Gardening

One of the main advantages of vegetable container gardening is its adaptability. You can grow a variety of vegetables in contain-ers, including tomatoes, peppers, lettuce, and herbs. This allows you to cultivate a diverse range of produce even if you don't have a large garden space.

Container gardening also provides excellent control over soil quality. You can tailor the soil mix to the specific needs of your plants, which can lead to better growth and productivity. More-over, it's easier to manage pests and diseases because they're less likely to spread across containers than they would in a tradi-tional garden bed.

Another benefit of container gardening is its mobility. If certain plants aren't thriving in their current location, you can easily move them to a different spot with more suitable light conditions. Additionally, during harsh weather conditions, containers can be moved indoors to protect the plants.

Disadvantages Of Vegetable Container Gardening

Despite the many benefits, there are also some drawbacks to consider when it comes to vegetable container gardening. One of the main disadvantages is the need for frequent watering. Containers tend to dry out faster than traditional garden beds, so you'll need to monitor the soil moisture levels closely, especially in hot weather.

Another potential downside is the limited root space. Some vegetables have extensive root systems and may not perform as well in a container as they would in a traditional garden. Overcrowding can also be an issue if too many plants are placed in a single container.

Lastly, the initial setup cost for container gardening can be high, especially if you're purchasing high-quality containers and soil. However, many of these costs are one-time expenses, and with proper care, containers can be used for several seasons.

Vegetable container gardening offers convenience and versatility, making it a great option for those with limited space or wanting to experiment with different types of vegetables. However, it also requires close attention to watering and can involve higher upfront costs. As with any gardening method, it's important to consider both the benefits and disadvantages to determine if it's the right fit for you.

BENEFITS & DISADVANTAGES OF VEGETABLE RAISED BED GARDENING

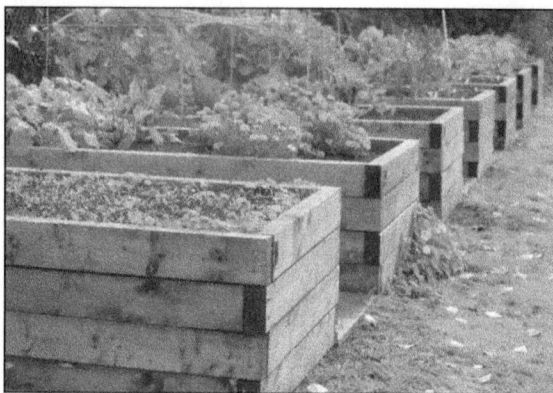

Understanding the benefits and disadvantages of vegetable raised bed gardening is essential for a variety of reasons. Firstly, it can help you evaluate whether this method aligns with your gardening goals and resources. Raised beds offer many advantages, such as improved soil conditions, better drainage, and easier accessibility, but they also require an initial investment in terms of time, effort, and money. By considering these factors, you can determine whether raised bed gardening is a feasible option for you.

Secondly, it can guide you in making informed decisions about the design and maintenance of your garden. For example, knowing that raised beds tend to dry out faster can prompt you to implement effective watering strategies or opt for drought-tolerant vegetables. Similarly, understanding that tall crops may become too high to manage comfortably in raised beds can influence your choice of plants.

Lastly, considering the pros and cons can help you maximize the potential benefits of raised bed gardening while mitigating its challenges. For instance, you can offset the higher initial costs by choosing cost-effective materials for your beds or by growing high-value crops. Overall, evaluating the benefits and disadvantages of raised bed gardening can contribute to a more successful and satisfying gardening experience.

Raised-bed gardening has become a popular choice for many vegetable gardeners due to its numerous advantages. However, like any gardening method, it also comes with its own set of challenges.

Benefits Of Vegetable Raised-Bed Gardening

One of the key benefits of raised-bed gardening is improved soil conditions. With raised beds, you have complete control over the soil used, allowing you to create the ideal environment for your vegetables to thrive. The soil in raised beds also tends to warm up faster in spring, which can give you a head start on the growing season.

Raised beds also offer better drainage compared to traditional in-ground gardens. This is particularly beneficial for crops that don't tolerate waterlogged soil. Moreover, because the soil is above ground level, it is less prone to compaction, promoting healthier root growth.

Another significant benefit of raised-bed gardening is its accessibility. The elevated design makes it easier to reach the plants, reducing the strain on your back and knees. This can make gardening a more enjoyable experience, especially for those with mobility issues.

Disadvantages Of Vegetable Raised-Bed Gardening

Despite the many advantages, there are also some drawbacks to raised-bed gardening. One of the primary disadvantages is the initial cost and labor involved. Building or buying raised beds, filling them with high-quality soil and compost, can be quite expensive and time-consuming.

Another potential challenge is that raised beds can dry out faster than in-ground gardens. This means they may require more frequent watering, especially during hot, dry periods. In regions with water restrictions, this could be a significant drawback.

Lastly, while the elevated design of raised beds can be an advantage in terms of accessibility, it can also be a disadvantage when it comes to certain crops. Tall crops, like corn or climbing beans, may become too high to comfortably tend when grown in raised beds.

Overall vegetable raised-bed gardening offers many benefits, such as improved soil conditions, better drainage, and increased accessibility. However, it also presents some challenges, including higher initial costs, potentially increased watering needs, and limitations with tall crops. As always, it's important to weigh both the benefits and disadvantages to determine if this method is suitable for your gardening needs.

TYPES OF CONTAINERS FOR VEGETABLE GARDENING

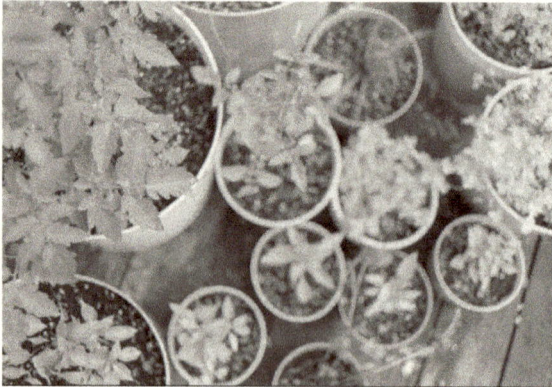

Terracotta Pots

Terracotta pots are a classic choice for vegetable container gardening. Made from baked clay, they offer a charming, rustic aesthetic that blends well with natural surroundings. Terracotta pots are porous, meaning they allow water and air to pass through their walls, which can be beneficial for the root health of your vegetables. They can host a wide variety of vegetables, from tomatoes and cucumbers to various herbs and more.

Benefits Of Using Terracotta Pots In Vegetable Container Gardening

There are several benefits to using terracotta pots in vegetable gardening.

- First, their porosity helps prevent overwatering by allowing excess water to evaporate out of the pot, reducing the risk of root rot.
- Second, they are generally heavy, making them stable and unlikely to tip over in windy conditions.
- Third, the natural, earthy color of terracotta pots can blend well with any garden design, adding a touch of elegance and timeless appeal.

Disadvantage Of Using Terracotta Pots In Vegetable Container Gardening

- Due to their porous nature, terracotta pots can dry out quickly, especially in hot, sunny weather, requiring more frequent watering.
- Second, they are prone to cracking or breaking in cold temperatures, so they may need to be stored indoors during winter in colder climates.

- Lastly, terracotta pots can be quite heavy, making them less ideal if you need to move your containers around frequently.

Plastic Containers

Plastic containers are another popular choice for vegetable container gardening. They are available in a wide range of sizes, shapes, and colors, providing flexibility and versatility in designing your garden. These lightweight containers can be easily moved around, making them a great choice for balconies, patios, or small spaces.

Benefits Of Using Plastic Containers In Vegetable Container Gardening

- The main benefits of using plastic containers for vegetable gardening include their lightweight, which makes them easy to handle and move around. They retain moisture better than terracotta pots due to their non-porous nature, meaning you won't need to water your plants as often.
- Plastic containers are also quite durable and can withstand varying weather conditions without cracking or breaking.

Disadvantage Of Using Plastic Containers In Vegetable Container Gardening

However, plastic containers also come with some disadvantages.

- Unlike terracotta pots, they do not allow air to pass through, which could potentially lead to waterlogging and root rot if not properly managed.

- Additionally, they can degrade over time when exposed to sunlight, and lower quality plastics may release harmful chemicals into the soil.
- Lastly, while plastic pots are practical, they may not offer the same aesthetic appeal as more natural materials like terracotta or wood.

Ceramic Pots

Ceramic pots, often glazed and exceptionally decorative, are a popular choice for vegetable container gardening. These pots, made from baked clay, come in a variety of sizes, shapes, and designs, offering both functionality and aesthetic appeal to your garden space. They can be used to grow a wide range of vegetables, from leafy greens to tomatoes, peppers, and more.

Benefits Of Using Ceramic Pots In Vegetable Container Gardening

- One of the main benefits of using ceramic pots in vegetable gardening is their porosity. This feature allows air and water to move through the walls of the pot, providing excellent breathability for plant roots and helping to prevent problems such as root rot and overwatering.
- Additionally, the substantial weight of ceramic pots can provide stability for top-heavy plants or in areas with high winds.

Disadvantage Of Using Ceramic Pots In Vegetable Container Gardening

- They are typically more expensive than plastic or terracotta pots, and their heavy weight can make them difficult to move around.

- Ceramic pots can also crack or break if exposed to freezing temperatures, so they may need to be moved indoors or protected during the winter months.
- Finally, due to their porous nature, ceramic pots can dry out quickly, requiring more frequent watering compared to non-porous containers.

Vertical Gardens

Vertical gardens, also known as green walls or living walls, are an innovative approach to vegetable container gardening. Instead of spreading out horizontally, plants in vertical gardens grow upwards, typically on trellises, fences, wall-mounted containers, or specially-designed vertical garden systems. This method can accommodate a variety of vegetables such as beans, cucumbers, tomatoes, and various herbs.

Benefits Of Using Vertical Gardens In Vegetable Container Gardening

- One of the main benefits of vertical gardening is its space-saving nature. Vertical gardens are ideal for urban environments or smaller spaces like balconies and patios where ground space is limited.
- They also provide easier access to the plants, reducing the need for bending and kneeling, which can make maintenance and harvesting easier.
- Additionally, growing plants vertically can improve air circulation around the plants, which can help prevent fungal diseases.

Disadvantage Of Using Vertical Gardens In Vegetable Container Gardening

- They may require more frequent watering as gravity can cause water to flow downwards, potentially leaving the top plants dry.
- The growth of some plants could be limited due to the lack of horizontal space, and not all types of vegetables are suited for vertical growth.
- Lastly, setting up a vertical garden may require more initial effort and resources compared to traditional ground-level gardens.

Hanging Baskets

Hanging baskets are a unique form of vegetable container gardening where plants are grown in containers that are suspended from the ceiling, often from hooks, chains or ropes. They are typically used for small, trailing vegetables and herbs such as cherry tomatoes, strawberries, or various types of herbs.

Benefits Of Using Hanging Baskets In Vegetable Container Gardening

- One of the key benefits of using hanging baskets in vegetable gardening is that they make excellent use of vertical space, which can be particularly useful in smaller areas or urban environments.
- Hanging baskets can also add a decorative element to your garden or balcony and can keep your plants safe from some ground-dwelling pests.
- Additionally, they provide good drainage and air circulation, which can contribute to the overall health of your plants.

Disadvantages Of Using Hanging Baskets In Vegetable Container Gardening

- They tend to dry out quickly due to their exposure to air from all sides, requiring regular watering, sometimes even daily during hot weather.
- The limited soil volume can also mean that plants may require more frequent feeding compared to those grown in larger containers or the ground.
- Lastly, not all vegetables are suitable for hanging baskets - they are best suited to smaller, lighter plants that have a trailing or cascading growth habit.

Window Boxes

Window boxes are a form of container gardening where shallow, elongated boxes are attached to the exterior side of a window, often via brackets. They can be used to grow a variety of small vegetables and herbs, such as lettuce, radishes, chives, and parsley.

Benefits Of Using Window Boxes In Vegetable Container Gardening

- One of the main advantages of window boxes is their space-saving design. They are a great option for those living in apartments or homes with limited outdoor space.
- Window boxes also offer easy access for watering, pruning, and harvesting right from your window.
- Furthermore, they add aesthetic appeal to your home's exterior and can provide extra insulation and shade to your windows.

Disadvantages Of Using Window Boxes In Vegetable Container Gardening

- The limited soil volume can restrict the size and number of plants you can grow and may require more frequent watering and fertilizing than traditional gardens.

- Additionally, window boxes need to be securely fastened, as they can become quite heavy when filled with soil and water.
- Lastly, plants in window boxes may be exposed to harsh weather conditions, including wind and intense sunlight, which can affect their growth and health.

TYPES OF RAISED BED'S FOR VEGETABLE GARDENING

Wooden Raised Beds

Wooden raised beds are a type of vegetable gardening setup where soil and plants are contained within a wooden frame elevated above the ground level. They can accommodate a variety of vegetables such as tomatoes, peppers, zucchinis, and more.

Benefits Of Using Wooden Raised-Beds In Vegetable Raised-Bed Gardening

- One of the most significant benefits of wooden raised beds is their ability to provide better control over the soil environment.

- Gardeners can tailor the soil mix to suit specific plant needs, which can lead to healthier, more productive plants.
- Raised beds also offer improved drainage, which is beneficial for preventing saturated soil conditions.
- They can also reduce the need for bending over during planting and maintenance, making them an excellent choice for individuals with mobility issues.
- Additionally, wooden raised beds can act as a barrier to some pests.

Disadvantages Of Using Wooden Raised-Beds In Vegetable Raised-Bed Gardening

- Wooden raised beds can be more expensive and time-consuming to set up compared to traditional in-ground gardens.
- The wood can eventually rot over time, requiring replacement.
- Because they warm up and cool down more quickly than the ground, they might require more careful monitoring of temperature changes, particularly in early spring and late fall.
- Lastly, they may require more frequent watering due to enhanced drainage.

Metal Or Plastic Raised Beds

Metal or plastic raised beds are another form of vegetable gardening where the soil and plants are contained within a metal or plastic frame elevated above the ground. They can host a variety of vegetables, from leafy greens to root vegetables and herbs.

Benefits Of Using Metal Or Plastic Raised-Beds In Vegetable Raised-Bed Gardening

- One of the primary advantages of metal or plastic raised beds is their durability. Unlike wooden beds, they don't rot over time, making them a more long-lasting option.
- They also offer excellent drainage and allow for better control over the soil environment, similar to wooden raised beds.
- These beds are typically easier to assemble than wooden ones and come in various sizes and shapes to accommodate different gardening needs.
- They can also be more pest-resistant, as some pests find it harder to climb slick metal or plastic surfaces.

Disadvantages Of Using Metal Or Plastic Raised-Beds In Vegetable Raised-Bed Gardening

- Metal can rust over time, especially if scratched or chipped, and can heat up quickly in direct sunlight, potentially affecting the soil temperature.
- Plastic, on the other hand, may degrade with prolonged exposure to sunlight and might not be as environmentally friendly.
- Like other types of raised beds, those made from metal or plastic can require more frequent watering due to improved drainage.
- Finally, some gardeners feel that metal and plastic beds don't blend as naturally into the garden landscape as wooden ones.

Stone Or Brick Raised Beds

Stone or brick raised beds are a style of vegetable gardening where the soil and plants are contained within a frame made from stone or bricks, elevated above the ground. These types of raised beds can be used to grow a wide variety of vegetables, including carrots, beetroot, beans, and peas.

Benefits Of Using Stone Or Brick Raised-Beds In Vegetable Raised-Bed Gardening

- One of the main benefits of stone or brick-raised beds is their aesthetic appeal. They can add a rustic charm to your garden and blend naturally with the landscape.
- Additionally, they are incredibly durable and long-lasting, as they are resistant to rot and decay.
- Like other forms of raised beds, they offer excellent drainage and allow for better control over the soil environment.
- The thermal mass of the stones or bricks can also help regulate soil temperature by absorbing heat during the day and releasing it at night.

Disadvantages Of Using Stone Or Brick Raised-Beds In Vegetable Raised-Bed Gardening

- Stone or brick raised beds can be quite expensive and time-consuming to construct, especially if mortar is used to secure the structure.
- They are also permanent and cannot be easily moved or resized once constructed. While the thermal mass can be an advantage, it can also cause the soil to heat up too much in very hot weather.
- Lastly, these types of raised beds may require more watering due to the enhanced drainage, and the rough edges of stone or bricks can make gardening tasks a bit more challenging.

Fabric Raised Beds

Fabric raised beds are a unique form of vegetable gardening where the soil and plants are contained within a fabric bag or container elevated above the ground. These types of raised beds can house an array of vegetables, such as lettuce, radishes, and spinach.

Benefits Of Using Fabric Raised-Beds In Vegetable Raised-Bed Gardening

- One of the key benefits of fabric-raised beds is their portability. They are lightweight and can be moved around easily, allowing you to change your garden layout whenever you want.
- The fabric material provides excellent drainage and aeration to the roots, which can promote healthier and more vigorous plant growth.
- Fabric raised beds are also relatively easy to set up and store away when not in use, making them an ideal choice for those with limited space or for seasonal gardening.

Disadvantages Of Using Fabric Raised-Beds In Vegetable Raised-Bed Gardening

- They may not be as durable as other types of raised beds, especially when exposed to harsh weather conditions over time.
- The fabric material can also heat up quickly in the sun, potentially leading to faster evaporation and requiring more frequent watering.
- Additionally, some gardeners may find that the aesthetic of fabric raised beds does not blend as naturally into the garden landscape compared to more traditional materials like wood or stone.
- Finally, fabric beds might need more regular replacement due to wear and tear compared to other more durable materials.

Tiered Raised Beds

Tiered raised beds are a unique style of vegetable gardening where multiple levels or "tiers" of beds are stacked on top of each other. Each tier can host a variety of vegetables, allowing for efficient use of space and creating an aesthetically pleasing structure in the garden.

Benefits Of Using Tiered Raised-Beds In Vegetable Raised-Bed Gardening

- One of the main advantages of tiered raised beds is their space-saving design. By growing vertically, you can cultivate more plants in a smaller area, making them ideal for urban gardens or small spaces.
- The different tiers also allow for better accessibility, as you can plant taller crops on the lower tiers and shorter ones on the higher tiers. This reduces the need for bending and reaching, making gardening tasks easier.
- Additionally, the tiered structure can provide good drainage, ensuring that excess water doesn't pool around plant roots.

Disadvantages Of Using Tiered Raised-Beds In Vegetable Raised-Bed Gardening

- Tiered raised beds can be more complex and time-consuming to construct compared to flat raised beds.
- They may also require more maintenance, as each tier might have different watering and soil needs.
- The higher tiers may dry out faster due to increased exposure to sun and wind, requiring more frequent watering.
- Plants on the lower tiers may receive less sunlight if the tiers above them are densely planted, which could impact their growth.

- Lastly, tiered beds might not be suitable for larger vegetables or those with deep root systems due to the limited depth of each tier.

Square Foot Gardening

Square Foot Gardening is a highly efficient method of vegetable raised bed gardening that optimizes space by dividing the growing area into square-foot sections. Each square foot is planted with a specific number of plants based on their mature size to ensure optimal growth.

Benefits Of Using Square Foot Gardening In Vegetable Raised-Bed Gardening

- One of the main benefits of Square Foot Gardening is its efficiency. It reduces the amount of space needed for growing crops, making it ideal for urban or small-space gardeners.
- This method also minimizes weeding and conserves water by concentrating resources where they are needed most.
- By separating each plant type into its own square, it can reduce the spread of disease and pests and make crop rotation simpler.

Disadvantage Of Using Square Foot Gardening In Vegetable Raised-Bed Gardening

- Setting up a square-foot garden can require a significant initial investment in terms of time and materials, particularly if you're building raised beds and purchasing soil mix.
- The system also requires careful planning and organization, especially when considering companion planting and crop rotation.

- Additionally, while the square foot method can work well for many vegetables, it may not be suitable for larger crops like pumpkins or corn that need more room to grow.
- Lastly, maintaining the structure and layout of the garden can be labor-intensive, as each square will have different planting and harvesting times.

SELECTING WHERE YOUR CONTAINER & RAISED BED VEGETABLE GARDENS WILL GROW

When it comes to growing your container and raised bed vegetable gardens, there are several factors to consider, including the location, soil quality, accessibility and much more. The importance of carefully selecting the location for your container and raised-bed gardening cannot be overstated. This decision significantly impacts the health and vitality of your plants. Here are some key factors to consider when choosing a location for your container and raised-bed gardening.

Sunlight Exposure

Sunlight exposure plays a pivotal role in the success of your container and raised-bed gardening. It's crucial because photosynthesis, the process through which plants convert light into chemical energy to fuel their growth, relies heavily on sunlight. Most vegetables and flowering plants require at least six to eight hours of direct sunlight each day for optimal growth. Without sufficient sunlight, plants may become weak and leggy as they stretch towards the light source, leading to poor yield or blooming. Some might not grow at all.

Therefore, when choosing a location for your garden, you need to observe the patterns of sunlight throughout the day. Note where the sun rises and sets and which areas are shaded during different parts of the day. This will help you identify spots that receive ample sunlight. Also, consider the changing seasons, as the sun's position and intensity can change dramatically across the year.

If you're growing in containers, one advantage is mobility - you can move your plants around to ensure they get enough sunlight. For raised beds, choose a sunny spot, ideally one that gets morning sun, which is less intense but effective for growth. Remember, some plants can tolerate or even prefer partial shade, so it's essential to understand the specific sunlight needs of the plants you want to grow.

Wind Exposure

Wind exposure is another critical factor to consider when selecting a location for your container and raised-bed gardening. Wind has both positive and negative effects on plants. On the positive side, wind can help to pollinate plants, aid in pest control by blowing away smaller pests, and improve air circulation, thereby reducing the risk of fungal diseases. On the negative side, strong winds can damage plants, causing breakage, desiccation, and even uprooting in severe cases. Young and delicate plants are particularly susceptible to wind damage.

Furthermore, winds can dry out soil quickly, leading to increased watering needs. Therefore, when choosing a garden location, observe the typical wind patterns in your area. If you live in a windy area, consider placing your garden in a location that's shielded from the wind, such as near a fence, wall, or hedge.

For container gardens, choose heavier containers that won't tip over easily, or consider using windbreaks to protect your plants. Additionally, select plants that are known for their wind tolerance if wind is a significant factor in your location. However, ensure that any barriers used do not block the essential sunlight. Balancing the benefits of wind with its potential damage is key to choosing the optimal location for your garden.

Accessibility

Accessibility is a vital component when determining the location for your container and raised-bed gardening. Having an easily accessible garden simplifies maintenance tasks such as watering, weeding, pest control, pruning, and harvesting. Regular interaction with your plants also allows you to spot potential problems early, such as signs of disease or pest infestation, and take necessary actions before they escalate.

Furthermore, if your garden isn't conveniently located, you might be less likely to spend time tending to it, which could negatively impact your plants' health and productivity.

Therefore, when choosing a location, consider its proximity to your house, the availability of a nearby water source, and the ease of access regardless of weather conditions. For raised beds, choose a flat area that's easy to navigate around, keeping in mind that you'll need to reach the center of the bed without stepping on the soil. For container gardens, ensure the containers are at a comfortable height and in a place where they can be easily moved if needed.

The path to the garden should be clear and safe to traverse, even with gardening tools or watering cans in hand. Prioritizing accessibility when selecting your garden location will make your gardening experience more enjoyable and less laborious.

Weight-Bearing Capacity

The weight-bearing capacity of the area you choose for your container and raised-bed gardening is of significant importance. The soil, compost, plants, and water combined can weigh quite a lot. A fully watered container or raised bed can be surprisingly heavy. If the surface underneath cannot support this weight, it could lead to structural damage or even collapse, possibly damaging your plants in the process. This is especially important if you're planning to place your garden on a deck, balcony, or rooftop.

Therefore, it's crucial to ensure that the chosen location has a solid base and can comfortably bear the weight of the fully-loaded garden. For container gardens, consider using lighter materials like plastic or resin for the pots, or use potting mixtures designed to be lighter than regular garden soil.

For raised beds, make sure the underlying surface is solid and stable. If you're placing the raised beds on grass or earth, ensure the ground is level and firm. If you're placing them on a harder surface, like concrete, remember to check the load-bearing capacity of the structure. Consulting with a structural engineer may be necessary if you're unsure about the weight-bearing capacity of your chosen location.

Water Source

Access to a reliable water source is crucial when determining the location for your container and raised-bed gardening. Plants require consistent watering to thrive, and hauling water over long distances can be labor-intensive and time-consuming. Containers and raised beds, due to their elevated nature and improved drainage, often require more frequent watering than in-ground gardens. This can become a significant concern during hot and dry weather conditions when plants may need watering daily.

Therefore, choosing a garden location near a water source, such as a hose, rain barrel, or irrigation system, can make a consider-able difference in maintaining the health and vitality of your plants. When selecting a location, consider its proximity to your house or an outdoor tap. If a nearby water source is not avail-able, you might need to think about installing an irrigation system that can reach your garden.

Keep in mind the length of your hose and the feasibility of running it from the tap to the garden without creating a tripping hazard or damaging other parts of your yard. Ensuring easy access to water will not only make your gardening tasks more manageable but also ensure that your plants get the necessary hydration they need to flourish.

Temperature & Microclimate

Understanding the temperature and microclimate of your garden area is vital when choosing the location for your container and raised-bed gardening. Microclimate refers to the specific climate conditions within a small, specific area, which can vary from the general climate of the region. It can be influenced by factors such as sunlight exposure, wind direction, proximity to buildings or bodies of water, and elevation.

Different plants have different temperature requirements for growth and fruit production. Some plants thrive in full sun, while others need partial shade. Similarly, some plants can tolerate cold, while others require warmer conditions.

Raised beds and containers can heat up and cool down more quickly than ground soil, which can be advantageous for warming the soil in spring, but may require additional watering in hot weather. Therefore, it's important to monitor the sunlight and shade patterns, wind exposure, and temperature fluctuations in your chosen location throughout the day and across the seasons.

Choose a location that best matches the needs of the plants you intend to grow. If your garden has varied microclimates, you can use this to your advantage by placing heat-loving plants in the sunniest spots and shade-tolerant plants in cooler, shaded areas. By understanding and working with your garden's microclimate, you can create an optimal growing environment for a wide variety of plants.

Pest Control

Effective pest control is a significant factor when choosing the location for your container and raised bed gardening. Pests can quickly decimate a garden, damaging or even killing plants. The location of your garden can either deter pests or attract them. For instance, placing your garden near compost piles, dense shrubs, or woodpiles can invite pests, as these areas provide shelter and breeding grounds for them. Similarly, gardens placed near light sources can attract nocturnal insects.

Therefore, it's important to choose a location that minimizes the risk of pest infestation. Consider placing your garden in an open area away from potential pest habitats. Raised beds and containers offer some natural protection against soil-borne pests and can be easily fitted with barriers to keep out larger pests like rabbits or deer. However, they can still be susceptible to flying insects or pests that climb. Regular monitoring is key to early detection and management of pest problems.

If pests are persistent in your area, consider using companion planting, natural repellents, or organic pesticides to protect your garden. Remember, a well-chosen location is the first step towards successful pest control in your garden.

Space – Room For Growth

Ensuring ample space and room for growth is an essential factor when choosing the location for your container and raised-bed gardening. Plants need adequate room to grow and spread out, both above and below ground, to reach their full potential. Over-crowding can lead to competition for resources like light, water, and nutrients, and it can also increase the risk of disease transmission between plants. Moreover, some vegetables, such as tomatoes, beans, and squash, require staking or trellising, which adds to their space requirements.

When planning your garden location, consider the mature size of each plant, including its height, spread, and root depth. Containers and raised beds offer the advantage of clear boundaries for plant spacing, but they still need to be large enough to accommodate the plants you want to grow.

Make sure there's enough space between the beds or containers for you to move around comfortably for planting, watering, weeding, and harvesting. If space is limited, choose dwarf or compact plant varieties, use vertical growing methods, or employ succession planting to make the most of the available area. Ultimately, providing enough space for your plants to grow will lead to healthier plants, better yields, and a more enjoyable gardening experience for you.

Aesthetics

Aesthetics play a key role when choosing the location for your container and raised-bed gardening. A well-placed, visually pleasing garden can enhance the beauty of your outdoor space, create a relaxing atmosphere, and even increase property value. The location of your garden can greatly affect its visual appeal. Consider the view from various points, both inside and outside your home. Your garden should be positioned where it can be easily seen and enjoyed but not where it might obstruct important views or pathways.

The design of your containers and raised beds can also contribute to the overall aesthetics. Choose materials and colors that complement the surrounding landscape and architectural style of your home. Arrange your plants in a way that takes into consideration their color, texture, size, and blooming period for a continuous display of beauty throughout the growing season.

Don't forget about adding elements like decorative pots, garden sculptures, or seating areas to enhance the aesthetic appeal. Also, consider how the garden fits into the broader landscape. A well-chosen and well-designed garden location can provide not just a source of fresh produce but also a beautiful and enjoyable outdoor living space.

Soil Quality

Soil quality is a critical factor when choosing the location for your container and raised bed gardening. Good soil is the foundation of any successful garden, as it provides the nutrients, water, and support that plants need to grow.

Soil quality can vary greatly from one location to another, even within the same yard, and poor soil can hinder plant growth and reduce yields. When planning your garden, take the time to assess the soil in potential locations. Look for soil that is rich in organic matter, well-draining, and free of contaminants.

If you're planning a raised bed garden, you'll be adding your own soil mix, but the underlying soil can still affect drainage and temperature. For container gardens, while you'll be using potting soil, the location can affect how quickly the soil dries out. Locations with intense sun or wind can cause containers to dry out quickly, requiring more frequent watering.

If the soil in your chosen location is not ideal, don't despair. Both containers and raised beds offer the opportunity to start with a perfect soil mix, regardless of the condition of the ground soil. By choosing the right location and ensuring good soil quality, you can create a productive and rewarding garden.

CHAPTER 2

CONTAINER & RAISED BED VEGETABLE GARDENING (PREPARATION)

Preparation for vegetable container and raised beds gardening is paramount for a successful yield. A well-prepared garden starts with the right selection of containers or raised beds, which should be large enough to accommodate plant growth and provide adequate drainage to avoid waterlogging.

The choice of soil mix also plays a pivotal role in the preparation process. It should be well-draining, rich in organic matter, and have the right pH level to support plant health. Preparing the garden also involves planning for the right placement of plants, based on their sunlight and space requirements. For instance, taller plants should be positioned so they don't overshadow smaller ones.

Furthermore, a good preparation includes having a watering and fertilizing schedule based on the specific needs of the plants. Lastly, preparing for potential pests and diseases through preventive measures can save a lot of trouble down the line. Overall, thorough preparation sets the stage for a flourishing vegetable garden, whether in containers or raised beds.

ESSENTIAL TOOLS FOR CONTAINER & RAISED BED VEGETABLE GARDENING

Understanding the need for essential tools in container and raised bed vegetable gardening is crucial for several reasons. First, these tools make the process of gardening more efficient and less physically demanding. For instance, using a trowel or a hand fork can significantly simplify the tasks of digging and planting. Secateurs are vital for pruning and maintaining plant health, while a watering can or hose with a sprinkler attachment ensures that your plants receive the right amount of water.

Secondly, certain tools are designed specifically for container and raised bed gardening. A soil scoop, for example, is particularly useful for filling containers with soil, and a dibber can help with precise seed and bulb planting. Thirdly, having the right tools can also contribute to the longevity of your garden. Tools like a soil pH tester can help monitor the soil condition and inform you when it's time to add fertilizer or adjust watering levels.

Finally, understanding the importance of these tools encourages responsible and sustainable gardening practices, as it promotes proper care and maintenance of your plants. Hence, essential tools are not just about convenience, they're about fostering a healthier, more productive garden.

Garden Trowel

A garden trowel is an indispensable tool for vegetable container and raised-bed gardens. This hand tool, which resembles a small shovel, is crucial for various gardening tasks, such as digging, transplanting, and smoothing soil. When planting vegetables in containers or raised beds, a trowel helps create the appropriate hole size, ensuring that the roots are adequately covered with soil for optimal growth. It's also ideal for adding compost or fertilizer to specific plants or areas within the garden bed.

Furthermore, a trowel is useful in weeding around plants, as it can get into tight spaces without damaging the surrounding vegetation. Therefore, its versatility, coupled with its easy handling, makes the garden trowel an essential tool for any gardener, whether beginner or experienced. It aids in making gardening tasks more efficient, precise, and enjoyable.

Hand Fork

A hand fork is a crucial tool for vegetable container and raised-bed gardens due to its versatility and effectiveness in small spaces. This three-pronged tool is perfect for loosening the soil, improving its aeration, and promoting better root growth, which are all key to healthy plant development. It's also excellent for mixing in compost or fertilizer, helping to evenly distribute these nutrients throughout your garden.

Furthermore, a hand fork is particularly effective for weed control. Its sharp tines can easily uproot weeds from the soil without damaging the surrounding plants. This is especially important in container and raised-bed gardening, where space is limited, and plants are closely spaced. Thus, a hand fork plays a vital role in maintaining the health and productivity of your vegetable garden, making it an essential tool for any gardener.

Secateurs (Pruning Shears)

Secateurs, also known as pruning shears, are an essential tool for vegetable container and raised-bed gardens. They are designed to make clean, sharp cuts on plant stems and branches, which is crucial for maintaining the health and productivity of your plants. Regular pruning with secateurs can help promote new growth, improve air circulation, and prevent disease spread by removing dead or diseased foliage.

For vegetable plants, this can translate into a larger, healthier yield. Furthermore, they are particularly useful in a container or raised-bed setting, where plants are often grown in close quarters. With secateurs, you can easily shape and manage your plants to ensure they don't overcrowd each other, allowing each plant to receive adequate sunlight and nutrients. Therefore, owning a good pair of secateurs is key to successful and efficient garden maintenance.

Watering Can/Hose With Sprinkler Attachment

A watering can or hose with a sprinkler attachment is an essential tool for vegetable container and raised-bed gardens. Adequate water supply is crucial for plant growth, and these tools provide a gentle and even distribution of water, mimicking natural rainfall. This is especially important in container and raised-bed gardening where the soil tends to dry out faster than in-ground gardens. A watering can is perfect for smaller gardens or for targeted watering of individual plants.

A hose with a sprinkler attachment, on the other hand, allows for efficient watering of larger areas, ensuring that all plants receive equal hydration. Furthermore, the sprinkler attachment minimizes the risk of water logging and erosion, as it disperses water over a wide area rather than concentrating it in one spot. Therefore, these watering tools are key to maintaining the right moisture balance in your garden, promoting healthy and productive plants.

Soil Scoop

A soil scoop is an indispensable tool for vegetable container and raised-bed gardens. Its deep, curved shape makes it ideal for digging holes for planting, moving soil into containers or beds, and adding compost or other organic matter to improve soil fertility. This tool is particularly valuable in a container or raised-bed setting where precision is key due to the limited space.

Using a soil scoop can minimize disturbance to surrounding plants while ensuring each plant has an adequately sized hole for root development. Additionally, the scoop can also be used for removing old, spent soil or for mixing in new, nutrient-rich soil, both of which are important for maintaining the health and productivity of your garden. Therefore, a soil scoop is a versatile and essential tool for any gardener focusing on container or raised-bed gardening.

Dibber

A dibber is a highly useful tool for vegetable container and raised-bed gardens. This pointed tool is designed to make holes in the soil for sowing seeds or transplanting seedlings. In a container or raised-bed setting, where space is often at a premium, a dibber allows for precise positioning of each plant, ensuring optimal use of the available area. It also helps create holes of the right depth, which is crucial for proper seed germination and root development.

Furthermore, using a dibber minimizes soil compaction compared to digging with larger tools, preserving the soil's structure and making it easier for roots to grow. Thus, a dibber is an essential tool for gardeners aiming for efficient planting and successful growth in their vegetable container and raised-bed gardens.

Gloves

Gloves are a fundamental tool for vegetable container and raised-bed gardening. They serve as a protective barrier, shielding your hands from dirt, thorns, sharp tools, and potential irritants or allergens present in the garden. This is particularly important in container and raised-bed gardening, where close contact with soil and plants is frequent.

Gloves also provide a better grip on tools and plants, reducing the risk of slips and accidents. Moreover, they prevent the transfer of harmful bacteria or fungi from your hands to the plants, helping to keep your garden healthy. High-quality gardening gloves can also lessen the fatigue and discomfort associated with prolonged hand use, making your gardening tasks more enjoyable. Therefore, gloves are an essential tool for any gardener, providing safety, comfort, and cleanliness in your vegetable container and raised-bed gardening endeavors.

Knee Pads or Kneeler

Knee pads or a kneeler are vital tools for vegetable container and raised-bed gardening. Gardening often involves kneeling or crouching, tasks that can put significant strain on your knees over time. Knee pads or a kneeler provide a cushioned surface that reduces the pressure and impact on your knees, making these positions more comfortable and sustainable. This is especially beneficial in container and raised-bed gardening, where the elevated nature of the garden might require you to kneel or bend down for extended periods.

By lessening the discomfort associated with these tasks, knee pads or a kneeler can help you spend longer periods in your garden without fatigue or pain. In addition, they can help prevent long-term joint problems that could arise from frequent kneeling. Therefore, a knee pad or kneeler is an essential tool for ensuring comfort, longevity, and health in your vegetable container and raised-bed gardening endeavors.

Garden Rake

A garden rake is an indispensable tool for vegetable container and raised-bed gardening. This tool is primarily used for preparing the soil before planting and maintaining it throughout the growing season. It helps to break up clumps of soil, remove rocks or debris, and level the soil surface, creating an ideal environment for seeds or seedlings.

In a container or raised-bed garden, where space might be limited, a smaller garden rake can offer precision in these tasks without disturbing existing plants. Additionally, a rake can be used to incorporate compost or other organic matter into the soil, improving its fertility and structure. During the growing season, a rake can help keep the soil surface loose, promoting air circulation and water penetration. Therefore, a garden rake plays a crucial role in both preparing your garden for planting and ensuring its ongoing health and productivity.

Garden Hoe

A garden hoe is a crucial tool for vegetable container and raised-bed gardening. It is a multi-purpose tool that aids in numerous gardening tasks, including weeding, soil preparation, and planting. A hoe can be used to dislodge and remove weeds from your garden, a task that is especially important in container and raised-bed gardening where weeds can quickly take over due to the close spacing of plants.

For soil preparation, the hoe can be used to break up compacted soil, allowing for better water absorption and root penetration. In terms of planting, a garden hoe can be used to create furrows or holes for seeds and seedlings. Given the elevated nature of container and raised-bed gardens, using a hoe can also reduce the physical strain involved in these tasks. Therefore, a garden hoe is an essential tool that can enhance the productivity and ease of maintenance of your vegetable container and raised-bed garden.

Spade

A spade is an essential tool for vegetable container and raised-bed gardening. It's primarily used for digging, but its versatility makes it useful for a variety of gardening tasks. In the initial stages of setting up your garden, a spade can be used to break up and turn soil, making it easier for roots to penetrate. It can also be used to mix in compost or other amendments, improving the soil's fertility and structure.

When it comes to planting, the sharp, flat blade of a spade is perfect for digging precise holes or trenches for your seeds or seedlings. Additionally, in a raised-bed or container garden, where space might be limited, a spade provides the control needed to work around existing plants without damaging them.

Finally, a spade can be useful for maintaining the edges of your raised beds, keeping them neat and tidy. Therefore, a spade is a vital tool that can significantly enhance the efficiency and productivity of your vegetable container and raised-bed garden.

Wheelbarrow Or Garden Cart

A wheelbarrow or garden cart is a significant tool for vegetable container and raised-bed gardening. Given the amount of soil, compost, mulch, or even plants that need to be moved around in a garden, these tools can save a lot of time and physical effort. In the initial stages of setting up your garden, a wheelbarrow or garden cart can be used to transport large volumes of soil or compost to fill your containers or raised beds.

During the growing season, they can be used to move heavy watering cans or bags of fertilizer, making routine maintenance tasks easier. Furthermore, when it comes to harvesting, a wheelbarrow or garden cart can be invaluable for collecting and transporting your produce. For gardeners with larger gardens or those with physical limitations, a wheelbarrow or garden cart is especially beneficial. Therefore, these tools are essential for improving the efficiency and ease of work in your vegetable container and raised-bed garden.

Compost Bin

A compost bin is an indispensable tool for vegetable container and raised-bed gardening. Composting is a process that turns kitchen and yard waste into rich, organic material that gardeners refer to as "black gold." This nutrient-packed compost can be used to improve the fertility and structure of the soil in your containers or raised beds.

Healthy soil is key to successful gardening, and adding compost can provide your plants with the nutrients they need to thrive. Additionally, composting can help reduce the amount of waste going to landfill, making it an environmentally friendly practice. A compost bin makes this process easy and convenient.

You can add waste materials to it regularly, and over time, these break down into compost. Therefore, a compost bin is an essential tool for enhancing the health and productivity of your vegetable container and raised-bed garden while promoting sustainable practices.

Soil pH Tester

A Soil pH Tester is a crucial tool for vegetable container and raised-bed gardening. The pH level of your soil can greatly affect the health and productivity of your plants. Different vegetables prefer different pH levels, and a slight variation in soil pH can impact nutrient availability, potentially leading to nutrient deficiencies or toxicities.

A Soil pH Tester allows gardeners to quickly and accurately measure the pH level of their soil, enabling them to adjust it accordingly, if necessary, using specific soil amendments. By ensuring that the soil pH is at the optimal level for the specific vegetables you are growing, you can maximize plant health and yield. Therefore, a Soil pH Tester is an essential tool for managing soil health and optimizing the growth and productivity of your vegetable container and raised-bed garden.

Garden Twine And Stakes

Garden twine and stakes are vital tools for vegetable container and raised-bed gardening. Many vegetables, such as tomatoes, cucumbers, peas, and beans, are vine plants that need support as they grow. Stakes provide the necessary support, keeping the plants upright, promoting healthier growth, and preventing the fruits from touching the ground where they might rot or be attacked by pests.

Garden twine is used to gently tie the plants to the stakes, providing additional support without damaging the plants. Using garden twine and stakes can also help to maximize space in your garden, allowing for better air circulation and sunlight exposure, which are crucial for the healthy growth of plants. Therefore, garden twine and stakes are essential tools for managing plant growth and maximizing yield in your vegetable container and raised-bed garden.

Fertilizer Spreader

A fertilizer spreader is a key tool for vegetable container and raised-bed gardening. Fertilizers are crucial for providing plants with the necessary nutrients they need for healthy growth, particularly in container and raised-bed gardens where soil nutrients can be depleted quickly.

A fertilizer spreader ensures that these nutrients are distributed evenly across your garden. Uneven application of fertilizer can lead to some areas receiving too much or too little, which can either cause nutrient burn or leave plants undernourished. Furthermore, a fertilizer spreader saves time and effort, making the process of fertilizing your garden more efficient. Therefore, a fertilizer spreader is an essential tool for maintaining soil health and promoting robust, productive growth in your vegetable container and raised-bed garden.

FUNDAMENTALS OF PREPARING YOUR CONTAINER & RAISED BED GARDEN SOIL

Understanding your garden soil is pivotal when growing vegetables in container and raised bed gardens. Soil is not just a medium to hold the plants, it's a living environment that provides nutrients, water, and aeration to your vegetable crops.

Different vegetables require different soil conditions to thrive - some prefer slightly acidic soil, others need more alkaline conditions. The physical structure of the soil also matters; it should be well-draining to prevent water-logging, yet capable of retaining enough moisture to sustain the plants.

Moreover, in container and raised bed gardening, the soil plays an even more critical role, as the roots are confined to a limited space and completely dependent on the provided soil for their needs. Thus, understanding the composition, pH level, and nutrient content of your soil can guide you in amending it appropriately for optimal growth, leading to healthier plants and a more bountiful harvest.

Choosing the right soil for container gardening and raised bed vegetable gardens is a crucial step towards a bountiful harvest. Start by determining the specific needs of the plants you intend to grow, as different vegetables have varying preferences for soil type and pH.

For most vegetables, a well-draining soil is essential to prevent waterlogging and root rot. A mix of loamy soil, which is rich in nutrients and has excellent moisture retention and drainage properties, is often recommended. If you're using commercial potting mix, ensure it's specifically designed for edible plants, as some mixes may contain chemical fertilizers or water-retaining crystals that aren't suitable for vegetable gardening. The soil should also be rich in organic matter like compost or well-rotted manure, which improves soil structure, enhances water and nutrient holding capacity, and provides a slow-release source of nutrients.

Regularly testing your soil's pH and nutrient levels is also advisable, as this can guide you in making necessary amendments. For instance, adding lime can raise soil pH (making it more alkaline), while adding sulfur lowers it (making it more acidic). By understanding these principles, you can make informed decisions on the best soil for your container or raised bed vegetable garden, setting the stage for a healthy, productive growing season.

CONTAINER & RAISED BED SOIL TYPES

Potting Soil

Potting soil, also known as potting mix, is a specially formulated medium that's used in container gardening. Unlike garden soil or topsoil, potting soil is typically soilless, lightweight, and designed to provide optimal conditions for plants grown in pots or containers. It's crafted to offer the right structure, drainage, and nutrient content for potted plants, making it an ideal choice for container gardening.

The composition of potting soil can vary, but it usually includes ingredients like peat moss, perlite, and vermiculite, each contributing unique benefits. Peat moss helps retain moisture and air, perlite improves aeration and drainage, and vermiculite aids in water retention and provides minerals. Some potting soils also include compost or other organic materials to boost nutrient content.

Benefits Of Potting Soil In Container & Raised Bed Gardening

- One of the main advantages of using potting soil for container gardening is its excellent drainage. Excess water can lead to root rot, a common problem in container gardening. The light, porous nature of potting soil allows water to drain quickly, preventing this issue.
- Another benefit is its sterility. Potting soil is free from weed seeds, pests, and diseases, reducing the risk of these common gardening problems.

- It also provides a consistent growing environment, which can be especially beneficial for novice gardeners or those new to container gardening.
- When it comes to raised bed gardening, potting soil can be mixed with topsoil or garden soil to create an ideal growing medium. This combination can provide the benefits of both types of soil - the nutrient content and natural microbiome of garden soil, and the drainage and structure of potting soil.

Disadvantages Of Potting Soil In Container & Raised Bed Gardening

Despite its many benefits, there are also some disadvantages to using potting soil.

- Firstly, it tends to dry out quickly and may require more frequent watering than garden soil.
- Secondly, potting soil is generally more expensive than topsoil or garden soil, which could be a significant factor for large containers or raised beds.
- Lastly, because potting soil is so lightweight, it may not provide enough support for larger plants or those with extensive root systems.

While potting soil has its drawbacks, its benefits make it an excellent choice for both container and raised bed gardening. By understanding its properties and how to use it effectively, gardeners can leverage potting soil to grow healthy, vibrant plants.

Topsoil

Topsoil is the uppermost layer of the earth's surface, typically the top two to eight inches. It's rich in organic matter and microorganisms, making it an essential element for plant life. Topsoil is the layer where most of the soil's biological activity occurs, as it's teeming with bacteria, fungi, insects, worms, and other organisms that contribute to a vibrant soil ecosystem.

Topsoil composition can vary widely based on location and is influenced by factors like climate, local flora and fauna, and human activity. Generally, good quality topsoil contains a balanced mix of sand, silt, and clay, along with organic matter, often in the form of decomposed plant material known as humus. This organic content is what gives topsoil its dark color and high nutrient content.

Benefits Of Topsoil In Container & Raised Bed Gardening

- It's usually locally available and more affordable than specialized soils, making it a cost-effective choice for filling large beds.
- Its high nutrient content can support robust plant growth, while its natural microbiome can help protect plants against certain diseases.
- When properly managed, topsoil in raised beds can support a wide variety of plants, from vegetables and herbs to ornamentals.

Disadvantages Of Topsoil In Container & Raised Bed Gardening

- Its dense structure and slower drainage can be problematic in a container environment, where good drainage is crucial.
- Without amendments to lighten its texture, topsoil in containers can become compacted, making it hard for roots to grow.
- Topsoil can contain weed seeds or disease organisms, which can be more difficult to manage in a container setting.

- The nutrient content, pH, and texture of topsoil can differ greatly from place to place, making it less consistent than commercial potting mixes. This can make it harder to provide the right growing conditions for certain plants.

While topsoil has its place in the gardener's toolkit, it's not always the best choice for every situation. In raised bed gardening, it can be a valuable component when mixed with other amendments to create a rich, well-draining soil blend. However, for container gardening, a lighter, faster-draining potting mix is usually a better option.

Compost

Compost is a rich, crumbly material that results from the natural decomposition of organic matter. Often referred to as "black gold" by gardeners, it's created through the process of composting, where kitchen scraps, yard waste, and other organic materials are broken down by microorganisms over time.

The composition of compost can vary widely depending on what materials were used in its creation. However, all good compost is high in organic matter and contains nutrients essential for plant growth, including nitrogen, phosphorus, and potassium. It also contains beneficial microorganisms that can help improve soil health and ward off plant diseases.

Benefits Of Compost In Container & Raised Bed Gardening

- One of the significant benefits of using compost in both container and raised bed gardening is its ability to improve soil structure. By adding compost to your garden, you can improve the soil's ability to retain moisture and nutrients while also enhancing drainage. This makes it an excellent amendment for both sandy soils (which drain too quickly) and clay soils (which drain too slowly).

- Compost also provides a slow-release source of nutrients to your plants, reducing the need for synthetic fertilizers.
- Furthermore, the microorganisms in compost can help suppress plant diseases and pests, promoting healthier plants overall.
- In container gardening, compost can be mixed with potting soil to provide a nutrient boost. However, it's important not to use compost alone in containers, as it can be too heavy and may not drain well, leading to waterlogged conditions that can harm plant roots.

Disadvantage Of Compost In Container & Raised Bed Gardening

While compost offers many benefits, there are also some potential disadvantages to consider.

- Creating compost at home requires time, effort, and space, which may not be available in all living situations.
- The nutrient content of compost can be variable, and it may not provide all the necessary nutrients for optimal plant growth. Over-reliance on compost could also lead to nutrient imbalances in the soil if not managed properly.
- If compost isn't fully decomposed, it can temporarily rob the soil of nitrogen as the decomposition process continues.
- While compost can help suppress some diseases and pests, poorly managed compost piles could potentially harbor unwanted seeds or disease organisms.

Despite the potential difficulties associated with using compost, its advantages render it an indispensable asset to any gardening endeavor. Be it in container plants or raised beds, incorporating compost into your soil can markedly enhance its richness and framework, thereby promoting the growth of more robust and fruitful plants.

Loamy Soil

Loamy soil is often heralded as the ideal garden soil. It's a well-balanced mix of sand, silt, and clay, providing an optimal balance of drainage and moisture retention. This type of soil also typically contains a good amount of organic matter, which contributes to its fertile nature and dark, crumbly appearance.

Benefits Of Loamy Soil In Container & Raised Bed Gardening

The benefits of using loamy soil in both container and raised bed gardening are numerous.

- The balanced texture of loamy soil means it has excellent structure, allowing plant roots to penetrate easily.
- It doesn't dry out quickly like sandy soils, yet drains more effectively than clay soils, reducing the risk of waterlogging.
- The organic matter found in loamy soil is also beneficial, as it provides a slow-release source of nutrients to plants and helps to maintain soil health by supporting beneficial microorganisms.
- In raised bed gardens, loamy soil can be an excellent choice because it's easy to work with and provides an ideal environment for many types of plants.
- Its well-draining yet moisture-retaining properties make it suitable for a wide range of plants, from deep-rooted vegetables to smaller herbs and flowers.

Disadvantages Of Loamy Soil In Container & Raised Bed Gardening

However, using loamy soil in containers can present some challenges.

- Loamy soil can be heavier than commercial potting mixes, potentially leading to poor aeration in a confined container environment. This could result in root stress or disease.
- If your existing garden soil is sandy or high in clay, you might need to purchase loamy soil or amend your existing soil, which can add to the cost and effort of setting up your garden.
- While loamy soil is generally nutrient-rich, it may still require additional amendments or fertilizers to supply specific nutrients needed by certain plants.

Despite the potential obstacles, such as its weight for container gardening and the possible extra effort or cost to obtain and upkeep, loamy soil's numerous benefits for gardening, owing to its balanced characteristics and high fertility, make it a popular choice among many gardeners. They believe that the advantages of using loamy soil in both raised bed and container gardens far outweigh any potential drawbacks.

Sandy Soil

Sandy soil, as the name suggests, has a high proportion of sand particles and is often recognized by its gritty texture. This type of soil is characterized by large, coarse particles that provide plenty of space for air and water to move around. Due to these properties, sandy soil warms up quickly in the spring and drains water faster than other types of soil.

Benefits Of Sandy Soil In Container & Raised Bed Gardening

- One of the main benefits of using sandy soil in container gardening is its excellent drainage. Overwatering is a common problem in container gardening, and using a soil that drains well can help prevent issues related to excess moisture, such as root rot or fungal diseases.
- Sandy soil also tends to be lighter than other types of soil, which can be an advantage when moving and handling containers.
- In raised bed gardens, sandy soil can be useful for growing plants that prefer well-drained conditions, such as certain herbs and succulents.
- Its ability to warm up quickly can also benefit early-season crops or heat-loving plants.
- Additionally, sandy soil is easy to work with, as it doesn't clump together as much as clay or loamy soils.

Disadvantages Of Sandy Soil In Container & Raised Bed Gardening

- The most significant disadvantage is its low nutrient-holding capacity. Because of the large, loose particles, water and nutrients can leach out of sandy soil quickly, making it less fertile than loamy or clay soils. This means that plants grown in sandy soil may require more frequent fertilization to maintain optimal growth.
- Another issue with sandy soil is its low water-holding capacity. While this can be an advantage in terms of preventing waterlogged conditions, it also means that plants grown in sandy soil may need to be watered more frequently, especially in hot or dry weather. In a container setting, where evaporation rates are already high, this could lead to increased maintenance.

While sandy soil has unique properties that can be advantageous in certain gardening situations, it also presents challenges in terms of nutrient and water management. However, with careful watering and fertilization practices, sandy soil can still be effectively used in both container and raised bed gardens. It's particularly well-suited to drought-tolerant plants or those that prefer well-drained conditions.

Peat Moss

Peat moss, also known as sphagnum peat, is a type of organic matter that is derived from decomposed plant materials in peat bogs. It is widely used in gardening for its unique properties, including its ability to retain water and slowly release nutrients. Peat moss has a fine, fibrous texture and is typically brown or dark red in color.

Benefits Of Peat Moss In Container & Raised Bed Gardening

- One of the primary benefits of using peat moss in container gardening is its excellent water retention capacity. This property can help prevent soil from drying out between waterings, which is especially beneficial in containers that dry out quickly.
- Additionally, peat moss is lightweight, making it easier to handle and move containers around.
- In raised bed gardens, peat moss can be used to improve the soil structure and increase its capacity to hold both water and nutrients.
- It can also help to acidify the soil, making it suitable for acid-loving plants like blueberries or azaleas.
- Because peat moss decomposes slowly, it can provide a long-term source of organic matter to the soil, enhancing its fertility over time.

Disadvantages Of Peat Moss In Container & Raised Bed

- One of the main criticisms is its environmental impact. Peat bogs are important carbon sinks, and the extraction of peat moss can contribute to greenhouse gas emissions.
- There are also concerns about the sustainability of peat moss harvesting, as peat bogs take thousands of years to form.
- Compared to other types of soil amendments, peat moss can be relatively expensive. This may be a consideration for gardeners working with large areas or on a tight budget.
- While the water-holding capacity of peat moss can be beneficial, it can also lead to waterlogged conditions if not managed properly. This is especially true in containers, where drainage is limited.
- Peat moss has a very low nutrient content, meaning that additional fertilizers will often need to be added to meet plant needs.

While peat moss offers several benefits for both container and raised bed gardening, including improved water and nutrient retention, it also has some significant drawbacks. These include environmental concerns, cost, potential for waterlogging, and low inherent fertility. As such, gardeners should weigh these factors before deciding to use peat moss in their gardens.

Coir (Coconut Fiber)

Coir, also known as coconut fiber, is a natural fiber product derived from the husk of the coconut. It consists of the coarse fibers extracted from the husk, the part of the coconut between the outer shell and the actual fruit. Coir has gained substantial popularity in the horticultural world due to its versatility and sustainability as a growing medium.

The process of obtaining coir involves removing the fibrous layer from the coconut and then soaking, beating, and drying it until it forms a light, airy medium. The end product is a soil-like substance that is rich in organic material and can hold a significant amount of water, making it an excellent choice for container gardening.

Benefits Of Coir In Container & Raised Bed Gardening

- One of the main advantages of using Coir in container gardening is its excellent water retention. This property helps prevent the soil from drying out quickly, which is particularly beneficial in containers as they often dry out faster than ground soil.
- Coir is relatively lightweight, which makes containers filled with it easier to move around.
- In raised bed gardening, Coir can help improve the structure of the soil, increasing its ability to retain water and nutrients. This can be particularly beneficial for growing plants that require a lot of moisture or nutrients.
- Coir is resistant to bacterial and fungal growth, reducing the risk of plant diseases.

Disadvantages Of Coir In Container & Raised Bed Gardening

- While it's excellent at retaining water, it can sometimes retain too much, leading to waterlogged conditions if not properly managed. This is especially true in containers where drainage is limited.
- While it's rich in organic material, Coir it's low in essential nutrients like nitrogen, phosphorus, and potassium. This means that gardeners will need to add additional fertilizers to the Coir to ensure that plants receive all the nutrients they need to grow.

- There are environmental concerns associated with its use of Coir. The process of extracting Coir from coconuts can lead to deforestation and habitat loss in the countries where coconuts are grown.

To sum up, while Coir provides numerous advantages as a planting medium for both container and raised bed gardening, it also comes with notable disadvantages. It's essential for gardeners to consider these strengths and weaknesses thoroughly before choosing to utilize Coir in their gardens.

Perlite

Perlite is a naturally occurring mineral that is often used as a soil amendment in gardening. It is derived from volcanic glass, specifically a glassy-looking rock known as obsidian, which forms when it comes into contact with water. When processed, perlite takes on a lightweight, granular form, often compared to small bits of styrofoam due to its white color and texture. Despite the comparison, it is worth noting that perlite is a completely natural material.

Benefits Of Perlite In Container & Raised Bed Gardening

- The primary benefit of perlite lies in its ability to improve soil aeration, water retention, and drainage.
- Its porous nature allows it to retain some moisture while also letting excess water drain away easily. This balance helps to prevent waterlogging and ensures that plant roots have access to both water and air - crucial elements for healthy growth.
- Perlite also acts as a natural filtration system, catching nutrients that plants need to thrive.
- In container gardening, perlite is particularly beneficial as it can help mitigate the challenges posed by limited space.

- It can improve the structure of potting compost mixes, enhancing aeration and drainage, key factors in preventing root rot and promoting robust plant growth.
- Similarly, in raised bed gardening, perlite can be used to open up the structure of ready-mixed loam or peat, improving overall soil texture and functionality.

Disadvantages Of Perlite In Container & Raised Bed Gardening

However, while perlite offers numerous benefits, it is not without potential drawbacks.

- It's lightweight nature, while beneficial for improving soil structure, can also mean it is easily washed away during heavy rain or watering. This could lead to a need for more frequent replenishment in outdoor gardening situations.
- Additionally, while perlite does retain some moisture, it does not contribute much in the way of nutrients to the soil. Therefore, gardeners using perlite will likely need to supplement with other nutrient-rich amendments to ensure plants receive all the nourishment they require.

Vermiculite

Vermiculite is a naturally occurring mineral that holds significant value in horticulture and gardening. This hydrous phyllosilicate mineral undergoes substantial expansion when subjected to heat, a process known as exfoliation. Its appearance varies from glossy flakes that can range in color from dark gray to sandy brown.

Benefits Of Vermiculite In Container & Raised Bed Gardening

- Vermiculite's unique properties make it an effective soil conditioner.
- It has the ability to loosen soil and improve aeration, which is crucial for plant root health.
- It has a high water retention capacity, meaning it can hold and slowly release moisture back into the soil as needed.
- In container gardening, vermiculite is especially useful. It promotes faster root growth and provides quick anchorage for young roots, an aspect that is particularly beneficial given the confined space of containers. This quality also helps in maintaining moisture levels in the soil, as containers can dry out quickly.
- Vermiculite aids in creating a light and fluffy soil mix, enhancing the soil's capacity to retain water and nutrients. This leads to an environment conducive to root spread and nutrient uptake, promoting overall plant health.

Disadvantage Of Vermiculite In Container & Raised Bed Gardening

- Due to its high water-retention capacity, it could lead to waterlogged conditions if used excessively, particularly in containers that lack adequate drainage. This can result in root rot and other moisture-related diseases.
- Additionally, while vermiculite is beneficial for retaining water and nutrients, it does not contribute much in terms of adding nutrients to the soil. Therefore, it is often necessary to supplement with additional fertilizers or compost to ensure plants receive the nourishment they need.

CREATING ORGANIC SOIL FOR RAISED BEDS AND CONTAINER VEGETABLE GARDENING

Creating organic soil for raised beds and container vegetable gardening is a rewarding process that can greatly enhance the health and productivity of your plants. The key to successful organic soil preparation lies in understanding its composition and the role each component plays in nurturing plant growth.

The first step in creating organic soil is selecting the right components. There are three primary ingredients to consider: topsoil, compost, and other soil amendments like perlite or vermiculite. Topsoil serves as the base of your mix. It's important to choose good quality, weed-free topsoil to avoid introducing unwanted seeds or pests into your garden.

Compost is the next crucial component. Compost enriches the soil by adding a wealth of beneficial microorganisms and nutrients. You can make your own compost from kitchen scraps, yard waste, and other organic materials, or purchase it from a reliable source. Composting not only improves soil fertility but also promotes sustainable waste management practices.

Perlite and vermiculite are optional additions often used to improve soil aeration and water retention, respectively. While they do not contribute nutrients, they significantly enhance the physical properties of the soil, promoting better root growth and overall plant health.

Once you have gathered your ingredients, the next step is to combine them. A common ratio used by many gardeners is 60% topsoil, 30% compost, and 10% other amendments, but feel free to adjust based on your specific needs. Mix the components thoroughly to ensure a uniform blend, then add the mixture to your raised beds or containers.

After filling your containers or raised beds, give the soil a good watering. This will help it settle and will also indicate if any additional soil is needed. Once the soil is settled, you're ready to start planting!

Remember, creating organic soil is an ongoing process. As plants grow, they consume the nutrients in the soil, so it's important to replenish those nutrients regularly. This can be done by adding more compost or other organic matter each growing season.

Creating organic soil for raised beds and container vegetable gardening involves careful selection of quality components, thorough mixing, and regular maintenance. With time and care, you'll cultivate a thriving garden that not only produces abundant crops but also contributes to a healthier environment.

HOW TO CHOOSE THE RIGHT CONTAINER FOR VEGETABLE GARDENING

Choosing the right container for vegetable gardening is a critical step in ensuring the success and yield of your garden. The type, size, and material of the container you select can significantly influence the health and growth of your plants.

The first consideration when choosing a container is its size. As a general rule, the more space you can offer your plant's roots, the better. Smaller containers limit root growth, which can stunt the overall growth of the plant and reduce its productivity. For instance, deep-rooted vegetables like tomatoes and cucumbers will require larger, deeper pots, while leafy greens or herbs can thrive in smaller, shallower containers. It's important to match the size of the container to the mature size of the plant you intend to grow.

The material of the container is another key factor. Plastic containers can be a good choice, provided they are food-grade and BPA-free. A food-grade designation means that the plastic does not contain harmful chemicals that could leach into the soil and be absorbed by the plants. Clay or ceramic pots are also popular choices due to their aesthetic appeal and ability to regulate soil temperature. However, they are heavier and more fragile than plastic counterparts. Wooden boxes or barrels can add a rustic charm to your garden, but ensure the wood hasn't been treated with harmful chemicals.

The shape of the container also matters. Square, rectangular, or cylindrical containers tend to need less frequent watering than tapered pots. This is because the larger soil volume in these shapes retains moisture for longer periods.

Finally, always ensure that your chosen container has adequate drainage. Poor drainage can lead to waterlogged soil and root rot, which can quickly kill your plants. If your container doesn't have drainage holes, you can drill some yourself.

Choosing the right container for vegetable gardening requires careful consideration of the plant's needs, the material, size, and shape of the container, and its drainage capabilities. With the right container, your vegetable garden can thrive, providing you with a bountiful harvest.

HOW TO CHOOSE & BUILD THE RIGHT RAISED BED FOR VEGETABLE GARDENING

Choosing and building the right raised bed for vegetable gardening can greatly enhance your gardening experience by improving productivity and making the process more manageable. The key to success lies in careful planning and consideration of factors such as size, location, materials, and soil requirements.

The first step is determining the right size for your raised bed. This depends on the space you have available and the types of vegetables you plan to grow. As a general guideline, raised beds are typically 3 to 4 feet wide — this width allows you to reach into the center from either side without stepping on the soil. The length can vary, but bear in mind that longer beds may be harder to navigate around. The height of the bed should be at least 6 inches, but if your native soil is poor or you want less bending, consider making it between 12 and 24 inches high. Different configurations, such as rectangular, square, or circular, can be chosen based on your garden space and personal preference.

Next, choosing the right location is crucial. Most vegetables need at least six to eight hours of sunlight each day, so find the sunniest spot in your yard. Also, ensure the location has good drainage to prevent waterlogging and is protected from harsh winds or other environmental factors. Proximity to a water source is also beneficial for easy watering.

The material for your raised bed can range from wood, concrete blocks, bricks, to recycled plastic based on your budget, aesthetic preference, and durability needs. Wood, especially cedar or redwood, is a popular choice due to its natural look and afford-ability, but remember that untreated wood may decay over time. Concrete blocks or bricks offer greater longevity and can also create an attractive look.

Lastly, preparing the right soil for your raised bed is essential for successful vegetable growth. A good mix often comprises 60% topsoil, 30% compost, and 10% potting soil. This blend provides a fertile and well-draining environment ideal for most vegeta-bles. Remember to replenish the nutrients in your soil by adding compost or other organic matter each season.

Choosing and building the right raised bed for vegetable gardening involves careful planning and consideration. With the right size, location, materials, and soil, you can enjoy a bountiful harvest from your own backyard.

DECIDING WHAT VEGETABLES TO GROW IN CONTAINERS & RAISED BED GARDENS

Deciding what vegetables to grow in containers and raised bed gardens depends on a variety of factors. These include your local climate, the size of your container or bed, the amount of available sunlight, and your personal preferences and goals.

Climate plays a pivotal role in determining what you can grow. Some vegetables prefer cooler weather (like lettuce, spinach, and peas), while others thrive in the heat (tomatoes, peppers, and cucumbers). Understanding your region's growing season can help guide your vegetable selection.

The size of your container or raised bed is another crucial consideration. Larger vegetables like tomatoes, cucumbers, and eggplants require more space and may be better suited to raised beds. On the other hand, smaller vegetables and herbs like radishes, carrots, lettuce, and basil can do well in containers.

Sunlight is a critical factor for plant health. Most vegetables need at least six hours of sunlight each day. If your space doesn't get much sun, consider growing vegetables that tolerate shade, such as leafy greens or root vegetables.

For beginners, it's advisable to start with easy-to-grow vegetables. Lettuce, radishes, and cherry tomatoes are great choices that require minimal care and provide quick results. More experienced gardeners might want to try growing more challenging crops like bell peppers or zucchini.

If space or time is limited, focus on high-yield and fast-growing vegetables. Leafy greens, bush beans, and cherry tomatoes can produce a lot in a small space over a short period.

When planning your garden, think about your goals. Are you aiming for a bountiful harvest, or do you just enjoy the process of gardening? If your goal is a high yield, opt for prolific producers like zucchini, tomatoes, and cucumbers. If you're in it for the joy of gardening, choose vegetables that you love to grow and eat, regardless of their yield.

Choosing what vegetables to grow in containers and raised beds should be a thoughtful process that considers your climate, space, sunlight, experience level, and gardening goals. With careful planning and selection, you can create a garden that is both productive and enjoyable.

PLANTING & SOWING SEEDS IN CONTAINER & RAISED BED GARDENS

The importance of choosing the right planting and sowing methods in container and raised bed gardening is paramount to achieving a successful garden. These methods have the potential to dictate the overall health, growth, and productivity of your plants.

One key reason why the right planting and sowing methods are crucial is due to the nature of container and raised bed gardening themselves. Unlike traditional in-ground gardens, these types of gardens have limited space and resources. The soil depth and volume, the nutrients available, and the space for root expansion are all restricted. Therefore, using appropriate planting methods that consider these limitations is vital. For instance, understanding the right depth at which to sow seeds, the correct spacing between plants, or the suitable soil type for each plant can dramatically impact their growth and yield.

Secondly, the right planting and sowing methods can help prevent common gardening problems such as diseases and pests. Overcrowding of plants in containers or raised beds can lead to poor air circulation and increased humidity around plants, which are ideal conditions for the spread of fungal diseases. Proper spacing of plants, therefore, is not just about maximizing productivity, but also about maintaining the health of your garden.

Moreover, some plants may be more susceptible to certain pests when grown in containers or raised beds. Implementing techniques such as companion planting - where certain plants are grown together for mutual benefit - can help deter pests naturally. For example, marigolds can be planted alongside tomatoes to repel harmful nematodes.

Lastly, selecting the right planting and sowing methods can enhance the efficiency of your gardening efforts. By choosing plants that are naturally suited to container or raised bed conditions, you can ensure that your time and effort are invested wisely. Some plants, due to their growth habits and size, are better adapted to these conditions and require less intensive care than others.

The right planting and sowing methods are integral to the success of container and raised bed gardening. They not only ensure the healthy growth of plants but also help in disease and pest prevention, and improve overall gardening efficiency. With careful planning and execution, you can harness these methods to create a thriving, productive garden in even the smallest spaces.

TYPES OF PLANTING & SOWING METHODS IN CONTAINER & RAISED BED GARDENS

Gardening in containers and raised beds offers a range of benefits, from space efficiency to improved control over soil conditions. However, understanding the various types of planting and sowing methods can enhance these benefits further and help ensure a successful vegetable garden.

So in the following we'll discuss the different types of planting and sowing methods that can be used in both container and raised bed vegetable gardens.

Direct Sowing

Direct sowing is a gardening method that involves planting seeds directly into the soil of your garden. Instead of starting seeds indoors and then transplanting them into the garden once they've sprouted, seeds are placed into the ground where they will ultimately grow to maturity. This method is commonly used for many types of vegetables and flowers, and can be used in both container and raised bed gardening.

In container gardening, direct sowing entails planting seeds right into the pots or containers where they will grow. This technique eliminates the need for transplanting, which can sometimes stress plants. In raised bed gardening, direct sowing means spreading the seeds on the topsoil of the raised bed, then covering them with a layer of soil or compost.

Benefits Of Direct Sowing

There are several benefits to using the direct sowing method in container and raised bed gardening.

- One of the main advantages is its simplicity. It's a straightforward process that doesn't require much equipment or technical skills.
- Direct sowing is also more cost-effective than buying young plants from a nursery. You can purchase a packet of seeds for a fraction of the cost of a single plant.
- Direct sowing allows plants to establish their roots early in their preferred growing location, which can lead to stronger, healthier plants.
- Another advantage of direct sowing is that it allows for flexibility in planting times. You can adjust your sowing

schedule based on the specific needs of each plant variety, ensuring optimal growing conditions for each type of seed you plant.

Disadvantages Of Direct Sowing

Despite its advantages, direct sowing does come with some challenges.

- One of the main disadvantages is that seeds planted directly in the garden are more susceptible to pests, diseases, and harsh weather conditions compared to seeds started indoors. This could potentially lead to lower germination rates and weaker seedlings.
- Another challenge with direct sowing is the need for careful management of planting depths and spacing. Seeds that are planted too deep might not germinate, while those planted too close together might compete for resources.
- In container gardening, direct sowing requires a commitment to the container you choose, as it can be challenging to transplant a seedling once it's begun to establish its root system in the pot.
- Similarly, in raised bed gardening, you'll need to be sure that your beds are prepared with nutrient-rich soil to support seed growth, as it will be harder to amend the soil once seeds have been sown.

While direct sowing is a simple and cost-effective method of planting, it does require careful planning and management to ensure success. By understanding the benefits and challenges of this method, gardeners can make informed decisions about whether it's the right approach for their particular situation.

Transplanting

Transplanting is a gardening technique that involves starting seeds indoors or in a controlled environment, allowing them to sprout and grow into seedlings before they are moved to their final growing location outdoors. This method is particularly useful for plants that have a long growing season or those that require special care during their early stages of growth. In both container and raised bed gardening, transplanting can be an effective way to get a head start on the growing season.

In container gardening, transplanting involves moving a young plant from its initial pot or tray into a larger, permanent container where it will continue to grow. In raised bed gardening, the process is similar, but instead of moving the plant to a new container, it's transferred to a prepared bed.

Benefits Of Transplanting

There are several advantages to using the transplanting method in both container and raised bed gardening.

- One of the main benefits is that it allows you to begin the growing season earlier. By starting seeds indoors while it's still too cold outside for germination, you can give your plants a head start. This is especially beneficial for plants with a long growing season, as it ensures they will reach maturity before the end of the growing period.
- Transplanting also offers the advantage of control. By starting your seeds indoors, you can control the conditions in which your plants germinate and begin their growth. This can result in healthier, stronger seedlings, as they are protected from pests, diseases, and harsh weather conditions during their most vulnerable stage.

Disadvantages Of Transplanting

Despite its benefits, transplanting also has some disadvantages.

- One of the main ones is the risk of transplant shock, a condition that can occur when a plant is moved from one location to another. Symptoms of transplant shock include wilting, yellowing leaves, and stunted growth. However, this can often be mitigated by carefully hardening off plants (gradually acclimating them to outdoor conditions) before transplanting them.
- Another disadvantage of transplanting is the extra time and resources it requires. Starting seeds indoors means you will need space, equipment (like grow lights and seed trays), and the time to care for the seedlings. Not all gardeners have these resources readily available.
- In container gardening, another challenge is ensuring the new container is large enough to accommodate the growing plant and also has adequate drainage.
- In raised bed gardening, preparing the beds to receive the transplants can be labor-intensive, especially if amending the soil is necessary.

To sum it up, even though transplanting demands more work than direct sowing, it can result in robust, vigorous plants that get an early start on the growing season. By weighing the advantages and potential hurdles of transplanting, gardeners can make a knowledgeable choice about the most suitable planting technique for their unique requirements and situations.

Square Foot Gardening

Square Foot Gardening is a gardening method that maximizes the use of space by dividing the garden area into square-foot sections, typically in a 4x4-foot block. Each block is further subdivided into one-foot squares, and different crops are planted in each square according to their size requirements. This approach is a solution for people who don't have a lot of space but still want to grow their own vegetables and little fruits.

In container gardening, Square Foot Gardening involves using containers that are divided into square-foot sections. Similarly, in raised bed gardening, the raised beds are divided into square-foot sections. The goal is to make the most efficient use of space while still providing plants with the nutrients and room they need to grow.

Benefits Of Square Foot Gardening

- One of the main benefits of Square Foot Gardening is its efficiency. By dividing the garden into square-foot sections, you can maximize your yield while minimizing the amount of space required. This method is particularly beneficial for those with limited gardening space, as it allows for a wide variety of plants to be grown in a small area.
- Another advantage of Square Foot Gardening is that it reduces the amount of work required. Because plants are closely spaced, there's less room for weeds to grow, reducing the need for weeding.
- Because each square foot is planted with a different crop, there's less risk of disease or pest infestation spreading throughout the entire garden.

Disadvantages Of Square Foot Gardening

Despite its advantages, Square Foot Gardening does have some drawbacks.

- One of the main challenges is the need for careful planning and organization. Each square foot must be planned out according to what plants will be grown, and considerations must be made for crop rotation and companion planting.

- Another disadvantage is that this method can require a significant initial investment of time and resources to set up the garden, especially if using raised beds or containers. The beds or containers must be filled with a nutrient-rich soil mix, and a grid must be created to divide the garden into square-foot sections.
- In container gardening, Square Foot Gardening can be challenging due to the limited amount of soil available for roots to spread out.
- In raised bed gardening, the close spacing of plants can sometimes lead to competition for nutrients and water, although this can be mitigated by careful planning and management.

In summary, square-foot gardening is a method that optimizes space and can generate a significant quantity of produce, though it demands thorough planning and oversight. By comprehending the pros and cons of this technique, gardeners can make a knowledgeable determination about whether it suits their specific needs and circumstances.

Vertical Gardening

Vertical gardening is a method of growing plants upwards instead of outwards. It's a technique often used in urban areas where horizontal space is limited. This type of gardening involves using various structures, such as trellises, stakes, cages, or walls, to provide support for plants to grow vertically[2]. Vertical gardening can be applied to both container gardening and raised bed gardening, as long as the appropriate supporting structures are used.

In container gardening, vertical gardening might involve stacking containers on top of each other or using hanging baskets. In raised bed gardening, vertical structures like trellises or stakes are often added to the bed to allow plants to climb.

Benefits Of Vertical Gardening

- One of the main benefits of vertical gardening is the efficient use of space. By growing plants upwards, you can fit more plants into a smaller area. This is particularly beneficial in urban environments, where horizontal space is often limited.
- Vertical gardening can also improve plant health. By lifting plants off the ground, it reduces their exposure to pests and diseases. Moreover, it can improve air circulation around the plants, which can help prevent fungal diseases.
- Additionally, vertical gardening can make the gardening process easier and more accessible. It eliminates the need for bending over to tend to plants, making it a good option for those with mobility issues.
- Harvesting is also often easier with vertical gardening, as fruits and vegetables are more visible and within reach.

Disadvantages Of Vertical Gardening

Despite its many benefits, vertical gardening does have some drawbacks.

- One of the main challenges is providing adequate support for the plants. Large or heavy plants will require sturdy supports, which can be difficult to install and maintain.
- Watering can be another challenge, especially in container vertical gardens. Water tends to flow downwards, so the top containers might get dry while the bottom ones become waterlogged.

- In raised bed gardening, vertical structures can cast shadows on the rest of the garden, potentially affecting the growth of sun-loving plants. Careful planning is required to ensure all plants receive adequate sunlight.

To sum it up, vertical gardening is an efficient technique that provides numerous advantages, such as enhanced plant health and simplified upkeep. Nonetheless, it comes with its own set of challenges related to providing adequate support, ensuring proper watering, and managing light exposure. Those contemplating the use of vertical gardening should consider these strengths and weaknesses to ascertain whether this approach aligns well with their unique needs and situations.

Interplanting Or Intercropping

Interplanting, also known as intercropping, is a gardening strategy that involves planting different crops in close proximity to each other. The core idea is that the different plants can benefit each other by maximizing the use of resources such as sunlight, water, and nutrients. For instance, tall plants can provide shade for shorter, shade-loving plants, while root vegetables can be grown alongside leafy greens that utilize more surface space. Interplanting can be done in both container gardening and raised bed gardening.

In container gardening, interplanting might involve planting a tall plant in the center of the container, surrounded by shorter plants. In raised bed gardening, plants can be intermixed throughout the bed, or planted in rows or blocks where they can complement each other.

Benefits Of Interplanting

- One of the main advantages of interplanting is that it can increase yield from a given space. By growing multiple types of plants in the same area, gardeners can make the most of their available space. This is especially beneficial in small gardens or urban environments where space is limited.

- Interplanting can also improve plant health. Different plants have different nutrient needs, so they can effectively share the available nutrients in the soil without competing with each other.
- Additionally, certain plant combinations can deter pests or attract beneficial insects, reducing the need for chemical pesticides.
- Interplanting can enhance the aesthetic appeal of a garden. By mixing different types of plants, gardeners can create a more varied and visually interesting landscape.

Disadvantages Of Interplanting

- One key issue is managing different watering and nutritional needs. Some plants require more water or specific nutrients than others, which can make it difficult to meet all plants' needs when they are grown together.
- Interplanting can also make maintenance more challenging. It can be harder to manage weeds or harvest crops when different types of plants are mixed together.
- In terms of container gardening, interplanting can lead to overcrowding if not carefully planned and managed. Overcrowded plants may compete for light, water, and nutrients, which can impact their overall health and yield.

While interplanting can offer benefits in terms of increased yield, improved plant health, and aesthetic appeal, it also presents challenges related to watering, nutrition management, and maintenance. Gardeners considering this method should carefully plan and monitor their garden to ensure all plants' needs are met.

Succession Planting

Succession planting is a strategic gardening method that involves planting crops in a sequential manner so that as soon as one crop is harvested, another can be planted in its place. This practice ensures a continuous harvest throughout the growing season. Succession planting can be applied in different types of gardens, including container and raised bed gardening.

In container gardening, succession planting might involve growing cool-season crops like lettuce or radishes early in the spring and then replacing them with warm-season crops like tomatoes or peppers once the weather warms up.

In raised bed gardening, gardeners can take advantage of the larger space to plan a more complex succession planting schedule, alternating between different types of crops throughout the season.

Benefits Of Succession Planting

- The most apparent benefit of succession planting is that it maximizes the productivity of a garden. By continuously planting crops, gardeners can make the most of their available space and extend the harvest period. This is particularly beneficial in smaller gardens or urban environments, where space may be at a premium.
- Additionally, succession planting can help maintain soil health. Different crops have different nutrient needs and can help balance the soil's nutrient levels over time. For example, legumes can fix nitrogen in the soil, providing a natural fertilizer for subsequent crops.

- Succession planting can help manage pests and diseases. By regularly changing the types of crops grown in a particular area, gardeners can disrupt the life cycles of certain pests and diseases, reducing their impact on the garden.

Disadvantages Of Succession Planting

- One of the main difficulties is the need for careful planning and organization. Gardeners must consider the growing conditions and life cycles of different crops to ensure a successful succession planting schedule.
- Another challenge is the increased labor and maintenance required. Succession planting often involves more frequent planting, weeding, and harvesting, which can be time-consuming.
- For container gardeners, there's the added challenge of ensuring the container's soil remains fertile and well-drained, as continuous planting can deplete nutrients and lead to compacted soil.

Succession planting is a beneficial strategy that can enhance productivity and soil health while helping manage pests and diseases. However, it requires careful planning and increased labor. Gardeners interested in this method should consider these factors to determine if it's the right fit for their gardening needs.

Companion Planting

Companion planting is a gardening strategy that involves growing different types of plants together based on their complementary characteristics. The idea is that certain plants can benefit each other when grown in close proximity, whether by deterring pests, improving soil health, or providing physical support. This approach can be applied in both container and raised bed gardening.

In container gardening, companion planting might involve growing a tall plant with a shorter one that thrives in the shade, or combining plants that deter each other's pests. In raised bed gardening, companion planting can be incorporated into the overall garden design, with different combinations of plants arranged together based on their mutual benefits.

Benefits Of Companion Planting

- One major advantage of companion planting is its potential to naturally control pests. Certain plant combinations can deter harmful insects or attract beneficial ones, reducing the need for chemical pesticides. For example, marigolds are known to repel several types of pests and are often planted alongside vegetables for this reason.
- Companion planting can also improve soil health. Different plants have different nutrient needs, and by growing them together, they can help balance the soil's nutrient levels. For instance, legumes can fix nitrogen in the soil, benefiting neighboring plants that require this nutrient.
- Additionally, companion planting can increase the biodiversity of a garden, which can enhance its resilience and aesthetic appeal.

Disadvantages Of Companion Planting

- One key challenge is the need for careful planning and knowledge about different plant species. Not all plants make good companions, and some combinations can even be detrimental.
- Another potential disadvantage is the increased complexity of garden maintenance. Managing different

watering and nutritional needs can be more difficult when multiple types of plants are grown together.

- For container gardens, there's the added challenge of limited space. Overcrowding can lead to competition for resources and potentially hinder plant growth.

While companion planting can offer benefits in terms of pest control, soil health, and biodiversity, it also requires careful planning and increased maintenance. Gardeners considering this method should be prepared to invest time in learning about compatible plant species and managing their garden's needs.

Broadcast Sowing

Broadcast sowing is a method of planting seeds by scattering them over a broad area rather than placing them in individual holes or rows. This technique can be used for a variety of plants, including many types of vegetables, flowers, and cover crops. It's a relatively simple and quick method of sowing, but it does require some care to ensure even distribution of seeds. Broadcast sowing can be employed in both container and raised bed gardening.

In container gardening, broadcast sowing might be used for small, fast-growing plants like lettuce or radishes, which can be scattered across the surface of the soil. For raised bed gardening, broadcast sowing can be used to quickly cover a large area with a single type of plant or a mix of compatible species.

Benefits Of Broadcast Sowing

- One of the main benefits of broadcast sowing is its simplicity and speed. Rather than meticulously placing each seed in its own hole or row, gardeners can simply scatter the seeds over the soil. This can save time and effort, especially when planting a large area.

- Broadcast sowing also allows for a denser planting, which can help suppress weeds by reducing the amount of bare soil exposed to sunlight. This can be particularly beneficial in raised bed gardens, where weed control can be a challenge.
- Further, broadcast sowing can create a more natural, less structured look in the garden, which some gardeners might prefer over the orderly lines of row planting.

Disadvantages Of Broadcast Sowing

- One key challenge is ensuring an even distribution of seeds. If seeds are clustered too closely together, they may compete for resources, leading to weaker plants.
- Another potential downside is the difficulty in controlling the depth at which seeds are planted. Some seeds may end up too shallow or too deep, affecting their ability to germinate effectively.
- For container gardens, the issue of space becomes even more critical. Overcrowding can lead to competition for light, water, and nutrients, potentially hindering plant growth.

To sum up, broadcast sowing presents a swift and straightforward planting approach. However, it mandates meticulous management to guarantee uniform seed dispersal and prevent excessive density. Those pondering the use of this method should balance these considerations with their unique gardening requirements and circumstances.

CHAPTER 3

VEGETABLE CONTAINER GARDENING - TOMATOES

T omatoes are a quintessential choice for vegetable container gardening, offering both versatility and a rewarding yield. As sun-loving plants, they thrive in container environments where their exposure to sunlight can be easily controlled. Their vibrant colors, ranging from classic red to yellow, orange, and even purple, add aesthetic appeal to any patio or balcony. Beyond their visual allure, tomatoes grown in containers boast a flavor profile that is often superior to their commercially grown counterparts.

Whether you're an urban gardener with limited space or simply someone seeking the satisfaction of growing your own produce, diving into the world of tomato container gardening can be a delightful and fruitful endeavor. This chapter will provide you with all the necessary knowledge and tips to successfully grow tomatoes in containers, from choosing the right variety and size of container to understanding watering and fertilizing needs.

THE RIGHT SOIL TO GROW TOMATOES IN CONTAINERS

Selecting the right soil for growing tomatoes in container gardens is a crucial step in ensuring a healthy and bountiful harvest. Unlike in-ground gardening, where the plants have access to the earth's natural reservoir of nutrients, container-grown tomatoes rely completely on the medium in which they are planted. Therefore, it's essential to provide them with nutrient-rich, well-draining soil.

Start with a high-quality potting mix as your base. These mixes are typically composed of peat moss, compost or composted bark, and perlite or vermiculite. The peat moss provides a light, fluffy texture that allows roots to grow easily, while the compost offers a rich source of nutrients. Perlite or vermiculite help improve drainage, ensuring that water flows freely and doesn't saturate the roots.

Avoid using garden soil or topsoil in your containers. These types of soil are often too heavy for container use and can lead to poor drainage, which increases the risk of root diseases. Moreover, they may contain weed seeds or disease organisms that could harm your plants.

For tomatoes, consider adding some organic matter to your potting mix. Compost, well-rotted manure, or worm castings can provide additional nutrients and help retain moisture in the soil. Tomatoes are heavy feeders, so they'll benefit from this nutrient boost.

It's also important to maintain the correct pH level in your soil. Tomatoes prefer slightly acidic conditions, with a pH between 6.0 and 6.8. Most potting mixes already come with a pH within this range, but if you're unsure, you can test the soil using a pH testing kit.

Lastly, remember that container-grown plants dry out more quickly than those in the ground. Check the soil moisture regularly, and water thoroughly when the top inch of soil feels dry to the touch. However, avoid overwatering as this can lead to root rot and other problems.

By carefully selecting and preparing your soil, you can create the ideal growing conditions for your container tomatoes, setting the stage for a successful growing season.

HOW TO SOW TOMATOES IN CONTAINERS GARDENS

Correct Season To Sow Tomatoes In Containers Gardens

Tomatoes are warm-weather crops that thrive in the growing season from spring to fall. The correct time to sow tomatoes in vegetable container gardens is after the last frost date of your area, as they are susceptible to frost damage. It's crucial to ensure the soil has warmed up before setting out plants. Tomatoes function best when the temperature is warm and will stop producing flowers and fruit if temperatures soar above 90 degrees, hence the need for a proper balance.

A rule of thumb for selecting containers is to choose ones that can hold at least 5 gallons of soil and measure 20 inches wide or more. Depending on the climate you live in, your tomato crop might thrive differently, but generally, the growing season spans from the beginning of spring through to the end of fall. Remember to fertilize, water, and monitor your tomatoes regularly for optimal results.

Plant Needs & Requirements

Germinating tomato plants from seeds to seedlings correctly is a critical step when growing in vegetable container gardens. The germination process sets the foundation for the plant's overall health, vigor, and productivity. Proper germination ensures that the seedlings develop a strong root system, which is essential for absorbing water and nutrients from the soil. It also promotes vigorous top growth, leading to a robust plant that can support a heavy crop load.

Moreover, healthy seedlings are more resistant to pests and diseases, reducing the likelihood of issues later in the plant's life cycle. Additionally, correct germination allows for better control over the growing conditions, such as light, temperature, and humidity, all of which can significantly impact the quality of the final harvest. Therefore, taking the time to properly germinate your tomato seeds can result in healthier plants, higher yields, and ultimately, a more successful container garden.

Germinating tomato plants from seeds to seedlings is a rewarding process that involves several steps. Firstly, you'll need to select the right kind of tomato seeds. There's a wide variety available, each with different growth habits, fruit types, and disease resistance. Choose one that suits your climate, taste preference, and gardening goals.

Start by filling a seed tray or small pots with a good quality seed compost. Sow the tomato seeds thinly on the surface, about 1/4 inch deep. Cover them lightly with compost or vermiculite, which helps retain moisture and allow light to penetrate, aiding germination. Water the compost well but avoid soaking it.

Next step is to place the tray or pots in a warm spot, ideally at a temperature of around 70-75°F (21-24°C). Tomato seeds require warmth more than light to germinate. You can use a heat mat to maintain consistent soil temperature. Cover the tray or pots with a plastic cover or bag to create a mini greenhouse effect, keeping the environment humid for the seeds.

After approximately 5-14 days, depending on the variety and conditions, the tomato seeds should start to sprout. Once the seedlings have emerged, remove the plastic cover and move them to a bright location but out of direct sunlight.

Ensure that the seedlings receive enough light, ideally 14-16 hours a day. Lack of sufficient light can lead to leggy and weak plants. Regularly check the moisture level of the compost and water when needed to keep it consistently moist but not waterlogged.

When the seedlings have developed their first true leaves (the second set of leaves that appear after the initial seed leaves), they're ready to be transplanted into individual pots. This usually happens when the plant is about 2-3 inches tall. Gently remove the seedling, taking care not to damage the delicate roots, and plant it in a pot filled with fresh compost.

Once the risk of frost has passed and the plants have grown to about 6-8 inches tall, they're ready to be transplanted into larger containers.

Spacing & Measurement

Spacing and measurements when transplanting tomato seedlings into container gardens are vital for several reasons. Firstly, it provides each plant with sufficient space to grow and develop without competition for essential resources such as sunlight, water, and nutrients. Overcrowding can result in stunted growth and a reduced yield as plants compete for these vital necessities.

Secondly, appropriate spacing promotes good air circulation around each plant. This is crucial in preventing the spread of diseases that can devastate your crop. Diseases often thrive in damp, poorly ventilated conditions, so ensuring that air can circulate freely between your plants helps to keep them healthy.

Finally, well-spaced plants have more room to develop a robust root system, which is key to their overall health and productivity. Therefore, taking the time to correctly space your tomato seedlings when you transplant them into container gardens can significantly improve their growth and yield.

When planning to plant tomato seedlings in container gardening, it's crucial to consider the desired spacing and measurements to ensure your plants thrive. Proper spacing is not merely a matter of aesthetics, but a practical consideration that can have a significant impact on the health and productivity of your plants.

The ideal spacing for tomato plants largely depends on the variety you're growing. As a general rule, most tomato plants should be spaced about 24 to 36 inches apart. This allows each plant ample room to grow and develop without competition for essential resources such as sunlight, water, and nutrients.

When plants are too closely spaced, they may compete for these necessities, leading to stunted growth and reduced yield. Moreover, proper spacing promotes good air circulation around each plant, which is critical in preventing the spread of diseases that can decimate your crop. Diseases often thrive in damp, poorly ventilated conditions, so ensuring that air can circulate freely between your plants helps to keep them healthy.

When it comes to container size, it's important to remember that tomatoes are deep-rooted plants that benefit from plenty of space to grow. Generally, a 5-gallon container is the minimum size recommended for a single tomato plant. The larger the container, the more room there is for root development, leading to a stronger, more productive plant.

In terms of depth, tomato seedlings should be planted deep in the soil. This encourages the formation of additional roots along the buried portion of the stem, resulting in a stronger, more stable plant. When planting your seedlings, dig a hole deep enough so that two-thirds of the plant is buried in the soil.

When planting tomato seedlings in containers, taking into account the desired spacing and measurements is crucial. By giving each plant sufficient space, choosing an appropriately sized container, and planting your seedlings deep in the soil, you can create an optimal environment for your tomatoes to thrive and produce a bountiful harvest.

Ideal Temperatures & Sun Requirements

The ideal temperatures and sun requirements are vital for successful tomato cultivation in container gardens. Tomatoes are warm-season plants that prefer daytime temperatures between 65°F and 85°F (18°C - 29°C) and nighttime temperatures that don't dip below 55°F (13°C). They can tolerate higher temperatures up to 95°F (35°C), but beyond this, the plants may experience stress and their blossoms might drop off, leading to reduced fruit set. If temperatures fall below 50°F (10°C), growth can be stunted and fruit production can slow down or stop.

Sunlight is another crucial factor for tomatoes. These plants require a minimum of six to eight hours of direct sunlight each day. This ample sun exposure is essential for photosynthesis, the process by which plants convert sunlight into the energy they need for growth. Lack of sufficient sunlight can lead to leggy plants, delayed ripening, and lower yields.

In a container garden, you have the advantage of mobility. You can move your plants around to ensure they get the necessary sun exposure. However, during the hottest part of the day, especially in summer, providing some shade can prevent the plants from overheating and the soil from drying out too quickly.

Remember, meeting these ideal temperature and sun requirements will help ensure that your tomato plants are healthy and productive, providing you with a bountiful harvest.

MAINTAINING YOUR CONTAINER GROWN TOMATO'S

Maintaining your container-grown tomatoes is pivotal in vegetable container gardening for several reasons. First, consistent maintenance ensures that your plants are growing in optimal conditions, which directly affects their health and productivity. Regular watering, for example, is crucial as container plants can dry out quickly, especially in hot weather. However, overwatering can lead to problems like root rot, so monitoring soil moisture is key.

Similarly, regular feeding with a balanced tomato fertilizer can help provide the necessary nutrients that may be lacking in the potting mix. Pruning, or removing unnecessary growth, can help direct the plant's energy towards producing larger, healthier fruits instead of excessive foliage. Additionally, maintenance activities like staking or caging help support the plant as it grows and prevent it from toppling over under the weight of the fruit. Regularly checking for pests and diseases allows for early detection and control, preventing potential devastation of your entire crop. Hence, maintaining your container-grown tomatoes not only enhances their health and yield but also extends their lifespan, ensuring a prolonged harvest period.

Pruning & Thinning Your Tomatoes

Pruning and thinning container-grown tomatoes in vegetable container gardening are essential practices that contribute significantly to the overall health and productivity of your plants. These procedures are not just about maintaining a neat appearance; they have direct benefits for the growth, yield, and disease prevention of your tomato plants.

Pruning involves removing unnecessary leaves and stems, particularly those at the bottom of the plant that do not receive much sunlight. This practice helps direct the plant's energy towards producing larger and more flavorful fruits rather than excessive foliage.

Moreover, pruning improves air circulation within the plant, which is crucial in preventing fungal diseases that thrive in damp, poorly ventilated conditions. It also allows more light to penetrate deeper into the plant, benefiting the photosynthesis process and promoting better fruit development.

Thinning, on the other hand, refers to the removal of some fruits, particularly when they are still small. This may seem counterproductive when the goal is to maximize yield, but thinning actually has long-term benefits. When a tomato plant has too many fruits, it may not have enough resources to fully develop all of them, resulting in a multitude of small, subpar tomatoes.

By thinning out the fruits, you allow the plant to focus its energy on the remaining ones, leading to larger, tastier tomatoes. Thinning also reduces the weight burden on the branches, preventing them from breaking.

Pruning typically begins once your tomato plants have grown tall enough that they have several branches or 'suckers'. These are the small shoots that appear in the joint where a branch meets the stem. Left unchecked, these suckers will grow into full branches, diverting the plant's energy away from fruit production.

To prune, simply pinch off these suckers when they're small, using your fingers or a pair of clean, sharp scissors. Pruning is generally best done in the morning when plants are less stressed, and it's important to avoid pruning on overly humid or wet days as this can expose the plants to fungal diseases.

In addition to removing suckers, you'll also want to remove any leaves that touch the soil to prevent soil-borne diseases from splashing onto the plant. You may also choose to remove some of the lower branches to improve air circulation around the base of the plant. However, remember not to over-prune, as leaves are necessary for photosynthesis and too much pruning can stress the plant.

Thinning, on the other hand, involves removing some of the fruits from your tomato plant. This is particularly important for larger tomato varieties that produce heavy fruits. When your plant has set its first fruits, assess the number and size of them. If there are too many or they are growing large, select the smallest or least developed fruits and remove them by cutting the stem above the fruit with a pair of sharp, clean scissors.

Thinning should be done carefully and thoughtfully, as removing too many fruits can lead to fewer tomatoes, even if they are larger. A good rule of thumb is to leave enough space so that each remaining tomato has enough room to grow without touching its neighbors. This not only allows the remaining fruits to receive more nutrients for growth but also helps prevent the spread of diseases that can occur when fruits are touching and moisture is trapped between them.

Both pruning and thinning are integral parts of maintaining container-grown tomatoes in vegetable container gardening. These practices not only enhance the quality of the fruits but also contribute to the overall health and longevity of the plants. They are worthwhile efforts that can significantly improve your gardening success.

Watering Your Container Grown Tomatoes

Watering is a fundamental aspect of maintaining healthy container-grown tomatoes in vegetable container gardens. Unlike in-ground plants, which can spread their roots deep into the soil to access water, container-grown tomatoes rely solely on the moisture available within the confined space of the pot. This makes them more susceptible to both overwatering and under-watering. Adequate watering is crucial for several reasons.

Firstly, water is essential for the plant's physiological processes, including photosynthesis and nutrient absorption. Without sufficient water, these processes are hindered, leading to stunted growth, wilting, and potentially death.

Secondly, consistent watering helps prevent Blossom End Rot, a common tomato disease associated with irregular watering and calcium deficiency.

Lastly, water plays a key role in fruit development. Insufficient watering can result in smaller, less juicy fruits, while overwatering can lead to split fruits and increased susceptibility to diseases. Therefore, ensuring your container-grown tomatoes receive the right amount of water at the right time is key to a healthy and productive harvest.

Watering container-grown tomatoes in vegetable container gardens is a delicate balance. Both the amount of water and the timing are crucial to ensure your plants stay healthy and productive.

The amount of water your tomato plants need will largely depend on the size of the plant and the pot, the type of soil used, the local climate, and the particular stage of growth the plant is in. As a general rule, tomatoes prefer deep watering, which encourages the roots to grow deep and strong.

This typically means watering until you see water coming out of the drainage holes at the bottom of the pot. However, it's important not to let your plants sit in water, as this can lead to root rot. Always ensure that excess water can drain away easily.

In terms of frequency, a common guide is to water your container-grown tomatoes whenever the top inch of soil feels dry to the touch. In hot weather, this may mean watering daily or even twice a day, while in cooler or cloudy weather, watering may be needed only every two to three days. It's also worth noting that smaller pots will dry out faster than larger ones and will therefore require more frequent watering.

When watering, aim to do so early in the morning. This gives the plants plenty of moisture to get through the heat of the day and allows any excess water on the leaves to evaporate before nightfall, reducing the risk of fungal diseases. Avoid watering in the evening, as this can leave the plants damp overnight, creating ideal conditions for disease development.

It's also important to water your tomatoes at the base of the plant rather than from above. Wet leaves can lead to the spread of diseases, and direct sunlight can cause spots of sunburn on wet foliage. By watering at the base, you ensure that the water goes straight to the roots where it's needed most, while keeping the foliage dry.

While there's no one-size-fits-all answer to how much and when to water container-grown tomatoes, these guidelines provide a good starting point. Always observe your plants closely for signs of overwatering or underwatering, such as yellowing leaves or wilting, and adjust your watering practices accordingly.

Organic Fertilization For Container Grown Tomatoes

Organic fertilization plays a vital role in the health and productivity of container-grown tomatoes in vegetable container gardens. Unlike in-ground plants that have access to a vast range of nutrients from the soil, container-grown tomatoes are limited to the nutrients provided in their confined environment.

Organic fertilizers, made from natural materials like compost, bone meal, or seaweed, provide a wide spectrum of essential nutrients that tomatoes need to grow strong and bear fruit. These nutrients are released gradually into the soil, ensuring a steady supply for the plants. This slow-release characteristic of organic fertilizers also reduces the risk of nutrient burn that can occur with synthetic fertilizers.

Additionally, organic fertilizers contribute to the overall health of the soil by improving its structure, enhancing moisture retention, and promoting beneficial microbial activity. This creates a healthier root environment, leading to more robust tomato plants. Moreover, using organic fertilizers aligns with sustainable gardening practices, reducing the chemical load on the environment. Therefore, organic fertilization is not just crucial for the immediate growth of your tomatoes but also contributes to long-term soil health and environmental sustainability.

Choosing the right organic fertilizer for your container-grown tomatoes in vegetable container gardens can make a significant difference to their health and productivity. There are several types of organic fertilizers that can be beneficial for tomatoes.

Compost is one of the most commonly used organic fertilizers. It's rich in nutrients, improves soil structure, and enhances its ability to hold water and air. You can add compost to the potting mix when planting and top up throughout the growing season. Worm castings, another excellent organic fertilizer, are full of beneficial microbes and nutrients. They can be mixed into the potting soil or used as a top dressing.

Bone meal is high in phosphorus, which is essential for healthy root development and fruiting. It's a slow-release fertilizer, meaning it provides nutrients over an extended period. It can be mixed into the potting soil at planting time. Similarly, blood meal is high in nitrogen, promoting lush, green growth. It can be used in moderation at the start of the growing season to encourage leafy growth.

Seaweed extracts or kelp meal are also great organic fertilizers for tomatoes. They contain trace minerals and growth-promoting substances that help boost the overall vitality of the plants. They can be used as a foliar spray or added to the watering can every few weeks during the growing season.

When it comes to applying these fertilizers, timing is crucial. At the beginning of the growing season, when the plants are focusing on developing foliage, a higher nitrogen content can be beneficial. As the plants start to flower and set fruit, however they need more phosphorus and potassium, so switching to a fertilizer with higher amounts of these nutrients can be beneficial.

Always remember to water thoroughly after applying any fertilizer to ensure it's well distributed in the soil and readily available to the plant roots. Also, it's important not to over-fertilize, as this can lead to nutrient burn or excessive leafy growth at the expense of fruit production. It's better to apply small amounts of fertilizer regularly rather than a large amount all at once.

Using organic fertilizers for container-grown tomatoes can enhance the health and productivity of your plants while also contributing to environmental sustainability. The key is to choose the right type of fertilizer, apply it at the right time, and in the correct quantities.

PROTECTING YOUR CONTAINER GROWN TOMATOES

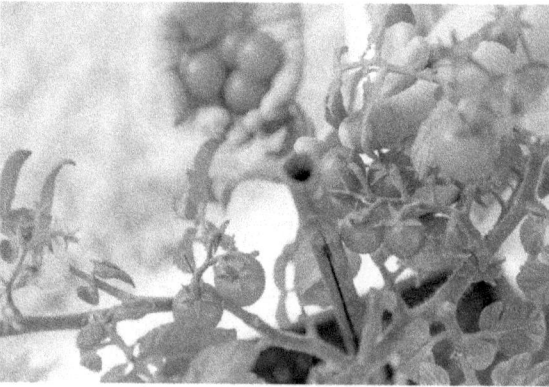

Extreme Temperatures

Protecting container-grown tomatoes from extreme temperatures in vegetable container gardens is crucial for their health and productivity. Tomatoes are warm-season crops that thrive in temperatures between 55°F and 85°F. Exposure to temperature extremes, either too hot or too cold, can stress the plants, impede their growth, affect fruit set, and even cause them to die. There-fore, implementing strategies to shield your tomatoes from harsh temperatures is imperative.

During periods of excessive heat, tomato plants can wilt, blos-soms may drop off, and fruits can get sunscald. One way to protect tomatoes from extreme heat is by providing shade. This can be achieved by using shade cloth, an umbrella, or by placing the containers in a location that receives some afternoon shade. Watering is also vital during hot weather. Container plants dry out more quickly than those in the ground, so check the soil moisture daily and water thoroughly as needed. However, avoid watering in the heat of the day to prevent evaporation.

On the other hand, cold temperatures can be just as damaging. If the temperature drops below 50°F, tomato plants can exhibit signs of stress, and frost can kill them. To protect your container tomatoes from chilly temperatures, consider moving the containers indoors or into a greenhouse at night when frost is forecasted. If moving the containers isn't feasible, you can cover them with frost blankets or cloches to trap heat.

Another strategy is to use dark-colored containers for growing your tomatoes. These will absorb heat during the day and release it slowly at night, providing some protection against temperature drops. Using a layer of mulch on the soil surface can also help regulate soil temperature and retain moisture, benefiting the plants in both hot and cold conditions.

Safeguarding your container-grown tomatoes from extreme temperatures is not only crucial for their survival but also for ensuring a good harvest. By monitoring weather forecasts and being proactive about applying protective measures, you can help your tomatoes navigate through periods of temperature extremes and continue to thrive.

Protecting Container Grown Tomatoes From Pests

Protecting container-grown tomatoes from pests in vegetable container gardens is of paramount importance to ensure a healthy and productive crop. Pests, such as aphids, whiteflies, and hornworms, can cause significant damage, stunting growth, spreading disease, and even killing plants if left unchecked.

They can rapidly multiply and infest the entire garden, posing a threat not only to your tomato plants but also to other vegetables growing nearby.

Furthermore, the confined environment of a container can intensify pest problems, as it provides an easy pathway for pests to spread from one plant to another. Pest damage can also negatively affect the quality of the fruits, making them unappealing or unsuitable for consumption. Implementing effective pest management strategies is thus essential to maintaining the health and vitality of your container-grown tomatoes, maximizing their yield, and ensuring you enjoy a bountiful harvest.

Container-grown tomatoes can be susceptible to various pests, including aphids, whiteflies, spider mites, and tomato hornworms. Aphids are small, soft-bodied insects that suck the sap from tomato plants, weakening them and potentially spreading diseases. Whiteflies, similar to aphids, feed on plant sap and can cause yellowing or wilting of leaves. Spider mites are tiny pests that also feed on plant sap, causing stippling or bronzing of the leaves. Tomato hornworms are large caterpillars that can cause significant defoliation and fruit damage.

Protecting container-grown tomatoes from these pests involves several critical steps. The first is prevention, which begins with selecting disease-resistant tomato varieties when available. These varieties have been bred to resist common pests and diseases, providing an excellent initial defense.

Proper plant care is another essential preventative measure. Healthy plants are generally less attractive to pests. This includes giving your tomatoes the appropriate amount of water, sunlight, and nutrients. Overwatering or underwatering, as well as nutrient imbalances, can weaken your plants and make them more prone to pest infestations. Additionally, overcrowding can create a humid environment that many pests find appealing, so ensure you provide adequate spacing between your containers for good air circulation.

Regularly inspecting your plants is crucial for early detection of pests. Look for signs such as leaf damage, discoloration, or the presence of the pests themselves. Check the undersides of leaves, where many pests prefer to hide. If you spot pests early, you can often manually remove them before they become a significant problem.

If you discover a substantial pest infestation, there are various control methods you can use. One option is biological control, which involves introducing beneficial insects that prey on the pests. For example, ladybugs and lacewings are natural predators of aphids.

Another control method is the use of organic pesticides. These are made from naturally occurring substances and are generally less harmful to the environment and non-target organisms than synthetic pesticides. Neem oil is a popular organic pesticide effective against a wide range of pests.

Remember, even with the best preventative measures and control strategies, it's nearly impossible to completely avoid pests in your garden. However, by regularly monitoring your plants and responding quickly at the first sign of trouble, you can keep pest populations manageable and ensure a successful harvest from your container-grown tomatoes.

Protecting Container Grown Tomatoes From Diseases

Protecting container-grown tomatoes from diseases in vegetable container gardens is of utmost importance for maintaining the health and productivity of your plants. Diseases can rapidly spread and cause significant damage, often resulting in a reduced yield or even total loss of the crop. Certain diseases, such as blight or fusarium wilt, can cause wilting, yellowing, or browning of the leaves, stunted growth, and rotting of the fruit.

Moreover, once a disease has taken hold, it can be incredibly difficult to control or eradicate. Many pathogens can survive in the soil or plant debris between growing seasons, causing recurring problems.

By taking steps to prevent and control diseases, you not only ensure the health and vitality of your individual tomato plants but also help maintain the overall health of your garden ecosystem, preventing the spread of diseases to other plants.

Container-grown tomatoes can be vulnerable to a variety of diseases, many of which can significantly impact the plant's health and productivity. Some of the most common diseases include Late Blight, Verticillium Wilt, Early Blight, and Septoria Leaf Spot. Late Blight, caused by the water mold pathogen Phytophthora infestans, can be particularly devastating, affecting both the leaves and fruit of the tomato plant.

Verticillium Wilt is another common disease, caused by a fungus that thrives in warm, wet conditions. Early Blight, caused by the fungus Alternaria, results in brown or black spots on the lower leaves. Septoria Leaf Spot is another common disease in humid conditions, causing spots on the leaves.

Organic methods of protecting your container-grown tomatoes from these diseases primarily involve prevention and early detection. One of the main advantages of container gardening is that it reduces the risk of soil-borne diseases. However, it's still important to ensure that the containers and tools you use are clean, as diseases can be spread by contaminated tools or pots.

Choosing disease-resistant tomato varieties can also be an effective preventative measure. Many modern tomato varieties have been bred for resistance to common diseases like blight and wilt. It's also crucial to provide your plants with the right growing conditions — adequate sunlight, water, and nutrients — as healthy plants are less susceptible to diseases.

For fungal diseases like blight and wilt, applying organic fungicides can be an effective control measure. These can be made from ingredients like copper or sulfur, which are toxic to fungi but generally safe for humans and the environment. For bacterial diseases, spraying the plants with a diluted solution of hydrogen peroxide can help kill the bacteria without harming the plant.

Crop rotation - changing the location of your tomato plants each year - can also help prevent the build-up of diseases in the soil. Even in a container garden, switching out the soil each year can be beneficial.

Protecting your container-grown tomatoes from diseases involves a combination of good cultural practices and organic disease control methods. With careful monitoring and proactive management, you can keep your tomatoes healthy and productive.

HARVESTING CONTAINER GROWN TOMATOES

The timeline for growing and harvesting container-grown tomatoes can vary widely depending on the variety of tomato you choose to grow. Generally speaking, most tomato plants will take between 60 to 80 days from transplanting to start producing mature fruit. Smaller, determinate varieties, also known as bush tomatoes, often mature faster than larger, indeterminate varieties, or vining tomatoes.

When you plant your tomato seedlings in the container, check the seed packet or plant tag for the expected days to maturity. This will give you an estimate of when you can expect to start harvesting tomatoes. Keep in mind, however, that these estimates are just that – estimates. The actual time to maturity can be influenced by a variety of factors, including the growing conditions and the care the plants receive.

Harvesting tomatoes properly is crucial to maintaining the health of the plant and ensuring a continuous yield. Tomatoes should be harvested when they are fully colored and slightly soft to the touch. For example, red tomatoes should be harvested when they are fully red. However, don't wait too long to harvest ripe tomatoes, as overripe tomatoes can attract pests and diseases.

To harvest a tomato, hold the fruit firmly but gently and twist it until it snaps off from the stem. Alternatively, you can use a pair of gardening shears to cut the stem above the fruit. Avoid tugging or pulling the fruit, as this can damage the plant. After harvesting, handle the tomatoes gently to avoid bruising them, and use or store them as soon as possible for the best flavor.

Remember, regular harvesting encourages more production. If you leave ripe tomatoes on the vine, the plant receives a signal that its job is done for the season and it doesn't need to produce more. By picking the ripe tomatoes, you're encouraging the plant to continue producing fruit for as long as the growing season allows.

Growing and harvesting container-grown tomatoes can be a rewarding endeavor. With the proper care and attention, you can enjoy fresh, homegrown tomatoes straight from your container garden.

CONTAINER GROWN TOMATO NOTES

Start: Seeds or Seedlings

Germination: 5-14 days, 70-75°F (21-24°C)

Seed Life: 3 Years

Soil Type: High-quality potting mix with some organic matter - pH between 6.0 and 6.8

Seed Spacing: 1/4 inch deep (in potting pots)

Seedling Spacing: 24 to 36 inches apart (in permanent growing containers)

Sunlight: 6 – 8hrs full sunlight daily

Growing Temperatures: Daytime temperatures between 65°F and 85°F (18°C - 29°C) and nighttime temperatures no lower than 55°F (13°C)

Days To Harvest: 60 to 80 days

CHAPTER 4
VEGETABLE CONTAINER GARDENING – PEPPERS

P eppers, with their vibrant colors and diverse flavors, are a fantastic addition to any vegetable container garden. These versatile plants not only add a visual appeal to your patio or balcony but also offer a bounty of home-grown produce that can spice up your culinary endeavors. Whether you're a fan of the sweet bell pepper or prefer the fiery kick of jalapenos, growing peppers in containers is a rewarding experience. This method allows for better control over the growing conditions, making it suitable even for those with limited garden space. With some understanding of their basic needs and a little care, you can enjoy a plentiful harvest of fresh, tasty peppers right from your own container garden.

Incorporating peppers into your vegetable container garden can bring a multitude of benefits. Firstly, peppers are compact plants that adapt well to the confines of a container, making them an ideal choice for those with limited gardening space. Secondly, growing peppers in containers allows for greater control over their growing conditions. You can easily adjust the soil type, watering schedule, and sunlight exposure to suit the specific needs of your pepper plants.

This control can result in healthier plants and a more abundant harvest. Moreover, container gardening can reduce the risk of soil-borne diseases and pest infestations, as it provides a barrier between the plant and the ground. In addition to these practical benefits, peppers also add a vibrant splash of color to your garden. Their varied hues can enhance the visual appeal of your garden, making it not just a source of fresh produce, but also a delightful space to relax and enjoy.

THE RIGHT SOIL TO GROW PEPPERS IN CONTAINERS

When it comes to growing peppers in container gardens, choosing the right soil conditions is crucial for a successful harvest. Peppers prefer well-drained, nutrient-rich soil with a pH level between 6.0 and 6.5. This slightly acidic environment promotes optimal nutrient absorption and encourages healthy plant growth.

Starting with a high-quality potting mix is a good first step. These mixes are typically composed of ingredients like peat moss, compost, perlite, and vermiculite, all of which contribute to creating a well-draining and fertile environment. It's important to avoid garden soil or topsoil as they can compact in containers, leading to poor drainage and root health.

Adding organic matter like compost or well-rotted manure can further enrich the soil. These additions improve the soil's structure, increase its nutrient content, and enhance its moisture retention capabilities. They also introduce beneficial microbes that aid in nutrient breakdown, making it easier for the pepper plants to access essential nutrients.

If you're aiming for a bountiful pepper harvest, consider incorporating a slow-release fertilizer into the soil at planting time. This will provide a steady supply of nutrients throughout the growing season. Alternatively, you can use a water-soluble fertilizer every few weeks. Just remember, peppers are sensitive to over-fertilization, so it's important to follow the manufacturer's instructions carefully.

Lastly, regular monitoring of the soil's pH level is essential. If the soil becomes too acidic or alkaline, it can hinder nutrient uptake, leading to stunted growth or potential disease issues. You can easily test the pH level using a home testing kit and adjust it as needed with lime (to raise pH) or sulfur (to lower pH).

By creating the right soil conditions, you not only set the stage for your pepper plants to thrive but also maximize their yield potential, ensuring a plentiful and satisfying harvest from your container garden.

HOW TO SOW PEPPERS IN CONTAINERS GARDENS

Correct Season To Sow Peppers In Containers Gardens

Pepper plants require a specific planting season to ensure optimal growth and productivity in vegetable container gardens.

Pepper seeds should be started indoors to get a head start on the growing season. The seeds need to be sown in flats or pots 8 to 10 weeks prior to the expected outdoor planting date. This early start allows the pepper plants to mature and produce fruit within the growing season. Peppers require a long growing season and at least 6-8 hours of sunlight per day, hence starting them indoors ensures they have ample time to develop before being moved outside.

Once the risk of frost has passed and the soil temperatures have consistently reached 60-70 degrees Fahrenheit, the young plants can be transplanted outdoors in a sunny, well-drained spot. Therefore, depending on your local climate, the indoor sowing could take place anywhere from late winter to early spring. Remember to space them 18 to 24 inches apart when planting in the garden or in larger containers to ensure each plant has enough room to grow.

Plant Needs & Requirements

Germinating peppers from seeds to seedlings correctly is a crucial step when growing in vegetable container gardens. The germination process determines the early vigor and health of the plant, which in turn affects its overall growth and yield potential. When seeds are properly germinated, they will sprout into strong, healthy seedlings that can withstand the many challenges they might face as they grow, such as pest attacks, weather changes, and nutrient deficiency.

Furthermore, proper germination ensures the optimum use of seeds, reducing waste and saving resources. It also allows gardeners to select the best seedlings for transplanting into containers, ensuring that only the fittest and most robust plants are chosen. This ensures a higher chance of survival and productivity. These seedlings, having been nurtured from the beginning, are better equipped to handle the transition from indoor germination to outdoor growth and ultimately to yield a bountiful harvest. Therefore, correct germination is a vital foundation for successful pepper cultivation in vegetable container gardens.

Germinating pepper vegetable plants from seeds to seedlings involves several key steps. Initially, you should select a quality seed-starting mix, which is typically lighter and more sterile than regular potting soil, creating an ideal environment for the seeds to sprout. Fill your chosen containers or flats with this mix, then plant the pepper seeds about 1/4 inch deep.

After planting, cover the containers with a plastic wrap or a dome to maintain high humidity, which is necessary for pepper seed germination. Then, place the containers in a warm area. Pepper seeds require a constant temperature of 70-85 degrees Fahrenheit (21-29 degrees Celsius) to germinate properly. This warmth can be provided by a heat mat placed under the containers if your home is not naturally within this temperature range.

Watering is also crucial during this stage. The soil should be kept consistently moist but not waterlogged. Overwatering can lead to fungal diseases, which can kill the seedlings. Using a spray bottle to lightly mist the soil surface can help maintain proper moisture levels.

Once the seeds have been planted and cared for correctly, you should see sprouts within 7 to 14 days. However, some pepper varieties might take longer, so patience is key.

As the seedlings grow, they'll develop their first pair of leaves known as cotyledons, followed by their true leaves. When the seedlings have at least two sets of true leaves, they are ready to be transplanted into larger containers. This usually happens 6-8 weeks after sowing.

Transplanting should be done carefully to avoid damaging the young roots. Make sure the new containers have good drainage and are filled with a high-quality potting mix. After transplanting, place the containers in a sunny location, and continue to water and care for the plants as they grow.

Remember, every type of pepper may have slightly different requirements, so it's important to research the specific needs of your chosen variety. But with patience and care, you'll be able to successfully germinate peppers from seeds to thriving seedlings, ready for a productive life in your vegetable container garden.

Spacing & Measurement

Proper spacing and measurements when transplanting pepper seedlings into container gardens are of paramount importance for several reasons. Firstly, each pepper plant requires sufficient room to grow and spread its roots. Crowded plants can compete for essential resources such as sunlight, water, and nutrients, which can hinder their growth and productivity. Secondly, proper spacing promotes good air circulation, which is crucial in preventing the spread of diseases and pests.

Diseases often thrive in humid, stagnant conditions, so having enough space between plants can help keep them healthy. Furthermore, adequate spacing makes it easier to maintain your plants. It provides enough room for watering, pruning, and harvesting without damaging other plants. Lastly, well-spaced plants result in a more aesthetically pleasing garden. Therefore, ensuring the right measurements and spacing when transplanting your pepper seedlings can greatly contribute to their overall health, growth, and yield.

The desired spacing and measurements when planting pepper seedlings in container gardening are dependent on a few key factors such as the size of the container, the variety of the pepper, and its growth habit.

Firstly, the container's size plays a significant role in determining the appropriate spacing for your pepper plants. As a general rule, each pepper plant should be planted in a container that is at least 12 inches in diameter and 18 to 24 inches deep. This provides ample room for the plant's root system to expand and absorb nutrients efficiently. A larger pot also retains more moisture, reducing the frequency of watering and providing a more stable environment for the plant.

Regarding the number of plants per container, it's typically best to plant one pepper plant per pot. However, if you're using a particularly large container (like a half-barrel or a container with a diameter of 18 inches or more), you could potentially plant two pepper plants, but they should be spaced at least 18 to 24 inches apart to avoid competition for resources.

Secondly, the variety of the pepper plant can affect the spacing requirements. Different varieties of peppers can have different growth habits - some may grow taller and narrower, while others may be shorter and bushier. It's important to research the specific variety you're growing to understand its growth pattern and size at maturity. This will help you gauge the right spacing and avoid overcrowding.

Lastly, consider the growth habit of the pepper plant. Indeterminate varieties, which continue to grow and produce fruit until killed by frost, tend to get quite large and may need more space. Determinate varieties, which grow to a certain size and then stop, are generally smaller and can be successfully grown closer together.

The desired spacing and measurements when planting pepper seedlings in container gardening largely depend on the container's size and the specific characteristics of the pepper variety. By providing adequate space for each plant, you can ensure healthier growth and a more bountiful harvest.

Ideal Temperatures & Sun Requirements

Ideal temperatures and sun requirements play a significant role in the successful growth of pepper plants in container gardens.

Peppers are warm-season crops, and they thrive in temperatures between 70 to 85 degrees Fahrenheit (21-29 degrees Celsius). At these temperatures, peppers can effectively photosynthesize and produce fruit. Anything below 60 degrees Fahrenheit (15 degrees Celsius) can slow down their growth and anything above 90 degrees Fahrenheit (32 degrees Celsius) can cause the plants to drop their blossoms, leading to reduced yield.

In terms of sunlight, peppers require plenty of it for optimal growth. Ideally, they need at least 6 to 8 hours of full sun each day. Sunlight is crucial for photosynthesis, the process by which plants convert light energy into chemical energy for growth. Lack of sufficient sunlight can lead to weak, leggy plants and poor fruit production.

However, in very hot climates, peppers might benefit from some afternoon shade to prevent them from overheating or getting sunscald. When growing peppers in containers, it's convenient because you can move the containers around to ensure they get the right amount of sun exposure.

By maintaining the ideal temperatures and meeting the sun requirements, you can ensure your peppers grow strong and produce a bountiful harvest. It's important to keep in mind that these are general guidelines, and specific needs may vary based on the variety of pepper you're growing.

MAINTAINING YOUR CONTAINER GROWN PEPPER GARDEN

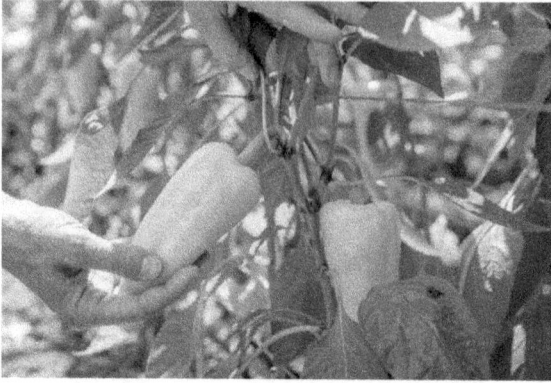

Maintaining your container-grown peppers is critically important in vegetable container gardening for several reasons. First, container plants are entirely dependent on the care they receive, as they cannot draw nutrients or water from the surrounding environment like in-ground plants can. Regular feeding and watering are crucial to ensure that the plants have all the nutrients they need for healthy growth.

Second, pests and diseases can swiftly affect container plants, so regular inspection and timely intervention can prevent minor issues from becoming major problems. Furthermore, because the root system of container plants is confined, they are more susceptible to becoming root-bound or suffering from temperature fluctuations. Regular maintenance, such as repotting when necessary and moving containers to more favorable conditions, can mitigate these issues.

Lastly, proper maintenance also includes pruning and staking as needed to support the plants' growth and productivity. In essence, regular and attentive maintenance is key to ensuring that your container-grown peppers thrive and yield a bountiful harvest.

Pruning & Thinning Your Pepper

Pruning and thinning container-grown peppers in vegetable container gardens are essential practices that significantly impact the health and productivity of your plants. Pruning involves removing specific parts of the plant, like some leaves or branches, to improve the plant's overall shape and growth. This practice helps to increase air circulation around the plant, reducing the risk of diseases that thrive in moist, stagnant conditions. It also allows more sunlight to reach the lower parts of the plant, promoting healthier and more balanced growth.

Thinning, on the other hand, involves removing some plants entirely to prevent overcrowding and ensure that each remaining plant has enough space to grow. In container gardening, space is often limited, and plants that are too close together can compete for resources, leading to stunted growth and reduced yields. Thinning ensures that each pepper plant has sufficient access to sunlight, water, and nutrients, allowing it to thrive.

Moreover, both pruning and thinning help to direct more of the plant's energy towards fruit production. By removing unnecessary foliage or competing plants, you allow the pepper plant to focus its resources on developing robust, healthy fruits. This can result in a higher yield and larger, more flavorful peppers.

While it may seem counterproductive to remove parts of your plants or entire plants, pruning and thinning are vital maintenance practices in container gardening. They help to optimize growing conditions, prevent disease, and ultimately enhance the quality and quantity of your harvest.

Pruning and thinning container-grown peppers in vegetable container gardens are essential practices that should ideally begin when the plants are young and continue throughout their growing season.

The exact timing can depend on the specific variety of pepper you're growing and local growing conditions, but generally, you should start to consider pruning and thinning when your plants are about 6-8 inches tall, or once they've developed a few sets of true leaves.

Pruning is best done in the morning when the plants are less stressed, using clean, sharp scissors or pruners to minimize damage to the plant and reduce the risk of disease transmission.

Start by removing any dead or yellowing leaves, as these can drain energy from the plant and potentially harbor diseases. Then, trim back the top of the plant, cutting just above a node where two leaves sprout. This will encourage the plant to grow bushier rather than taller, leading to a sturdier plant with more potential for fruit production.

Thinning, meanwhile, involves removing entire plants to reduce overcrowding. Look at your container and assess whether the plants have enough space to grow without competing for light, water, or nutrients.

A good rule of thumb is to allow at least 2-3 inches of space between each plant, but this can vary depending on the specific variety of pepper. Carefully pull out or cut off at the base any excess plants, focusing on those that look weaker or less healthy. Remember to water the remaining plants well after thinning to reduce stress.

Repeat these processes throughout the growing season as needed. Monitor your plants regularly and step in with pruning or thinning whenever you notice overcrowding, excessive height, or energy being wasted on unnecessary foliage. With these careful maintenance practices, your container-grown peppers will have the space and energy they need to produce a bountiful harvest.

Watering Your Container Grown Peppers

Watering your container-grown peppers in a vegetable container garden is of utmost importance for several reasons. First, unlike plants grown directly in the ground, container plants depend solely on the grower for their water supply. Their roots can't reach out further into the soil to access additional moisture. Therefore, consistent watering is crucial to keep them hydrated and healthy.

Second, water plays a pivotal role in nutrient absorption. It helps dissolve the nutrients present in the soil, enabling the roots to absorb and transport them to the rest of the plant. Without adequate watering, your pepper plants may suffer from nutrient deficiencies, impacting their growth and productivity.

Lastly, water aids in photosynthesis - the process by which plants convert light energy into chemical energy to fuel their growth. Without sufficient water, this process can be hindered, leading to stunted growth or even plant death. Therefore, proper watering is key to ensuring your container-grown peppers thrive and produce a bountiful harvest.

Watering container-grown peppers in vegetable container gardens requires attention to detail and understanding of the plant's needs. Peppers, like many plants, have specific watering needs that vary based on several factors including the size of the container, the type of soil used, and the current weather conditions.

The amount of water that your pepper plants need will depend on the size of the container they're growing in. Typically, a pepper plant in a 5-gallon container will need about 1-2 gallons of water per week. However, this can vary depending on the weather and the stage of growth the plant is in. During hot, dry periods, you may need to water your plants more often, possibly every day or every other day. In cooler, rainy periods, you might only need to water once a week.

When it comes to the timing of watering, it's generally best to water your peppers in the early morning. This allows the water to soak into the soil and reach the roots before the heat of the day causes evaporation. If you can't water in the morning, the next best time is in the late afternoon or early evening, giving the water a chance to soak in before nightfall. Avoid watering in the middle of the day when the sun is at its hottest, as this can cause the water to evaporate before it reaches the plant's roots.

The type of soil you use in your containers can also affect your watering schedule. Peppers prefer well-draining soil, so using a potting mix designed for containers can help ensure the right balance of moisture retention and drainage. If the soil is too compacted or doesn't drain well, the roots can become water-logged, and the plant can suffer from root rot.

Finally, remember that watering is just one part of maintaining healthy pepper plants. They also need regular feeding with a balanced vegetable fertilizer and plenty of sunlight – at least 6-8 hours a day. By providing the right care and attention, you can enjoy a plentiful harvest of fresh, homegrown peppers.

Watering container-grown peppers requires a balance between ensuring the plant has enough moisture to thrive without over-watering. The key is to monitor your plants closely and adjust your watering schedule as necessary based on the weather, the stage of growth, and the condition of the soil.

Organic Fertilization For Container Grown Peppers

Organic fertilization plays a crucial role in the growth and productivity of container-grown peppers in vegetable container gardens. Unlike plants grown in the ground, which can access a wide range of nutrients from the surrounding soil, container-grown plants are limited to the nutrients available in their potting soil. Over time, these nutrients get used up and need to be replenished, which is where organic fertilizers come in.

Organic fertilizers, derived from plant, animal, or mineral sources, provide a wide array of essential nutrients that promote healthy growth and high yields. They improve the structure and water-holding capacity of the soil, encouraging root development and enhancing the plant's ability to absorb nutrients. Furthermore, organic fertilizers release nutrients slowly, providing a steady supply over a long period and reducing the risk of over-fertilization.

They also contribute to the sustainability of gardening practices by recycling natural waste products and reducing dependence on synthetic chemicals. Therefore, using organic fertilizers is not just beneficial for the health and productivity of your peppers, but it's also an environmentally friendly choice.

Peppers are a popular choice for container gardening, and using organic fertilizers can significantly enhance their growth and productivity. There are several types of organic fertilizers that are well-suited for container-grown peppers.

Compost is one of the most commonly used organic fertilizers in vegetable container gardens. It is made from decomposed organic matter, such as kitchen scraps, garden waste, and manure. Compost provides a wide range of nutrients to the soil and improves its structure and water-holding capacity. It also introduces beneficial microorganisms that help break down organic matter into nutrients that plants can absorb. Compost can be mixed into the potting soil at the time of planting or used as a top dressing during the growing season.

Worm castings, the waste product of earthworms, are another excellent organic fertilizer for container-grown peppers. They are rich in nutrients and beneficial microbes and have a neutral pH, which is ideal for peppers. Worm castings can be mixed into the potting soil or added as a top dressing.

Bone meal and blood meal are other organic options. Bone meal is high in phosphorus, which promotes root development and fruiting, while blood meal is a good source of nitrogen, vital for leafy growth.

Fish emulsion and seaweed extracts are liquid organic fertilizers that provide a quick nutrient boost. They are typically diluted with water and applied to the soil or used as a foliar spray.

The timing and method of fertilization depend on the specific needs of your peppers. Generally, peppers should be fertilized when they are planted and again when they start to flower. The fertilizer should be mixed into the top layer of the soil or applied as a side dressing, taking care not to let it come into contact with the plant's stems or leaves, as this could cause burning.

When using organic fertilizers, it's essential to remember that they release nutrients slowly over time, so over-fertilization is less of a risk than with synthetic fertilizers. However, it's still important to follow the recommended application rates and not to overdo it, as too much of any nutrient can be harmful to plants.

Organic fertilizers offer a sustainable and effective way to nourish your container-grown peppers. By understanding the different types of organic fertilizers and how to use them, you can ensure that your peppers have all the nutrients they need to thrive.

PROTECTING YOUR CONTAINER GROWN PEPPERS

Extreme Temperatures

Growing peppers in containers offers many advantages, including the ability to control the growing environment more closely than in-ground gardening. However, container-grown peppers are also more susceptible to extreme temperatures, as their roots are confined to a limited space and cannot escape the heat or cold as easily as they could in the ground. Therefore, it's important to take steps to protect your peppers from temperature extremes.

Extreme heat can stress pepper plants, causing them to wilt, drop their flowers or fruit, or even die if the temperatures are high enough. To protect your peppers from heat, it's essential to ensure that they receive adequate water. Peppers require more water when it's hot, so check the soil moisture levels regularly and water thoroughly when the top inch of soil feels dry. However, avoid watering in the middle of the day when the sun is at its hottest, as this can cause the water to evaporate before it reaches the plant's roots.

Shade cloth can also be used to protect pepper plants from intense sunlight and heat. A shade cloth with a 30-50% shade rating can help reduce the intensity of the sun's rays without blocking out too much light. Simply drape the shade cloth over the plants during the hottest part of the day, ensuring that it doesn't touch the foliage, as this can cause scorching.

Extreme cold can be just as damaging to peppers, which are warm-season plants and cannot tolerate frost. When cold weather is forecasted, consider moving your containers to a sheltered location, such as a garage, shed, or indoors if possible. If moving the containers isn't practical, you can wrap them in burlap or bubble wrap to insulate the soil and protect the roots from freezing. Using a cloche or garden fleece to cover the plants can also help keep them warm.

Another critical aspect of protecting peppers from cold is timing your planting correctly. Peppers should be planted after the risk of frost has passed, and young plants should be hardened off gradually before being left outside full time.

Protecting your container-grown peppers from extreme temperatures is vital for their health and productivity. Heat stress can cause poor fruit set and reduced yields, while frost can kill the plants outright. By taking steps to moderate the temperature of your containers and protect your plants from heat and cold, you can ensure that they have the best possible conditions for growth and fruit production.

Protecting Container Grown Peppers From Pests

Protecting container-grown peppers from pests is vital for several reasons. Pests can cause significant damage to peppers, affecting both their health and productivity. They can defoliate plants, stunt their growth, cause discoloration or deformities in the fruit, and even kill plants in severe cases. Pest infestations can also spread quickly in a container garden, as the close proximity of the plants makes it easy for pests to move from one plant to another. Moreover, some pests can carry diseases that can further harm your peppers or potentially spread to other plants in your garden. By actively protecting your peppers from pests, you can help ensure that they remain healthy, vigorous, and productive, maximizing your harvest and the enjoyment you get from your vegetable container garden.

Protecting container-grown peppers from pests is an essential aspect of maintaining a healthy and productive vegetable container garden. There are several strategies that you can use to prevent and control pest infestations.

First and foremost, good plant care is the best defense against pests. Healthy plants are less susceptible to pest damage and more able to recover if they do get attacked. Ensure your peppers have the right growing conditions - adequate light, the right temperature range, proper watering, and suitable soil. Regularly check your plants for signs of stress or disease, as these can make them more attractive to pests.

Secondly, regularly inspect your plants for signs of pests. Many pests can be controlled effectively if caught early before they have a chance to establish large populations and cause significant damage. Look for signs such as chewed leaves, discoloration, wilting, or unusual growth patterns. Also, check under leaves and around the base of the plant for pests or their eggs.

In terms of prevention, consider using a horticultural soap or neem oil spray, which can deter a wide range of pests. These sprays work by suffocating pests or disrupting their life cycles, and they are safe to use on edible plants. Apply according to the package instructions, typically in the early morning or late evening when beneficial insects are less active.

Introducing beneficial insects to your garden can also help control pests. Ladybugs, lacewings, and parasitic wasps are all natural predators of common pepper pests like aphids and whiteflies. You can attract these beneficial insects by planting flowers nearby or purchase them from gardening suppliers.

Physical barriers can be effective for certain pests. For example, a fine mesh netting can prevent flying insects from reaching your plants, while copper tape around the base of the container can deter slugs and snails.

If you do find pests on your plants, remove them by hand if the infestation is small or use a strong spray of water to dislodge them. For severe infestations, you may need to use a stronger pest control product. Choose one that is safe for use on edible plants and follow the package instructions carefully.

In summary, protecting your container-grown peppers from pests involves a combination of good plant care, regular monitoring, prevention strategies, and targeted control measures when necessary. By taking a proactive approach to pest management, you can help ensure that your peppers stay healthy and productive.

Protecting Container Grown Peppers From Diseases

Protecting container-grown peppers from diseases is vital for several reasons. Firstly, disease can significantly reduce the yield and quality of your pepper plants. Diseases such as bacterial leaf spot, blossom end rot, and various fungal infections can cause leaves to yellow and drop, flowers to abort, and fruits to develop unsightly blemishes or rot, rendering them inedible.

Secondly, some diseases can spread rapidly, not only affecting multiple plants within the same container but also potentially spreading to other containers or plants in your garden. This can lead to widespread damage and a significant loss of crops. Thirdly, certain diseases can persist in the soil or plant debris, posing a risk for future plantings.

Lastly, managing diseases after they've taken hold can be challenging and may require the use of chemical treatments, which some gardeners prefer to avoid. Therefore, taking steps to prevent disease in your container-grown peppers is an essential part of maintaining a healthy and productive vegetable container garden.

One common disease that affects pepper plants is Bacterial Leaf Spot, which presents as small, dark spots on the leaves, eventually leading to leaf drop. This disease thrives in wet, humid conditions. To prevent it, avoid overhead watering, and ensure your containers have adequate drainage. If you notice signs of this disease, remove and dispose of affected leaves immediately to prevent its spread.

Anthracnose, another common disease, causes large, sunken spots on fruits and can be devastating for pepper plants. To prevent anthracnose, practice crop rotation and avoid planting peppers in the same soil where diseased plants were previously grown. Also, maintain a regular fungicide spray program as a preventative measure.

Fusarium Wilt is a soil-borne fungus that causes yellowing and wilting of leaves, often leading to plant death. This disease is difficult to control once established, so prevention is key. Use sterilized potting soil, and ensure your containers are clean before planting. If a plant does become infected, remove it immediately to prevent the disease from spreading.

Phytophthora Blight is another disease that can affect both the roots and fruits of pepper plants. It causes damping-off in seedlings, root rot in adult plants, and fruit rot. Prevention methods include using well-draining soil and avoiding overwatering.

Blossom end rot is a physiological disorder caused by calcium deficiency and irregular watering, leading to dark, sunken areas at the blossom end of the fruit. To prevent blossom end rot, ensure a consistent watering schedule and use a calcium-rich fertilizer. Also, using a potting mix that drains well can help maintain the right moisture levels in the soil.

Pepper Mosaic Virus leads to mottled leaves and stunted growth. Unfortunately, there is no cure for this virus, so prevention is crucial. Regularly check plants for aphids, which spread the virus, and remove any infected plants immediately.

Verticillium Wilt is a soil-borne disease that causes wilting and yellowing of leaves, stunted growth, and eventually plant death. It's challenging to control once it's in the soil, so prevention is key. Using disease-resistant varieties, rotating crops, and avoiding overwatering can help prevent Verticillium wilt.

Remember, maintaining good gardening practices is the best defense against these diseases. This includes proper spacing of plants for good air circulation, watering at the base of the plant to keep the foliage dry, regular monitoring for early detection of problems, and immediate action at the first sign of disease. With these strategies, you can keep your container-grown peppers healthy and productive.

HARVESTING CONTAINER GROWN PEPPERS

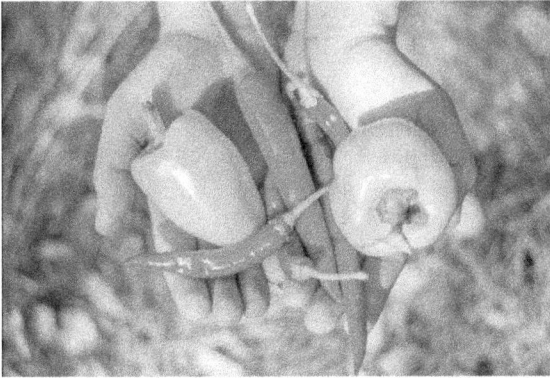

Growing peppers in containers is a rewarding endeavor, but it requires patience. The time it takes for container-grown peppers to be ready for harvest can vary widely depending on the variety of pepper and the growing conditions. Most sweet bell peppers mature in 60-90 days, while hot peppers can take anywhere from 60-150 days. These timelines start from transplanting seedlings into the container, not from sowing seeds.

Pepper plants will typically produce flowers before setting fruit. Once pollinated, these flowers will develop into small green peppers that gradually grow in size. Over time, the peppers will change color as they mature - from green to red, yellow, orange, or even purple, depending on the variety. While you can harvest peppers at any stage of maturity, they are often sweeter and more flavorful when allowed to fully ripen on the plant.

Harvesting your container-grown peppers is a straightforward process. Peppers should be cut off the vine rather than pulled. Tugging on the pepper could damage the plant or remove the entire fruit stem, which should remain on the plant. Use a sharp knife or scissors to cut the stem about an inch above the fruit. Be careful not to damage the branch or neighboring fruits.

When harvesting, it's important to handle the peppers gently to avoid bruising them. After picking, peppers can be stored at room temperature for a short period or refrigerated for longer storage. They can also be dried, frozen, or canned for preservation.

Remember, regular harvesting encourages the plant to produce more fruit. So, don't be afraid to pick your peppers as they ripen. This will ensure a continuous supply throughout the growing season.

CONTAINER GROWN PEPPERS NOTES

Start: Seeds or Seedlings

Germination: 7 to 14 days, 70-85 degrees Fahrenheit (21-29 degrees Celsius)

Seed Life: 2 Years

Soil Type: High-quality potting mix with some organic matter (compost or well-rotted manure) - pH level between 6.0 and 6.5.

Seed Spacing: 1/4 inch deep (in potting pots)

Seedling Spacing: 12 - 18 inches apart (depending on size of chosen container) and 18 to 24 inches deep (in permanent growing containers)

Sunlight: 6 – 8hrs full sunlight daily

Growing Temperatures: 70 to 85 degrees Fahrenheit (21-29 degrees Celsius). Anything below 60 degrees Fahrenheit (15 degrees Celsius) can slow down their growth and anything above 90 degrees Fahrenheit (32 degrees Celsius) can cause the plants to drop their blossoms.

Days To Harvest: 60 to 90 days / 60- 150 days (hot pepper variety)

CHAPTER 5
VEGETABLE CONTAINER GARDENING – GREEN ONIONS

G reen onions, also known as scallions, are a delightful addition to any vegetable container garden. Easy to grow and manage, these versatile vegetables not only add a distinct flavor and crunch to a variety of dishes, but they also beautify your garden with their vibrant green hues. With minimal space requirements and quick growth cycles, green onions are an ideal choice for container gardening.

Whether you're a seasoned gardener or a beginner looking to experiment with urban farming, cultivating green onions in containers can be a rewarding and fruitful endeavor. In this chapter, we'll explore the ins and outs of successfully growing green onions in your container garden, from planting and care to harvest and usage.

Incorporating green onions into your vegetable container garden can bring about numerous benefits. For starters, green onions are a compact plant, making them an ideal choice for container gardening where space may be limited. They grow vertically and don't require much room, allowing you to maximize the use of your container space.

Additionally, green onions have a relatively short growing cycle, meaning you can enjoy the fruits of your labor sooner compared to other vegetables. They're also a hardy plant, resistant to many common pests and diseases that could otherwise harm your garden. Furthermore, green onions are a companion plant, helping protect other plants in your container garden by repelling certain pests with their strong scent.

Lastly, green onions are a cut-and-come-again plant; you can harvest them continuously throughout the growing season by cutting the tops and leaving the bulbs in the soil to regrow. This not only provides you with a steady supply of fresh greens but also increases the efficiency of your garden.

THE RIGHT SOIL TO GROW GREEN ONIONS IN CONTAINERS

Choosing the right soil conditions for growing green onions in container gardens is a key factor to ensure their healthy growth and abundant harvest. Green onions prefer well-draining, fertile soil with a neutral pH of around 6.0 to 7.0. They are not particularly picky about their soil type, but they do thrive in soil that's rich in organic matter. Therefore, incorporating compost or well-rotted manure into your soil can greatly boost the nutrient content and improve the overall soil structure, promoting robust onion growth.

The soil's drainage capacity is another crucial aspect to consider when growing green onions in containers. Onions are prone to rot if they sit in waterlogged soil. Therefore, a well-draining potting mix is essential to prevent water from accumulating and causing root damage. You can enhance the drainage of your soil by adding materials like perlite or sand. Additionally, ensure your container has adequate drainage holes to allow excess water to escape.

Apart from these, it's also important to maintain a steady supply of nutrients to your green onions throughout their growth. Regularly applying a balanced vegetable fertilizer can help supplement the necessary nutrients and promote healthy, vigorous growth. Remember to follow the manufacturer's instructions when applying fertilizer to avoid over-fertilization, which can harm your plants.

In summary, creating the right soil conditions for your green onions involves selecting a fertile, well-draining soil, ensuring proper drainage in your container, and providing regular feedings with a balanced fertilizer. With these steps, you can create an optimal growing environment for your green onions to thrive in your container garden.

HOW TO SOW GREEN ONIONS IN CONTAINERS GARDENS

Correct Season To Sow Green Onions In Containers Gardens

Green onions are versatile plants that can be grown in various seasons, making them ideal for container gardening. The optimal time to sow green onion seeds is in early spring as soon as the soil can be worked, with temperatures above 40°F being conducive for germination. However, if you want a continuous supply of fresh green onions, it's recommended to sow a new batch of seeds every three weeks right up until July. This method ensures a constant supply throughout the growing season.

In colder climates, green onions can be grown from spring through to fall, thanks to the flexibility provided by container gardening. Containers can easily be moved indoors during harsh winter conditions, allowing the plants to continue growing year-round. Moreover, some varieties of green onions can be grown in spring or fall and can even be overwintered for cut-and-come-again production.

While early spring is often the best time to start sowing green onions, their adaptable nature allows for a wide planting window, especially when grown in containers. Regularly sowing new batches can ensure a steady supply of this useful and flavorful crop.

Plant Needs & Requirements

Germinating green onion vegetable plants from seeds to seedlings correctly is a vital step when growing in vegetable container gardens. The process of germination is the first stage of growth, and it sets the foundation for the health and productivity of your plants. Proper germination ensures that the seedlings have the best possible start, which translates into stronger, more robust plants that can resist pests and diseases better and yield a higher harvest.

During germination, seeds awaken from their dormant state and begin developing into plants. If this process is not carried out correctly, it may result in weak seedlings that struggle to thrive or even fail to grow at all. Factors such as planting depth, soil temperature, moisture levels, and light exposure all play a crucial role in successful germination.

For instance, planting seeds too deeply can make it difficult for the seedlings to break through the soil surface, while inadequate moisture can prevent the seeds from germinating altogether. Therefore, understanding and implementing the correct germination practices are key to successful green onion cultivation in vegetable container gardens.

Germinating green onions from seeds to seedlings involves several steps, and understanding these can help ensure your success when growing these flavorful plants in your vegetable container garden.

Step 1: Seed Selection and Preparation. Start by selecting high-quality seeds from a reputable source. This ensures that the seeds are viable and disease-free. If you wish, you can soak the seeds in water for a few hours before planting to help speed up germination, but this is not necessary.

Step 2: Planting the Seeds. Fill a seed tray or small pots with a good quality potting mix. The soil should be well-draining to prevent waterlogging. Sow the green onion seeds on the surface of the soil, then lightly cover them with a thin layer of soil. The seeds should be planted about 1/4 inch deep.

Step 3: Providing the Right Conditions. Green onion seeds germinate best at temperatures between 65 and 85 degrees Fahrenheit. Place the seed tray or pots in a warm location, such as a sunny windowsill or under grow lights. Keep the soil consistently moist, but not soggy. Covering the tray or pots with a plastic dome or wrap can help maintain humidity.

Step 4: Germination. With the right conditions, green onion seeds usually germinate within 7 to 10 days. Once the seeds sprout, remove the plastic covering (if used) and make sure the seedlings receive plenty of light to prevent them from becoming leggy.

Step 5: Transplanting the Seedlings. The green onion seedlings are ready to be transplanted into their final containers once they have at least two sets of true leaves, which typically occurs around 3 to 4 weeks after germination. To transplant, carefully lift the seedlings out of their initial containers, making sure to avoid damaging the roots. In the final container, make a hole deep enough to accommodate the root system, place the seedling in the hole, and gently fill in around it with soil. Water thoroughly after transplanting.

By following these steps, you can successfully germinate green onion seeds and grow them into healthy seedlings ready for transplanting into your vegetable container garden.

Spacing & Measurement

Proper spacing and measurements when transplanting green onion seedlings into container gardens are crucial for the optimal growth and productivity of the plants. Green onions, like all plants, need enough room to grow and spread without competing for resources. When seedlings are spaced correctly, they have ample room to develop robust root systems, which are essential for absorbing water and nutrients from the soil.

Spacing also ensures adequate airflow between the plants, reducing the risk of fungal diseases that can thrive in damp, crowded conditions. If green onions are planted too closely together, they may compete for sunlight, water, and nutrients, leading to stunted growth and lower yields.

Generally, green onions should be planted 1-2 inches apart in rows that are 12-18 inches apart. However, these measurements can be adjusted based on the size of your container and the specific variety of green onion you're growing. By providing the appropriate spacing and measurements, you can help ensure a healthy, bountiful harvest from your container garden.

When it comes to planting green onion seedlings in container gardens, the correct spacing and measurements are critical to ensure healthy growth and a generous harvest. Green onions don't need a lot of space, but they do need enough to develop a strong root system and sufficient foliage for photosynthesis.

As a rule, green onion seedlings should be planted about 1-2 inches apart. This allows each plant plenty of room to grow without crowding its neighbors. It also ensures that each plant has access to the nutrients it needs from the soil. If you're planting multiple rows of green onions in a larger container, maintain a distance of about 12-18 inches between each row. This will allow for sufficient airflow between the plants, reducing the risk of disease and pest infestation.

The depth at which you plant your green onion seedlings is also important. Generally, they should be planted at the same depth they were growing at before. You can tell this by looking for the soil line on the stem, which is usually a slightly different color. Planting at the correct depth will help the seedlings establish quickly and grow strong.

The size of your container will also impact the spacing of your green onions. For smaller containers, you may only be able to fit a few plants. But for larger containers, you can plant more rows of green onions, always keeping the recommended spacing in mind.

Remember that these are just guidelines. The specific variety of green onion you're growing might have slightly different requirements, so it's always a good idea to check the seed packet or source for the most accurate information.

By following these spacing and measurement guidelines, you'll give your green onion seedlings the best chance of thriving in their new container home, leading to a successful and satisfying harvest.

Ideal Temperatures & Sun Requirements

The importance of ideal temperatures and sun requirements when growing green onions in container gardens cannot be over-stated. Green onion seeds generally need a soil temperature of at least 45 degrees to germinate, although warmer conditions are typically more conducive to germination. Once the seeds have sprouted, maintaining an optimal temperature is crucial for the growth and development of the plants. Green onions are hardy and can tolerate a wide range of temperatures.

In addition to temperature, sunlight plays a significant role in the successful cultivation of green onions. Like most vegetables, green onions require full sun exposure for optimum growth. A site that receives at least 6 to 8 hours of direct sunlight each day is ideal. Full sun exposure encourages robust growth, helps the plants produce energy efficiently through photosynthesis, and promotes the formation of healthy bulbs.

Overcast skies and cool temperatures during the growing season can delay bulb formation. Therefore, when planning your container garden, ensure that your green onions are positioned in a location where they can receive sufficient sunlight and warmth. These factors combined will help maximize the yield and quality of your green onion crop.

MAINTAINING YOUR CONTAINER GROWN GREEN ONION

Maintaining your container-grown green onions in vegetable container gardening is crucial for a variety of reasons. First and foremost, regular maintenance ensures that the plants receive the necessary care and attention they need to grow healthily and productively. This includes tasks such as watering, feeding, weeding, and pest control.

Proper watering, for instance, helps to prevent issues like root rot and dehydration, which can significantly affect the growth and yield of your green onions. Regular feeding with a balanced fertilizer can provide the essential nutrients that your green onions need to thrive, especially considering that nutrients in containers can be quickly depleted. Regularly checking for and removing any weeds can help to ensure that your green onions aren't competing for resources.

Finally, monitoring for pests and diseases allows you to address any issues promptly before they can cause significant damage. Consistent maintenance, therefore, not only helps to maximize the quality and yield of your green onions but also contributes to the overall success of your vegetable container garden.

Pruning & Thinning Your Green Onions

Pruning and thinning container-grown green onions in vegetable container gardens are essential gardening practices that contribute significantly to the health and productivity of the plants.

Pruning, which involves removing the tips of the green parts, can encourage the plants to focus their energy on developing stronger roots and bulbs, leading to a more abundant harvest. It also helps maintain the size of the plants, making them more manageable, especially when grown in a confined space like a container. Moreover, pruning can improve air circulation around the plants, reducing the risk of fungal diseases that thrive in damp, stagnant conditions.

On the other hand, thinning is the process of removing some plants to reduce overcrowding. This practice is particularly important when growing green onions from seeds, as they are often sown densely.

By thinning out the seedlings, you allow each remaining plant sufficient room to grow and flourish without competing for resources such as sunlight, water, and nutrients. Thinning can also prevent disease spread by ensuring better airflow between the plants.

Both pruning and thinning play vital roles in maintaining the overall health and vigor of your green onion plants. They not only help to maximize the yield of your crop but also contribute to the success of your vegetable container garden.

Pruning and thinning container-grown green onions are crucial practices that aid in the overall health and productivity of these plants. The process can begin as early as when the green onions have grown to about 3-4 inches tall, usually a few weeks after planting. At this stage, you can start thinning the plants to prevent overcrowding and ensure they have ample space for growth.

To thin your green onions, carefully remove some plants from the densely populated areas of your container. Aim to leave about 1-2 inches of space between each remaining plant. This spacing allows each green onion to receive adequate light, water, and nutrients. The thinned plants don't need to go to waste; they can be used in salads or other dishes for a fresh, mild onion flavor.

As for pruning, it's not commonly required for green onions since they're often harvested before they become overly large. However, if you notice any dead, yellowing, or diseased leaves, they should be pruned to maintain plant health. Simply use a clean, sharp pair of scissors or pruning shears to cut off the affected foliage at its base. This removal can help prevent the spread of diseases and pests, and it encourages healthier, more vigorous growth.

Furthermore, regular check-ups on your green onions will help you spot any potential issues early on. Look out for signs of pests, diseases, or nutrient deficiencies, and address them promptly to keep your plants healthy. Remember, proper watering and feeding are also part of maintaining your container garden, contributing to the success of your green onions.

Knowing when and how to prune and thin your container-grown green onions can significantly enhance their health and yield. These simple practices can make a big difference in your vegetable container gardening experience.

Watering Your Container Grown Green Onions

Watering your container-grown green onions is vital for their growth and overall health. These plants, like all living organisms, need water to survive and thrive. Water serves several functions in green onions; it helps transport nutrients from the soil to the plant, aids in photosynthesis, and maintains the plant's structure by keeping the cells turgid. Furthermore, container gardening requires regular watering because containers often have good drainage and can dry out quickly, especially during hot weather.

Insufficient water can lead to stunted growth, wilting, and even death of the plants. However, it's also important not to over-water as this can lead to root rot and other diseases. Therefore, maintaining an optimum watering schedule, which keeps the soil consistently moist but not waterlogged, is crucial for the successful growth of green onions in container gardens.

Watering container-grown green onions in vegetable container gardens is a delicate balance. These plants like consistent moisture, but not waterlogged conditions. The amount and frequency of watering depend on several factors, including the size of the container, the type of soil, the weather, and the growth stage of the onions.

A general rule of thumb is to water your green onions when the top 1 inch of soil feels dry to the touch. This method ensures that the plants receive enough water without becoming waterlogged. In hot weather or during periods of rapid growth, you may need to water your green onions daily to maintain consistent soil moisture. In cooler weather or when the plants are not actively growing, watering may only be needed every few days.

When watering, aim to thoroughly saturate the soil. Water should be applied slowly until it begins to drain out of the bottom of the container. This technique ensures that the water reaches the root zone where it's most needed. Avoid watering the foliage as this can promote the growth of mold and other diseases.

It's also important to remember that green onions have shallow roots, so they can't access water deep in the soil like some other plants. This characteristic makes them more susceptible to drying out, particularly in containers where the soil can dry quickly. Therefore, regular checks of soil moisture are vital for maintaining the health of your container-grown green onions.

Watering your green onions correctly plays a crucial role in their overall growth and productivity. By understanding their watering needs and adjusting your practices accordingly, you can ensure that your green onions thrive in their container garden environment.

Organic Fertilization For Container Grown Green Onions

Organic fertilization plays a crucial role in the growth and health of container-grown green onions in vegetable gardens. Unlike traditional in-ground gardening, where plants have access to a vast amount of soil nutrients, container gardening confines the root systems to a limited amount of soil. This makes the plants more dependent on the gardener for their nutritional needs.

Organic fertilizers, derived from natural sources such as compost, manure, or bone meal, provide a wide range of essential nutrients in a form that plants can easily absorb. They also improve the structure and water-holding capacity of the soil, promoting healthier root development.

Moreover, organic fertilizers release nutrients slowly over time, ensuring a steady supply of nutrition to your plants. They also contribute to the sustainability of gardening by reducing reliance on synthetic fertilizers, which can cause environmental harm due to nutrient runoff. Therefore, the use of organic fertilization is not only beneficial for the growth of your green onions but also for the overall health of the environment.

Several types of organic fertilizers are suitable for container-grown green onions in vegetable container gardens. Each offers its unique set of benefits and nutrient profiles, so understanding their properties can help you choose the most appropriate one for your garden.

Compost is a gardener's gold and an excellent choice for green onions. It is rich in nutrients and helps improve soil structure, providing a slow-release source of nutrients over time. Adding compost to your container at the start of the growing season can give your green onions a healthy boost.

Worm castings, the waste product of worms, are another excellent option. They are rich in nitrogen, which is vital for leafy growth, making them ideal for green onion plants. Worm castings also improve soil structure and help retain moisture.

Fish emulsion is a water-soluble, quick-release organic fertilizer that's high in nitrogen. It's an excellent choice for providing a nutrient boost during the growing season. However, it's strong-smelling, so it's best used outdoors or in a well-ventilated area.

Bone meal is a slow-release fertilizer high in phosphorus, which promotes root and bulb development. It's an excellent supplement for green onions, particularly in the early stages of growth when root development is crucial.

In terms of when and how to fertilize, it's best to add compost or worm castings to your potting mix before planting your green onions. This step will ensure that the nutrients are available right from the start. For fish emulsion and bone meal, it's best to start applying these fertilizers a few weeks after planting. Follow the instructions on the package for how much to use, as over-fertilizing can harm your plants.

When applying fertilizer, be sure to spread it evenly over the soil surface. Avoid letting the fertilizer come into direct contact with the plant stems, as this can cause burning. After application, water thoroughly to help the nutrients seep into the soil and reach the root zone.

Using organic fertilizers in your container garden can significantly benefit your green onions. By understanding the different types of organic fertilizers and how to use them, you can ensure that your green onions receive the nutrients they need to thrive.

PROTECTING YOUR CONTAINER GROWN GREEN ONIONS

Extreme Temperatures

Protecting container-grown green onions from extreme temperatures in vegetable container gardens is a critical aspect of maintaining their health and productivity. Green onions can tolerate a wide range of temperatures, but extremes of heat or cold can cause stress and damage to the plants, affecting their growth and yield.

In hot weather, green onions can suffer from heat stress, leading to wilting, bolting (premature flowering), or even death of the plants. To protect your green onions from extreme heat, it's crucial to provide adequate watering, as evaporation rates can be high, especially in containers.

Watering should be done early in the morning or late in the evening to reduce water loss through evaporation. Mulching the top of the soil with organic materials like straw or compost can also help retain moisture and keep the roots cool.

Shade cloth or umbrellas can be used to shield the plants from the intense afternoon sun. Alternatively, you can move the containers to a shaded location if the heat becomes too intense. This is one of the advantages of container gardening; the mobility of the containers allows for easy adjustment according to weather conditions.

In cold weather, green onions are at risk of frost damage. While they are somewhat frost-tolerant, extended periods of freezing temperatures can harm or kill the plants. To protect your green onions from frost, you can move the containers indoors or into a greenhouse.

If that's not possible, wrapping the containers with insulating materials like burlap or bubble wrap can help keep the soil from freezing. Covering the plants with a frost cloth or a plastic cover can also provide some protection.

Understanding why it's important to protect green onions from extreme temperatures comes down to their health and productivity. Stress from high or low temperatures can weaken the plants, making them more susceptible to diseases and pests.

It can also negatively affect their growth, reducing the quantity and quality of your harvest. By taking measures to moderate the temperature conditions of your container-grown green onions, you can ensure their healthy growth and a bountiful yield.

Protecting Container Grown Green Onions From Pests

Protecting container-grown green onions from pests in vegetable container gardens is vital for several reasons. Pests can significantly damage or even destroy your green onion plants, hampering their growth and reducing their yield. They can cause visible harm, such as chewing leaves or bulbs, or invisible

CHAPTER 5

damage by spreading diseases. Moreover, some pests can multiply quickly, infesting your entire container garden in a short period if left unchecked.

This can put all your plants at risk, not just your green onions. Additionally, many pests can overwinter in the soil or plant debris, causing recurring problems in subsequent growing seasons. Therefore, implementing effective pest management strategies is crucial to maintaining the health and productivity of your container-grown green onions.

Green onions grown in containers can be vulnerable to a variety of pests that can cause significant damage if left unchecked. Some of the common pests that attack green onions include aphids, onion maggot flies, thrips, slugs, and cutworms.

Aphids are small, soft-bodied insects that can be green, yellow, brown, red, or black. They feed by sucking sap from plants, which can lead to yellowed, curled leaves, stunted growth, and reduced yield. Aphids also excrete a sticky substance known as honeydew, which can encourage the growth of sooty mold.

Onion maggot flies lay their eggs at the base of the onion plant. The larvae burrow into the bulb, causing it to rot. These pests can be particularly destructive, leading to significant crop losses. Thrips, meanwhile, are tiny insects that feed on the leaves of green onions, causing silvery-white streaks or blotches. In severe infestations, they can cause leaves to turn brown and die.

Slugs and cutworms are other pests that can pose a threat to container-grown green onions. Slugs feed on the leaves and bulbs of the plant, while cutworms, which are the larvae of certain species of moths, can cut young plants off at the base.

Protecting your green onions from these pests involves a combination of preventative measures and active interventions. Regularly inspect your plants for signs of pests and remove any that you find. You can also use traps or barriers to prevent pests from reaching your plants. For example, placing copper tape around the rim of your container can deter slugs, while diatomaceous earth sprinkled around the base of the plants can help control cutworms.

Introducing beneficial insects, such as ladybugs and lacewings, can also help keep pest populations in check. These insects are natural predators of many common garden pests, including aphids and thrips.

For more stubborn infestations, consider using organic pesticides, such as neem oil or insecticidal soap. These can be effective against a variety of pests but should be used sparingly to avoid harming beneficial insects.

While several pests can pose a threat to container-grown green onions, there are many strategies you can employ to protect your plants and ensure a healthy harvest.

Protecting Container Grown Green Onions From Diseases

Protecting container-grown green onions from diseases in vegetable container gardens is of paramount importance for a multitude of reasons. Diseases can drastically affect the health, productivity, and overall yield of your green onions.

They can cause symptoms ranging from discoloration and wilting to stunted growth and eventual plant death. Moreover, once established, many plant diseases can be challenging to control or eradicate, potentially leading to recurring issues over multiple growing seasons. Also, diseases can quickly spread from plant to plant, especially in the close quarters of a container garden, putting all your vegetables at risk.

Therefore, proactive disease prevention and timely management are critical to ensure the vitality of your green onions and the overall health of your vegetable container garden.

One common disease that affects green onions is Onion Smudge, caused by the fungus Colletotrichum circinans. This disease manifests as dark spots on the bulbs and can lead to rot. To prevent Onion Smudge, ensure good air circulation around your plants, avoid overwatering, and dispose of any infected plants immediately to prevent the spread of the fungus.

Another disease that can affect green onions is Downy Mildew, caused by the fungus Peronospora destructor. This disease results in yellow or white patches on the leaves, which can eventually kill the plant. Prevent Downy Mildew by watering your plants at the base rather than from above to keep the leaves dry and avoid planting your green onions too closely together to ensure proper air circulation.

Bacterial Soft Rot, caused by various bacteria, is another disease that can affect green onions. It leads to soft, rotten bulbs and can spread quickly in wet conditions. To prevent this disease, avoid overwatering and ensure your soil has good drainage. Also, practice crop rotation even in your containers, as this can help prevent the build-up of disease-causing organisms in the soil.

In addition to these, Fusarium Basal Rot, caused by the fungus Fusarium oxysporum, can also affect green onions. It leads to yellowing and wilting of leaves and decay of the bulb base. To prevent this disease, use disease-free bulbs and compost, maintain a balanced soil pH, and ensure proper watering and drainage.

Finally, Thrips, tiny insects that suck sap from the plant, can also cause damage to green onions. They cause white patches on leaves and can spread viral diseases. Regularly check your plants for signs of thrips and use insecticidal soap or neem oil to control them.

While green onions can be affected by several plant diseases, maintaining good gardening practices like proper watering, ensuring air circulation, using disease-free planting material, and keeping a close eye for any signs of diseases can help you prevent these problems and ensure a healthy, bountiful harvest.

HARVESTING CONTAINER GROWN GREEN ONIONS

Container-grown green onions are a wonderful addition to any vegetable garden due to their relatively quick growth cycle and easy harvesting process. Depending on the variety, green onions are typically ready for harvest in about six to eight weeks after planting. This short growing season makes them an excellent choice for gardeners who want to see quick results from their efforts.

The exact timing of the harvest can depend on several factors, including the specific variety of onion, the growing conditions, and your personal preference for the size and flavor of the onions. Green onions can be harvested when they reach about 6 inches tall and the bulbs are slightly swollen. At this stage, they will have a mild flavor, perfect for salads and garnishes. If you prefer a stronger flavor, you can wait a bit longer until the bulbs are more developed.

Harvesting container-grown green onions is a simple and straightforward process. Start by watering the soil well to soften it. This will make it easier to pull the onions out without damaging them. Then, grasp the green onions at their base and gently pull upwards. If they resist, use a hand trowel to loosen the soil around them before pulling again. Make sure to pull gently to avoid breaking the stalks or damaging the bulbs.

Once you've harvested the green onions, rinse them well to remove any soil. You can then trim the roots and any damaged or yellowed leaves. Freshly harvested green onions can be used immediately in your meals or stored in the refrigerator for up to a week.

A benefit of container-grown green onions is that they can be harvested as needed, providing a fresh supply of green onions throughout their growing season. If you only need a few green onions for a meal, simply harvest what you need and leave the rest to continue growing. This "cut and come again" method allows you to maximize your harvest from a single planting.

Growing green onions in containers is a quick and rewarding gardening project. With minimal effort, you can enjoy fresh, homegrown green onions in just a few weeks.

CONTAINER GROWN GREEN ONIONS NOTES

Start: Seeds or Seedlings

Germination: 7 to 10 days, 65 and 85 degrees Fahrenheit

Seed Life: 1 Years

Soil Type: Well-draining, fertile soil with some organic matter (compost or well-rotted manure) - pH level between 6.0 to 7.0.

Seed Spacing: 1/4 inch deep (in potting pots)

Seedling Spacing: 1-2 inches apart in rows that are 12-18 inches apart. Measurements can be adjusted based on the size of your container and the specific variety.

Sunlight: 6 – 8hrs full sunlight daily.

Growing Temperatures: 65 and 85 degrees Fahrenheit.

Days To Harvest: 6-8 weeks after planting.

CHAPTER 6
VEGETABLE CONTAINER GARDENING – LETTUCE

L ettuce is a fantastic choice for vegetable container gardening due to its compact size, quick growth cycle, and versatile use in the kitchen. As a cool-season crop, it thrives in spring and fall, making it a great candidate for successive plantings throughout these seasons. Its shallow root system means it can be grown in relatively shallow containers, making it an ideal choice for gardeners with limited space.

Whether you're looking to grow crispy romaine for Caesar salad, buttery bibb for sandwiches, or mixed leaf lettuces for a vibrant salad bowl, container-grown lettuce allows you to enjoy fresh, homegrown greens just steps from your kitchen door. With a variety of colors, shapes, and textures available, lettuce can also add visual interest to your container garden, making it as decorative as it is delicious.

Planting lettuce using vegetable container gardening offers a multitude of benefits for your garden. Firstly, it allows for better control over the growing conditions, including soil quality, water, and even pest management. Lettuce prefers cool weather and can bolt or become bitter in high heat; growing in containers allows you to easily move your plants to shadier spots if temperatures spike.

Secondly, container gardening reduces the risk of soil-borne diseases and pests that can affect lettuce. It also makes it easier to implement companion planting strategies, as you can position containers with compatible plants next to each other to deter pests and encourage growth. Moreover, growing lettuce in containers is an excellent way to maximize space, especially for those with limited gardening areas.

You can grow a surprising amount of lettuce in a small container, providing fresh salads right from your balcony or patio. Lastly, container gardening allows for successive planting. As soon as one crop of lettuce is harvested, another can be planted in its place, providing a continuous harvest throughout the season.

THE RIGHT SOIL TO GROW LETTUCE IN CONTAINERS

Choosing the right soil is crucial for growing lettuce successfully in container gardens. Lettuce, like many other leafy greens, prefers a well-draining soil that's rich in organic matter. The soil should be loose and friable, allowing the roots to penetrate easily and access the necessary nutrients for growth. Moreover, it's important to ensure the soil doesn't become waterlogged, as this can lead to root rot and other diseases.

A good-quality potting mix is usually the best choice for container gardening. These mixes are designed to hold moisture while still providing excellent drainage. They also tend to be lightweight, which is essential for container gardening as it allows for easy movement of your pots. You can further improve the quality of your potting mix by adding compost or well-rotted manure, which will enrich the soil with additional nutrients.

The pH level of the soil can also impact the health of your lettuce plants. Lettuce prefers slightly acidic to neutral soil, with a pH range of 6.0 to 7.0. If needed, you can adjust the pH of your soil using lime to raise it or sulfur to lower it. Regularly testing your soil's pH can help you maintain optimal conditions for your lettuce.

Lastly, remember that container-grown plants rely entirely on their growers for nutrients. Regular feeding with a balanced liquid fertilizer will help keep your lettuce thriving. Be sure to follow the manufacturer's instructions for application rates and frequencies.

Creating the right soil conditions for your lettuce involves choosing a well-draining, nutrient-rich potting mix, maintaining a suitable pH level, and providing regular feedings. With these steps, you can create an ideal environment for growing healthy, productive lettuce plants in your container garden.

HOW TO SOW LETTUCE IN CONTAINERS GARDENS

Correct Season To Sow Lettuce In Containers Gardens

Growing lettuce in container gardens is an excellent way to have a constant supply of fresh, leafy greens. Lettuce is a cool-season crop that thrives best in cool but not freezing temperatures, making spring and fall the ideal seasons for sowing lettuce seeds.

You can choose to start the seeds indoors on a plastic garden tray about 3-4 weeks before the last frost or plant them directly in your containers. This flexibility allows you to extend the growing season by bringing pots indoors, letting you sow lettuce seeds earlier in the year.

Under the right conditions, these seeds can germinate in as little as two days, with the average time being more like 4-10 days. Lettuce's compact size and short growing time make it one of the best vegetables to grow in containers, and you can start harvesting in just a few weeks. Moreover, growing lettuce in winter is also possible by selecting frost-tolerant varieties and pairing them with a season extender like a cold frame.

Regardless of the season, lettuce plants prefer moist soil but do not enjoy being waterlogged. Therefore, ensure your container has adequate drainage. By understanding the growth preferences of lettuce and adjusting for your local climate, you can enjoy a bountiful harvest of homegrown lettuce throughout the year.

Plant Needs & Requirements

The process of correctly germinating lettuce plants from seeds to seedlings is a crucial step when growing them in vegetable container gardens. Germination is the first stage of a plant's life, and a successful start can significantly impact its overall growth and productivity. Proper germination ensures that the lettuce seedlings develop robust root systems, which are critical for absorbing nutrients and water from the soil. This leads to healthier, stronger plants that can resist pests and diseases more effectively.

Furthermore, well-germinated lettuce seedlings are more likely to mature into productive plants, yielding a plentiful harvest of crisp, flavorful leaves. In a container garden context, where space is often limited, maximizing each plant's potential is essential to get the most out of your garden. Therefore, investing time and effort in correctly germinating your lettuce seeds can result in a more successful, bountiful crop.

Germinating lettuce plants from seeds to seedlings involves several crucial steps. The process begins with selecting high-quality seeds from a reputable source. It's important to choose a variety that suits your climate and the time of year you're planting, as lettuce is a cool-season crop.

Firstly, you need to prepare a seed tray or a shallow container filled with a mixture of soil and compost. This provides a nutrient-rich environment for the seeds to germinate. Moisten the soil mixture, but ensure it's not waterlogged. Sprinkle the lettuce seeds evenly over the surface of the soil and lightly cover them with a thin layer of the same soil mixture. Covering the seeds helps maintain moisture around them and protects them from being washed away during watering.

Place the seed tray in a location where it will receive plenty of indirect light. Most lettuce varieties require light to germinate, so placing the tray near a window or under a grow light can be beneficial. However, avoid direct sunlight as it may cause the soil to dry out too quickly.

The optimal temperature for lettuce seed germination is between 40°F (4°C) and 80°F (27°C). The seeds can germinate at temperatures as low as 40°F, but they germinate best at around 75°F. If you're starting your seeds indoors and your house is cooler than this, you might consider using a heat mat to provide additional warmth.

It's essential to keep the soil consistently moist during the germination process. Use a fine mist sprayer to water the seeds, ensuring the soil doesn't dry out but also isn't waterlogged. Overwatering can lead to damping off, a fungal disease that can kill seedlings.

Lettuce seeds typically germinate within 2-10 days, depending on the variety and conditions. Once the seeds have sprouted, continue to keep the soil lightly moist and provide plenty of light.

When the lettuce seedlings have produced their first set of true leaves (the second set of leaves that appear after the initial seed leaves), they're ready to be transplanted into individual containers. At this stage, the plants are strong enough to handle being moved and will benefit from having more space to grow. Be gentle during the transplanting process to avoid damaging the delicate root system. After transplanting, keep the seedlings in a sunny spot and continue to water them regularly.

Properly germinating lettuce seeds and nurturing the resulting seedlings is a rewarding process that leads to a bountiful harvest. By understanding the requirements of lettuce plants and providing them with the right conditions, you can enjoy fresh, homegrown lettuce throughout the season.

Spacing & Measurement

The importance of proper spacing and measurements when transplanting lettuce seedlings into container gardens cannot be overstated. Each seedling needs an adequate amount of space to grow and develop without competition for resources such as light, water, and nutrients. When seedlings are overcrowded, they may become weak and spindly as they stretch for light, reducing their overall health and productivity.

Furthermore, crowded plants can create a humid environment that is conducive to the spread of diseases and pests. For lettuce, generally, each plant should be given about 6-8 inches of space on all sides, although this can vary depending on the specific variety. The size of the container also plays a role in determining how many plants it can support.

A larger container can hold more plants, but each plant still needs its own space. Proper spacing ensures that each lettuce plant can fully mature and produce the maximum yield, resulting in a more bountiful and successful harvest from your container garden.

When it comes to planting lettuce seedlings in container gardens, understanding the desired spacing and measurements is essential for optimal growth. Proper spacing not only ensures that each plant has enough room to develop fully but also reduces competition for resources and helps prevent the spread of diseases.

A standard rule of thumb for lettuce plants is to allow for 6-8 inches of space between each plant. This distance allows each lettuce plant sufficient space to grow and expand without encroaching on its neighbour's territory. This spacing also provides adequate airflow around each plant, reducing the risk of fungal diseases that can thrive in damp, stagnant conditions.

The size of the container you choose will also determine how many lettuce plants it can comfortably accommodate. As a general guideline, a container with a diameter of 12 inches can support about 2-3 lettuce plants. A larger container, say 18 inches in diameter, can accommodate up to 5 plants. However, these are rough estimates and can vary depending on the specific variety of lettuce you're growing.

The depth of the container is another crucial factor. Lettuce has relatively shallow roots compared to other vegetables, so a depth of 6-8 inches should be sufficient for most varieties. This depth provides ample room for the roots to spread and absorb nutrients while also ensuring that the soil doesn't dry out too quickly.

When transplanting your lettuce seedlings into their containers, it's important to position them at the correct depth. The top of the root ball should be level with or slightly below the surface of the soil. Planting too deep can lead to rot, while planting too shallow can expose the roots to drying out.

In summary, proper spacing and measurements when planting lettuce seedlings in container gardening are key factors in ensuring healthy growth and a productive harvest. By giving each plant the space, it needs and choosing an appropriately sized and depth container, you can set the stage for a successful growing season.

Ideal Temperatures & Sun Requirements

The ideal temperatures and sun requirements play a vital role in successfully growing lettuce in container gardens. Lettuce is known as a cool-season crop, preferring temperatures between 35 – 75 degrees F for optimum growth, with the sweet spot being around 60 to 65°F.

As temperatures rise towards 70 to 80°F, lettuce plants tend to bolt, meaning they start to flower and produce seeds, which can result in bitter-tasting leaves. Therefore, maintaining a cooler environment is crucial for producing flavorful lettuce.

In terms of sunlight, lettuce requires a fair amount but doesn't need full, intense sun all day. It thrives best with about 4-6 hours of direct sunlight each day. However, lettuce is somewhat shade-tolerant and can grow in spots that receive closer to three or four hours of sunlight per day. This flexibility makes it an excellent plant for container gardening, where you can move the pots around to ensure they get the right amount of light.

In hotter climates or during summer months, lettuce can benefit from some afternoon shade to protect it from extreme heat. In contrast, in cooler seasons or climates, positioning the containers to maximize sunlight exposure can help keep the plants warm.

Paying attention to the ideal temperatures and sun requirements is key to successful lettuce cultivation in container gardens. By providing the right conditions, you can enjoy a bountiful, tasty harvest from your homegrown lettuce plants.

MAINTAINING YOUR CONTAINER GROWN LETTUCE

Maintaining your container-grown lettuce is vital for ensuring a healthy, productive crop. In container gardening, plants rely entirely on you to provide the nutrients, water, and care they need. Without proper maintenance, lettuce plants can suffer from nutrient deficiencies, inadequate watering, or pest issues, all of which can negatively impact their growth and yield.

Regular watering is critical as containers can dry out quickly, especially in hot weather.

However, overwatering should also be avoided as it can lead to root rot. Nutrient-rich soil and occasional fertilizing can help provide the necessary nutrients for your lettuce's growth. Regularly checking for pests and diseases allows for early detection and treatment, preventing potential devastation of your crop.

Lastly, rotating your crops in container gardening can help prevent the build-up of soil-borne diseases and pests. Overall, diligent maintenance of your container-grown lettuce not only leads to healthier plants but also maximizes your harvest, making your gardening efforts worthwhile.

Pruning & Thinning Your Lettuce

Pruning and thinning container-grown lettuce in vegetable container gardens are essential practices that significantly contribute to the health and productivity of your plants. Thinning is the process of removing some plants to make room for others to grow. When lettuce seedlings are too close together, they compete for sunlight, water, and nutrients, which can stunt their growth and lead to smaller, less vigorous plants.

By thinning your lettuce, you ensure that each plant has enough space to grow to its full potential. This not only results in larger, healthier plants but also improves air circulation, reducing the risk of diseases caused by excess moisture and poor ventilation.

Pruning, on the other hand, involves removing dead or damaged leaves from your lettuce plants. This practice helps to maintain the overall health of the plant. Dead or damaged leaves can attract pests and diseases, which can spread to healthy parts of the plant if not promptly addressed. Pruning these leaves allows the plant to direct more energy towards growing new, healthy leaves. Additionally, it improves the plant's appearance and makes harvesting easier.

In addition to these benefits, both pruning and thinning can help to improve the quality of your harvest. Thinned seedlings are often perfectly good to eat and can be used in salads or as a garnish. Regularly pruning your lettuce plants encourages a continual harvest by stimulating new growth. Therefore, these practices not only enhance the health and productivity of your lettuce plants but also provide you with a steady supply of fresh, homegrown lettuce.

Pruning and thinning container-grown lettuce are essential steps in the cultivation process to ensure healthy plant growth and a good harvest. The timing and method for both practices depend on the growth stage of your lettuce plants.

Thinning typically occurs early in the plant's life cycle, once the lettuce seedlings have sprouted and developed their first true leaves – these are the leaves that appear after the initial seed leaves. At this point, you'll likely notice that the plants are too close together, which can hinder their growth by causing competition for resources.

To thin your lettuce, carefully remove seedlings to create space around remaining plants. The goal is to leave at least 4-6 inches of space between each plant, allowing them room to grow and mature. You can simply cut the unwanted seedlings at soil level with a pair of scissors to avoid disturbing the roots of the remaining plants. Remember, thinned lettuce seedlings are edible and can be added to salads or sandwiches.

Pruning, on the other hand, is an ongoing process throughout the life of your lettuce plants. Lettuce pruning primarily involves removing dead or damaged leaves that can attract pests or diseases. Regularly inspect your plants, and if you see any leaves that are yellowing, wilted, or showing signs of disease, remove them promptly. You can do this by hand or with a pair of clean, sharp gardening shears. Cut the leaf off where it joins the main stem, taking care not to damage the rest of the plant.

Additionally, some gardeners practice a form of pruning known as "cut-and-come-again." This method involves cutting the entire plant about an inch above the soil when the leaves are mature but before the plant has bolted or started to flower. This encourages the plant to produce a second growth of leaves, extending your harvest period.

Both thinning and pruning are vital for maintaining the health and productivity of your container-grown lettuce. By providing your plants with the space and care they need, you can enjoy a bountiful harvest of fresh, homegrown lettuce.

Watering Your Container Grown Lettuce

Watering is a fundamental aspect of maintaining your container-grown lettuce in vegetable gardens. Unlike plants grown directly in the ground, container plants rely entirely on you for their water supply. Lettuce, in particular, is a moisture-loving plant and requires consistent watering to thrive. Adequate hydration ensures that the lettuce grows quickly, resulting in tender and flavorful leaves.

Moreover, steady water levels help to prevent the plant from bolting - a survival mechanism where the plant rapidly produces flowers and seeds, often resulting in bitter tasting leaves. Inconsistent watering can stress the plant, leading to poor growth and susceptibility to pests and diseases.

However, it's also essential to avoid overwatering, as soggy conditions can lead to root rot or other fungal diseases. Therefore, providing the right amount of water - not too much and not too little - is crucial for the health and productivity of your container-grown lettuce.

Watering container-grown lettuce in vegetable container gardens is a careful balance. As lettuce is composed of over 80 percent water, it requires a consistent supply of moisture to thrive 1. However, while lettuce needs regular watering, it cannot tolerate overly wet conditions, emphasizing the need for well-drained soil and careful watering practices 2.

During the initial stages of growth, right after sowing the seeds, it's crucial to keep the soil moist until the seeds germinate. This might require watering once or twice daily, depending on the weather and the container's exposure to sun and wind. However, beware of overwatering, as soggy conditions can lead to root rot or other fungal diseases.

If you notice water sitting on the surface of the soil for a long time after watering, it may indicate that your soil is not draining well, and you are potentially overwatering.

Once the lettuce plants have established, they still need consistent watering, but the frequency may decrease. A general rule of thumb for container gardening is that plants in pots 24 inches deep require about 2 inches of water each week. However, this amount can vary depending on factors such as the size of the plant, the size of the container, the type of soil used, and the current weather conditions.

In hot weather, lettuce may need daily watering, as containers dry out more quickly than garden soil. In contrast, during cooler, cloudy weather, watering might be needed only every few days. The key is to monitor the soil moisture regularly. You can do this by sticking your finger about an inch into the soil. If it feels dry at that depth, it's time to water your lettuce.

Remember that it's better to water thoroughly less frequently than to give your plants a little water more often. Shallow watering can lead to shallow root systems and make your plants less resilient in the face of dry conditions. When you water, aim to moisten the entire root zone, which in a container is usually the whole pot.

By understanding the water needs of lettuce and adapting your watering practices to meet these needs, you can grow healthy, productive lettuce plants in your container garden.

Organic Fertilization For Container Grown Lettuce

Organic fertilization plays a crucial role in the successful growth of container-grown lettuce in vegetable gardens. Unlike in-ground gardens, where plants have access to a wide range of nutrients present in the native soil, container-grown plants are limited to what is available in their potting mix. Over time, as the lettuce plant grows and matures, it depletes these nutrients.

Organic fertilizers help replenish these essential nutrients, promoting healthy plant growth. They contain a wide range of macro and micronutrients, which are released slowly into the soil, ensuring a steady supply for the plant. Moreover, organic fertilizers improve the structure of the potting mix, enhancing its ability to hold water and air, both critical for root health.

They also increase the soil's biodiversity, encouraging the presence of beneficial microbes that aid in nutrient uptake. Overall, organic fertilization is a sustainable and eco-friendly practice that not only boosts your lettuce's growth and productivity but also contributes to the overall health of your container garden ecosystem.

Organic fertilizers are a great choice for container-grown lettuce in vegetable container gardens. They not only provide the necessary nutrients for plant growth but also improve soil structure and promote the growth of beneficial microorganisms.

One popular organic fertilizer option is compost. Compost is rich in nutrients and can be made at home from kitchen scraps and yard waste. It releases nutrients slowly over time, providing a long-term source of nourishment for your lettuce plants.

Before planting, mix compost into your potting soil. You can also add a layer of compost to the top of the soil once or twice during the growing season.

Worm castings, also known as vermicompost, are another excellent organic fertilizer for lettuce. They are full of nutrients and beneficial bacteria. Like compost, worm castings can be mixed into your soil before planting and added as a top-dressing partway through the growing season.

Sea-based products like fish emulsion and seaweed extract are also beneficial. Fish emulsion is high in nitrogen, which promotes leafy growth, making it ideal for lettuce. Seaweed extract contains a range of micronutrients and can help improve plant health and resistance to stress. These liquid fertilizers can be diluted with water and applied directly to the soil around your plants.

Bone meal and blood meal are other organic fertilizers that can be beneficial for lettuce. Bone meal is high in phosphorus, which is essential for root development and plant health. Blood meal is a high-nitrogen fertilizer, which is ideal for promoting the leafy growth desired in lettuce.

When it comes to timing, it's best to add your organic fertilizer at planting time. Mix it into the soil to ensure that the nutrients are available to the roots. After that, you can add more fertilizer as a top-dressing partway through the growing season. This is especially important for fast-growing crops like lettuce, which can quickly use up the available nutrients.

However, remember that over-fertilizing can be just as harmful as under-fertilizing. Too much nitrogen can lead to excessive leafy growth at the expense of root development, while too much phosphorus can interfere with the uptake of other nutrients. Always follow the manufacturer's instructions when applying any fertilizer and adjust based on the health and growth of your plants.

By choosing the right organic fertilizers and using them correctly, you can ensure that your container-grown lettuce is healthy, productive, and delicious.

PROTECTING YOUR CONTAINER GROWN LETTUCE

Extreme Temperatures

Protecting container-grown lettuce from extreme temperatures in vegetable container gardens is essential for a successful harvest. Lettuce, being a cool-season crop, thrives in temperatures between 60°F and 70°F. It can tolerate light frosts, but hot temperatures can cause the plants to bolt, or go to seed prematurely, resulting in bitter-tasting leaves. Similarly, hard freezes can damage or kill the plants. Therefore, managing temperature extremes is crucial to maintaining the health and productivity of your lettuce crop.

To protect your lettuce plants from the heat, consider providing them with some shade during the hottest part of the day. This could be accomplished by positioning them under a larger plant, using a shade cloth, or even moving them to a cooler location if they are in portable containers. Regular watering is also key during hot weather, as it helps to keep the plants cool and prevents them from drying out. However, be careful not to over-water as this can lead to root rot and other diseases.

For protection against freezing temperatures, one of the most effective strategies is to move the containers indoors or to a sheltered location. If that's not possible, you can cover the plants with a frost blanket or even an old sheet to provide a layer of insulation. Another technique is to wrap the containers themselves with bubble wrap or burlap to help keep the soil from freezing.

Mulching around the base of the lettuce plants can also help to regulate soil temperature and moisture levels. Organic mulches like straw, shredded leaves, or wood chips are excellent choices. They insulate the soil, keeping it warmer in winter and cooler in summer, and they also conserve moisture and suppress weeds. By taking steps to protect your lettuce from temperature extremes, you can ensure a healthy, productive crop that provides fresh, tasty leaves for your table.

Protecting Container Grown Lettuce From Pests

Protecting container-grown lettuce from pests in vegetable container gardens is crucial for several reasons. Firstly, pests can cause significant damage to your plants, potentially ruining your entire crop. Lettuce is particularly susceptible to a variety of pests, including aphids, slugs, and snails, which can quickly devour or damage the leaves. Furthermore, some pests can transmit diseases to your lettuce plants, exacerbating the damage and making it more difficult for the plants to recover.

Secondly, pests in a container garden can easily spread to other containers, threatening your whole collection of plants. Lastly, if you're growing lettuce with the intention of eating it, you'll want to avoid using harsh chemical pesticides that could leave residues on your food.

Therefore, keeping pests at bay from the outset is the best way to ensure healthy, edible lettuce. Implementing preventive measures and using organic pest control methods can help you maintain a healthy, productive lettuce crop in your container garden, free of harmful chemicals.

Container-grown lettuce can be susceptible to several pests that can significantly impact their growth and health. Some of the most common pests include slugs, snails, aphids, and fungus gnats.

Slugs and snails are particularly attracted to the tender leaves of lettuce, where they can cause extensive damage by chewing large, irregular holes. These pests are more active during cool, damp conditions, especially at night. To combat them, you can use a variety of methods.

One effective strategy is to use barriers around your containers, such as copper tape, which gives off a small electric charge when the slug or snail tries to cross it. Diatomaceous earth can also be sprinkled around the plants; its sharp particles deter these pests. Handpicking at night can also help keep their population in check.

Aphids are tiny insects that suck the sap from lettuce leaves, causing them to curl and become discolored. They can also transmit diseases between plants. Natural predators like lady-bugs and lacewings can help control aphid populations. You can also use insecticidal soaps or neem oil sprays that are safe for edible plants. It's important to spray the undersides of the leaves as well, as this is where aphids often hide.

Fungus gnats are small, fly-like insects that lay their eggs in the soil. While the adults don't cause damage to plants, their larvae can feed on the roots, potentially stunting growth or killing young plants. To prevent fungus gnat infestations, avoid over-watering your lettuce, as these pests thrive in damp conditions. Yellow sticky traps can also be effective in catching adult gnats.

One of the best ways to protect your lettuce from pests is to practice good garden sanitation. This includes removing plant debris that can harbor pests or disease, regularly inspecting your plants for signs of infestation, and isolating any affected plants to prevent the spread of pests.

Remember, while these pests can be a nuisance and cause damage, they don't spell the end for your lettuce crop. With vigilance and the proper preventative measures, you can successfully grow healthy, pest-free lettuce in your container garden.

Protecting Container Grown Lettuce From Diseases

Protecting container-grown lettuce from diseases in vegetable container gardens is crucial for a variety of reasons. Diseases can severely affect the health and productivity of your lettuce plants, leading to poor growth, discolored or wilting leaves, and even plant death in severe cases.

Many plant diseases are caused by fungi, bacteria, or viruses that thrive in specific conditions, such as high humidity or poor air circulation, which can be common in container gardens. Once established, these diseases can be difficult to eradicate and may spread to other plants in your garden, causing widespread damage. Moreover, some diseases can render the lettuce unsafe or unappetizing to eat.

By taking preventive measures to protect your lettuce from diseases, you can ensure a bountiful and healthy harvest, preserve the aesthetic appeal of your garden, and prevent potential losses from reduced yield.

Container-grown lettuce can be affected by several diseases, including Bacterial Leaf Spot, Bottom Rot, Damping Off, Downy

Mildew, Lettuce Mosaic, Anthracnose (Shot-hole), Leaf drop (Sclerotinia drop), and Powdery Mildew. These diseases can cause a range of symptoms, such as leaf spots, rotting, wilting, discoloration, and stunted growth, which can significantly impact the health and productivity of your lettuce plants.

Bacterial Leaf Spot, caused by the bacterium Xanthomonas campestris pv. vitians manifests as small, dark brown spots on the leaves. To manage this disease organically, avoid overhead watering to minimize leaf wetness and promote good air circulation around your plants. Planting resistant varieties can also help.

Bottom Rot is a soil-borne disease that causes browning and rotting at the base of the lettuce plant. It is often associated with high soil moisture and poor drainage. To prevent this, ensure that your containers have adequate drainage and avoid overwatering.

Damping Off is another soil-borne disease that can kill seedlings before they emerge or soon after. It is caused by several types of fungi, including Pythium and Rhizoctonia. Using sterile potting mix and avoiding overwatering can help prevent this disease.

Downy Mildew is caused by the fungus Bremia lactucae and can cause yellow to light green patches on the upper leaf surface and fluffy, white fungal growth on the underside. Good air circulation, proper spacing of plants, and preventive spraying with organic fungicides like copper or sulfur can help manage this disease.

Lettuce Mosaic is a viral disease that causes mottling and distortion of the leaves. It is often spread by aphids. Using virus-free seed and controlling aphid populations can help prevent this disease.

Anthracnose, caused by the fungus Microdochium panattonianum, creates small, sunken spots on the leaves. Leaf drop is caused by Sclerotinia spp. and can cause the lettuce plant to wilt and collapse. Powdery Mildew, caused by Erysiphe cichoracearum, results in white, powdery fungal growth on the leaf surface. These diseases can be managed by promoting good air circulation, proper sanitation practices, and using organic fungicides.

Remember that prevention is always the best strategy when it comes to managing diseases in your container garden. By maintaining good cultural practices, such as proper watering, sanitation, and spacing, you can keep most of these diseases at bay and enjoy a healthy, productive lettuce crop.

HARVESTING CONTAINER GROWN LETTUCE

Container-grown lettuce is a fast-growing cool-season crop that typically takes between 30 to 60 days to reach maturity, depending on the variety and the growing conditions. Leaf lettuce varieties, such as 'Black Seeded Simpson' and 'Oak Leaf,' are usually ready to harvest in about 30 to 45 days from planting.

Romaine types, like 'Parris Island Cos,' can take slightly longer, typically around 60 days. Butterhead lettuces, like 'Buttercrunch,' can also take around 60 to 70 days to mature. Crisphead or iceberg types take the longest, often requiring 70 to 80 days to fully mature.

The great thing about lettuce is that you don't have to wait until it's fully mature to start enjoying it. You can begin harvesting as soon as the leaves are large enough to eat. This is often just a few weeks after planting. For a continual harvest, consider using the "cut-and-come-again" method. This involves cutting the outer leaves of the plant at the base, leaving the inner leaves to continue growing. This way, you can enjoy a steady supply of fresh lettuce over a longer period.

When it comes to harvesting your lettuce, the time of day matters. It's best to harvest in the early morning when the leaves are crisp, hydrated, and full of nutrients. If you can't do it in the morning, late afternoon or evening is the next best option. Avoid harvesting in the heat of the day, as the leaves can wilt quickly.

To harvest, use clean, sharp scissors or a knife to cut the leaves. If you're harvesting individual leaves, cut them off at the base of the plant. Be careful not to damage the central growing point, as this is where new leaves sprout. If you're harvesting the entire head, cut it off at the base, leaving a bit of stem attached. This can sometimes encourage the plant to produce a second smaller crop.

After harvesting, rinse the leaves under cool water to remove any soil or pests. Pat them dry, or use a salad spinner to remove excess moisture. Freshly harvested lettuce can be stored in the refrigerator for about a week. It's best to store it in a plastic bag or container with a few paper towels to absorb any excess moisture.

CONTAINER GROWN LETTUCE NOTES

Start: Seeds or Seedlings

Germination: 4 to 10 days, 40°F (4°C) and 80°F (27°C).

Seed Life: 1 Years

Soil Type: Well-draining, fertile soil with some organic matter (compost or well-rotted manure) - pH level between 6.0 to 7.0.

Seed Spacing: 1/4 inch deep (in potting pots)

Seedling Spacing: 6-8 inches between each plant and depth of 6-8 inches. (The size of the container you choose will also determine how many lettuce plants it can comfortably accommodate.)

Sunlight: 4 – 6hrs full sunlight daily.

Growing Temperatures: Temperatures between 35 – 75 degrees F for optimum growth. Ideal temperatures around 60 to 65°F

Days To Harvest: Black Seeded Simpson and Oak Leaf varieties - 30 to 45 day. Parris Island Cos varieties – up to 60 days. Buttercrunch varieties - 60 to 70 days. Crisphead and iceberg varieties - 70 to 80 days.

CHAPTER 7
VEGETABLE CONTAINER GARDENING – CELERY

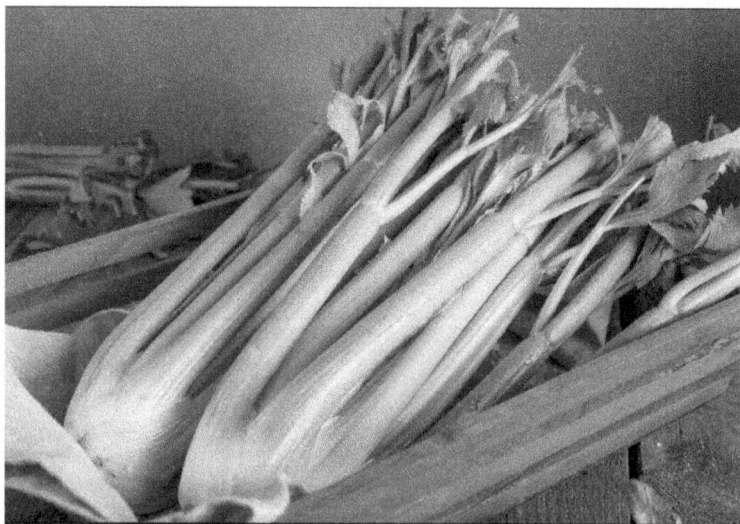

C elery, scientifically known as Apium graveolens, is a versatile vegetable that has been gaining popularity in container gardening due to its nutritional benefits and its adaptability to grow in small spaces. Known for its crunchy texture and distinctive flavor, celery is packed with essential vitamins and minerals, making it a favorite among health-conscious individuals.

Despite its reputation of requiring a bit more attention compared to other vegetables, with the right knowledge and care, growing celery in containers can be a rewarding endeavor. This method of gardening allows you to control the environment better, ensuring optimal growth conditions for your celery plants.

Whether you're an experienced gardener or a novice, cultivating celery in containers at home provides not only a constant supply of this nutritious vegetable but also adds a touch of deluxe greenery to your indoor or outdoor space.

Vegetable container gardening, especially with crops like celery, can bring numerous benefits to your gardening experience. Firstly, it maximizes the use of limited space, which is particularly advantageous for urban gardeners or those with smaller yards. Growing celery in containers allows you to cultivate this nutritious vegetable without needing a large plot of land.

Secondly, container gardening offers better control over the growing conditions, including soil quality, water, and light exposure. This means you can provide the ideal environment for your celery plants to thrive. Containers also make it easier to protect your celery from pests and diseases, as you can move the plants as needed.

Lastly, the mobility of containers allows you to extend the growing season by bringing the plants indoors during harsh weather conditions. Therefore, vegetable container gardening with celery not only gives you a fresh, home-grown supply of this healthy vegetable but also enhances your gardening flexibility and efficiency.

THE RIGHT SOIL TO GROW CELERY IN CONTAINERS

Choosing the right soil condition is essential for successfully growing celery in container gardens. Celery thrives best in rich, well-draining soil that can retain moisture without becoming waterlogged. This is because celery has shallow roots and requires consistent moisture to grow well. A soil mix that is too heavy or poorly draining can lead to waterlogging and root rot, while a mix that is too light may not retain enough moisture.

One of the best types of soil for celery is sandy loam soil. This type of soil is loose and drains well, preventing water from pooling around the plant's roots. It's also rich in nutrients, providing the celery with the essential elements it needs to grow strong and healthy.

If you're preparing your own soil mix for your container garden, consider combining two parts garden soil, one part compost or well-rotted manure, and one part coarse sand. The compost or manure adds nutrients to the soil, while the sand improves drainage.

It's also important to maintain the soil's pH level between 6.0 and 7.0, which is slightly acidic to neutral. Celery prefers this pH range and will struggle to absorb nutrients from the soil if the pH is too high or too low. You can test the soil pH using a home testing kit and adjust it as necessary using lime to raise the pH or sulfur to lower it.

Lastly, remember to regularly replenish the nutrients in your soil throughout the growing season. Celery is a heavy feeder, so it can quickly deplete the nutrients in the soil. Regular applications of a balanced, slow-release fertilizer can help maintain nutrient levels and promote healthy growth.

The right soil conditions for growing celery in container gardens include a well-draining, nutrient-rich soil with a slightly acidic to neutral pH. Regular watering and fertilization are also key to ensuring the success of your celery plants.

HOW TO SOW CELERY IN CONTAINERS GARDENS

Correct Season To Sow Celery In Containers Gardens

Celery is a cool-season crop that thrives when planted in the spring or fall, as it doesn't perform well in the heat of the summer. It has a long maturation period, generally requiring 130-140 days to fully mature, so planning your planting schedule accordingly is crucial. To get a head start on the growing season and ensure a strong, early start for your plants, it's recommended to sow celery seeds indoors.

Once the seedlings have developed and the threat of frost has passed, they can be transplanted into vegetable container gardens. Planting in containers allows for greater control over the growing conditions and bypasses the vagaries of weather, providing a more stable environment for celery to thrive.

Remember, celery needs moist, rich soil, so regular watering and feeding are essential to support its growth. As the season progresses into the hotter months, the containers can be moved to shadier locations to protect the celery from excessive heat. By understanding and adhering to the correct sowing season for celery, you can maximize your chances of a successful harvest.

Plant Needs & Requirements

Properly germinating celery vegetable plants from seeds to seedlings is crucial when growing in vegetable container gardens. Celery seeds are tiny and require special care to ensure successful germination. The process of germination is the first step in a plant's lifecycle and sets the stage for the plant's overall health and productivity. If the seeds are not germinated correctly, it can lead to weak or stunted seedlings that may not survive transplanting, let alone mature into productive plants.

Celery has a long growing season, so starting with robust seedlings is especially important to ensure they have enough time to mature before the end of the growing season.

Proper germination also helps to maximize the use of your seeds, reducing waste and saving resources. This is particularly important given that celery seeds can be relatively expensive compared to other vegetable seeds.

Finally, by carefully controlling the germination conditions, you can avoid many common problems such as damping off, a fungal disease that can kill seedlings before they have a chance to grow. Therefore, understanding and implementing correct germination techniques is key to successfully growing celery in vegetable container gardens.

Germinating celery vegetable plants from seeds to seedlings requires patience and attention to detail. The first step is to prepare your planting medium. Use a high-quality seed starting mix, which is typically lighter and more sterile than regular potting soil, reducing the risk of disease. Fill your seed trays or pots with the mix, leaving a little room at the top.

Next, sow the celery seeds. Celery seeds are tiny, so you'll need to be careful when handling them. Sprinkle the seeds lightly over the surface of the soil. Because they need light to germinate, do not cover them with soil.

Instead, gently press them into the surface of the soil to ensure good contact. Mist the surface with water to moisten the seeds and the soil around them. Cover the tray or pots with a clear plastic dome or plastic wrap to help retain moisture and warmth.

Celery seeds prefer a consistent temperature of around 70 degrees Fahrenheit (21 degrees Celsius) for germination. You can use a heat mat under your seed trays or pots to maintain this temperature if necessary. Place the trays or pots in a location that receives indirect sunlight. Check daily to ensure the soil remains moist, but not waterlogged. Germination of celery seeds can take anywhere from 10 to 21 days.

Once the celery seeds have sprouted and grown their first set of true leaves, they are ready to be transplanted into individual pots. At this point, they should be moved to a cooler location, ideally around 60-70 degrees Fahrenheit during the day and slightly cooler at night. Continue to keep the soil evenly moist and provide plenty of indirect sunlight.

When the seedlings have grown to about 2-3 inches tall and have at least three sets of true leaves, they are ready to be transplanted into their final container garden homes. This is typically about 5-6 weeks after germination.

Be sure to harden off the seedlings by gradually introducing them to outdoor conditions over a week or two before transplanting them permanently. Plant them at the same depth they were growing in their seedling pots, spaced about 8-10 inches apart. Continue to provide ample water and nutrients and protect them from extreme weather and pests to ensure a successful celery harvest.

Spacing & Measurement

Proper spacing and measurements when transplanting celery seedlings into container gardens are essential for a variety of reasons. Celery plants, like most vegetables, require ample space to grow and develop properly. Each plant needs enough room to spread out its roots and foliage without competition from its neighbors.

Overcrowding can lead to competition for resources such as light, water, and nutrients, which can stunt growth and reduce the overall health and productivity of the plants. Furthermore, adequate spacing helps promote good air circulation around the plants, which can help prevent fungal diseases that thrive in damp, stagnant conditions.

When it comes to measurements, ensuring your containers have sufficient depth is crucial, as celery has a strong root system that needs plenty of room to expand. A container that is too shallow could restrict root growth, affecting the plant's ability to take up water and nutrients efficiently, and ultimately limiting its growth and yield. Therefore, careful attention to spacing and measurements when transplanting celery seedlings can significantly impact the success of your celery crop in container gardens.

When it comes to planting celery seedlings in container gardens, understanding the desired spacing and measurements is crucial for the successful growth of your plants. The size of the container plays a significant role in this process.

The ideal depth of the container should be at least 8 inches. This depth allows for adequate room for the celery's robust root system to grow and expand, which is essential for the plant's ability to uptake water and nutrients efficiently.

As for the spacing between each celery plant, planting celery in a block rather than rows, with each plant spaced approximately 9 inches apart in each direction is recommended. This arrangement allows the plants to shade each other, which can help in blanching them. Similarly, transplanting seedlings outside 8-10 inches apart. This spacing helps ensure each plant has enough space to establish its roots and foliage without competing with its neighbors for resources.

However, if you're planting in rows, the rows should be spaced 2 feet apart, and the plants should be 12 inches apart within the row. This layout promotes good air circulation, reducing the risk of fungal diseases, and forces tall growth and long petioles.

In summary, when planting celery seedlings in container gardens, opting for containers with an 8-inch depth and maintaining a spacing of 8-12 inches between each plant can contribute significantly to your gardening success. It's also worth considering the arrangement of your plants; planting in blocks can aid in blanching, while row planting can encourage taller growth.

Ideal Temperatures & Sun Requirements

The ideal temperatures and sun requirements are crucial factors in ensuring the successful growth of celery in container gardens. Celery is a cool-season crop that thrives in temperatures between 60-70 degrees Fahrenheit (15-21 degrees Celsius). If the temperature rises above 75 degrees Fahrenheit (24 degrees Celsius), the plant may bolt, or prematurely go to seed, which can negatively affect the taste and texture of the stalks.

At the same time, if the temperatures drop below 55 degrees Fahrenheit (13 degrees Celsius), the growth of the plant can be significantly slowed down. Therefore, maintaining the optimal temperature range is vital for the healthy development of celery plants.

As for sun requirements, celery needs a good amount of sunlight to grow well. It requires around 6 hours of full sun each day, but it can also tolerate partial shade. In fact, in hot climates, a bit of afternoon shade can help prevent the plant from overheating. However, too much shade can lead to leggy growth and diminished flavor. Hence, finding the right balance of sunlight exposure is key.

To summarize, providing celery with the ideal temperature range of 60-70 degrees Fahrenheit and around 6 hours of sunlight daily is important for its growth and development. These conditions, coupled with proper care and maintenance, can lead to a bountiful harvest of crisp, tasty celery from your container garden.

MAINTAINING YOUR CONTAINER GROWN CELERY

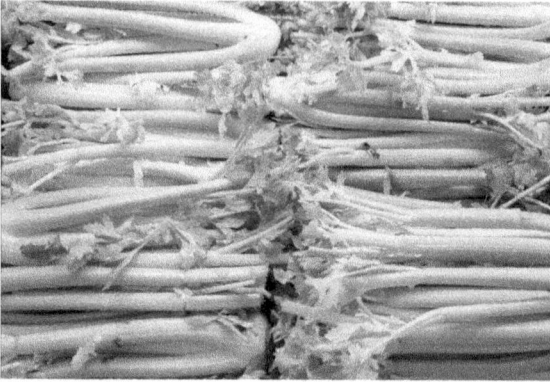

Maintaining your container-grown celery in vegetable container gardening is of paramount importance for several reasons.

Firstly, container-grown plants rely solely on the care provided by the gardener for their nutrient, water, and light needs since they don't have access to the broader resources available in a ground garden. Therefore, regular watering, feeding, and appropriate positioning are crucial for their survival and productivity.

Secondly, celery is a heavy feeder and requires consistent supply of nutrients to produce crisp, flavorful stalks. Regular application of a balanced fertilizer can help meet this need.

Thirdly, celery requires consistent moisture levels, and containers can dry out faster than ground soil, making daily monitoring necessary, especially in hot weather.

Lastly, growing in containers can make plants more susceptible to pests and diseases due to the close proximity of other plants. Regular maintenance includes checking for signs of disease or pests, which allows for early detection and treatment, preventing potential spread and severe damage. Thus, diligent maintenance is key to successful celery cultivation in container gardens.

Pruning & Thinning Your Celery

Pruning and thinning container-grown celery in vegetable container gardens is a vital practice for several reasons. Pruning, which involves removing the outer stalks of the celery plant, allows the inner stalks to receive more nutrients and grow larger. It also helps in maintaining the size of the plant, especially in a container garden where space is limited. Regular pruning can also help prevent disease by increasing air circulation and reducing the chances of fungal infections.

Thinning, on the other hand, involves removing weaker plants to allow stronger ones more room to grow. In the case of celery, thinning is typically done at the seedling stage.

Overcrowded plants can compete for nutrients, water, and sunlight, leading to stunted growth and lower yields. By thinning out the weaker plants, you ensure the remaining ones have enough space to grow and develop properly.

Moreover, both pruning and thinning can help deter pests. Dense foliage can create a humid environment that attracts pests like aphids and caterpillars. By maintaining proper spacing and removing excess foliage, you can reduce these risks.

Pruning and thinning practices are essential in managing the health and productivity of your celery plants. They ensure optimal growth conditions, prevent diseases, deter pests, and ultimately contribute to a successful harvest from your container garden.

Pruning and thinning container-grown celery should be done periodically to ensure healthy plant growth and an abundant harvest. The timing and method for each process, however, can vary based on the plant's growth stage and overall health.

Pruning is typically done throughout the growing season, but it's especially important during the initial stages of growth when the plants are establishing their roots and foliage. Start by inspecting the celery plant for any signs of disease or damage.

Look out for yellow or brown leaves, wilted stalks, or any signs of pest infestation. Once identified, use a clean, sharp pair of garden shears or scissors to remove these parts. Cut at the base of the stalk to avoid leaving stubs that could foster disease.

Remember to sanitize your tools before and after pruning to prevent the spread of diseases. Regular pruning not only helps maintain the plant's health but also encourages more vigorous growth.

Thinning, on the other hand, should ideally start when the celery plants have grown their first true leaves, typically a few weeks after planting. At this stage, the plants are strong enough to withstand the thinning process, and you can identify which ones are weak or underdeveloped.

To thin out your celery, identify the smallest or weakest-looking plants in the container and gently pull them out from the soil, taking care not to disturb the roots of neighboring plants. Aim to leave about 2-3 inches of space between each remaining plant. This ensures that each celery plant has enough room to grow and access to adequate sunlight and nutrients.

Performing these tasks regularly can greatly enhance the overall health and yield of your container-grown celery. However, be sure to monitor your plants closely after pruning or thinning to ensure they are responding well to these practices. Adjust as necessary based on your observations and the specific needs of your plants.

Watering Your Container Grown Celery

Watering your container-grown celery in vegetable container gardens is crucial for several reasons. Celery is a water-loving plant that thrives in consistently moist soil conditions. Lack of adequate water can lead to the development of stringy, tough, and bitter-tasting stalks. Moreover, containers tend to dry out more quickly than traditional garden beds due to their limited soil volume and exposure to wind and sun.

Therefore, regular watering is necessary to maintain the moisture levels in the soil. Additionally, water is a carrier of nutrients; it helps transport the essential nutrients from the soil to the plant cells where they are needed for growth. Proper watering also aids in maintaining the turgidity of the plant, keeping it upright and robust.

Consistent watering can prevent common problems associated with water stress, like wilting and yellowing of leaves. Therefore, regular and appropriate watering is a key factor in successfully growing healthy and flavorful celery in container gardens.

Watering container-grown celery plants requires a careful balance. These plants love moisture and require regular watering to thrive, but the amount and frequency of watering can greatly depend on several factors including the size of the container, the type of soil, weather conditions, and the growth stage of the plant.

In general, celery plants prefer consistently moist soil. One common recommendation is to water the plants deeply until water runs out of the drainage holes at the bottom of the container. This ensures that the water reaches the deeper roots and doesn't just wet the surface.

However, it's crucial to avoid waterlogging the soil, as this can lead to root rot and other fungal diseases. Using a well-draining soil mix and ensuring your container has adequate drainage holes can help prevent overwatering.

The frequency of watering can vary based on weather conditions and the size of your container. In hot, dry, or windy weather, you might need to water your celery plants daily, or even twice a day, as the containers can dry out quickly. On cooler or cloudy days, watering every 2-3 days might be enough. Smaller containers will also dry out faster than larger ones and may require more frequent watering.

It's important to check the soil moisture regularly to determine when to water. You can do this by sticking your finger an inch into the soil. If it feels dry at that depth, it's time to water. If it still feels moist, wait another day before checking again.

As the celery plants grow and their root systems develop, they may need more water to support their growth. However, towards the end of the growing season, as the plants begin to mature and the weather cools down, you may need to reduce the watering frequency slightly to prevent excess moisture from causing rot in the mature stalks.

While celery plants are thirsty crops, it's crucial to monitor the soil moisture closely and adjust your watering practices as needed to provide just the right amount of water. Overwatering and underwatering can both harm your plants, so finding that sweet spot is key to growing healthy, productive celery in your container garden.

Organic Fertilization For Container Grown Celery

Organic fertilization is a crucial component of growing container-grown celery in vegetable container gardens. Unlike in-ground plants that have access to a wide range of nutrients present in the earth, container plants are limited to what is available in the potting mix. Over time, as the plants absorb the nutrients, the soil can become depleted.

Organic fertilizers play a critical role in replenishing these nutrients and maintaining healthy soil. They provide a wide array of macro and micronutrients necessary for plant growth, including nitrogen, phosphorus, and potassium, which are vital for celery's cell structure, root development, and overall vitality. Besides, organic fertilizers improve soil structure, enhancing its ability to hold water and nutrients, thus benefiting the celery plants' overall health and productivity.

Furthermore, they introduce beneficial microorganisms into the soil, promoting a healthy soil ecosystem that can naturally suppress diseases and pests. Organic fertilizers also release nutrients slowly over time, providing a steady supply of nutrition to your celery plants throughout the growing season.

This gradual release helps prevent nutrient run-off, making organic fertilizers an environmentally friendly choice. Therefore, using organic fertilizers is not only essential for the health and yield of your celery plants but also contributes to sustainable gardening practices.

Container-grown celery in vegetable container gardens can greatly benefit from organic fertilizers. These fertilizers are rich in nutrients, improve soil structure, and promote a healthy soil ecosystem. There are several types of organic fertilizers that you can use for your celery plants.

Compost is one of the most commonly used organic fertilizers. It's rich in a wide range of nutrients and can help improve soil structure. Compost also introduces beneficial microorganisms into the soil, which can enhance nutrient availability to your plants and suppress diseases. You can mix compost into your potting soil before planting or use it as a top dressing throughout the growing season.

Worm castings, also known as vermicompost, are another excellent choice. They are packed with nutrients and beneficial microbes, and they have a slow-release nature that provides a steady supply of nutrients over time. Worm castings also help improve soil moisture retention, which is particularly beneficial for water-loving celery plants.

Bone meal and fish emulsion are other organic options that are high in phosphorus, which is crucial for root development and plant growth. Bone meal is a slow-release fertilizer that provides nutrients over a long period, while fish emulsion is water-soluble and provides quick nutrition.

When it comes to applying organic fertilizers to your celery plants, timing and method are important. Generally, you should start feeding your celery plants when you see the first true leaves, usually a few weeks after planting. After that, a regular feeding schedule of every 2-4 weeks can be beneficial.

Application methods can vary based on the type of fertilizer. For compost and worm castings, you can simply add them to the top of the soil and lightly mix them in. For bone meal, fish emulsion, or other granular or liquid fertilizers, follow the package instructions for application rates. Make sure to water thoroughly after applying fertilizers to help the nutrients seep into the soil.

Remember, while organic fertilizers are generally safe, over-fertilization can still harm your plants. It's always better to err on the side of under-fertilizing and adjust as needed based on your plants' growth and health. Regular monitoring of your celery plants will help you determine their nutrient needs and adjust your fertilization practices accordingly.

PROTECTING YOUR CONTAINER GROWN CELERY

Extreme Temperatures

Protecting container-grown celery from extreme temperatures in vegetable container gardens is essential for the plant's health and productivity. Celery plants are cool-season crops, which means they prefer a stable temperature range of about 60-70 degrees Fahrenheit. Therefore, they may struggle to survive and produce well during periods of extreme heat or cold.

During hot weather, celery plants can suffer from heat stress, which can result in wilting, yellowing leaves, and stunted growth. To protect your celery plants from extreme heat, consider moving your containers to a shaded area during the hottest part of the day, if possible.

If you can't move your containers, consider using shade cloth to provide some relief from the intense sun. Regular watering is also crucial during hot weather to prevent the soil from drying out. However, avoid watering in the middle of the day when evaporation rates are high. Early morning or late evening is the best time to water.

In cold weather, celery plants are at risk of frost damage, which can cause cell damage and even kill the plant. If frost or freezing temperatures are predicted, you can protect your celery plants by moving the containers indoors or into a greenhouse, if possible.

If moving the containers isn't an option, you can cover them with frost cloths or old blankets to provide some insulation. Adding a layer of mulch around the base of the plants can also help retain soil warmth and protect the roots from freezing temperatures.

Protecting your celery plants from extreme temperatures is important because it allows them to maintain their metabolic processes and continue growing and producing. Extreme temperatures can cause stress to the plants, leading to reduced growth, lower yields, and increased susceptibility to pests and diseases. By taking steps to moderate the temperature conditions around your celery plants, you can ensure they have the optimal environment to thrive and produce a bountiful harvest.

Whether it's scorching summer heat or frigid winter frost, extreme temperatures can pose a serious threat to your container-grown celery. But with careful monitoring, timely intervention, and the use of protective measures like shade cloths, frost covers, or even relocating your plants, you can help your celery weather these challenges and continue to flourish.

Protecting Container Grown Celery From Pests

Protecting container-grown celery from pests in vegetable container gardens is of utmost importance for several reasons. Firstly, pests can cause significant damage to the plants, affecting their health and reducing their productivity.

Common pests such as aphids, slugs, and celery leafminers can feed on the leaves, stems, or roots of the celery, leading to yellowing leaves, stunted growth, and in severe cases, plant death.

Secondly, some pests can transmit diseases to the celery plants, further impacting their health and yield. For instance, aphids spread viral diseases, which can be challenging to control once established.

Thirdly, pest infestations can spread quickly in a container garden due to the proximity of the plants, so early detection and control are critical to prevent widespread damage.

Lastly, managing pests organically in container gardens can contribute to a healthy ecosystem by reducing reliance on synthetic pesticides, which can harm beneficial insects and the environment. Therefore, protecting your celery plants from pests not only ensures the health and yield of your plants but also contributes to sustainable gardening practices.

Celery grown in container gardens can fall prey to a variety of pests, each posing unique challenges and requiring specific strategies for control. Some of the most common pests that attack celery include aphids, blister beetles, tomato hornworms, flea beetles, slugs, earwigs, and parsley worms.

Aphids, including carrot-willow aphids, peach aphids, hawthorn aphids, and melon aphids, are small soft-bodied insects that suck sap from celery plants, weakening them and potentially spreading diseases.

They can cause leaves to curl and yellow, and they excrete a sticky substance called honeydew that can lead to the growth of sooty mold. To manage aphids, regularly inspect your plants for signs of infestation. If you spot aphids, try washing them off with a strong jet of water or using insecticidal soap.

Blister beetles and tomato hornworms are larger pests that feed on celery leaves, causing noticeable defoliation. Handpicking can be an effective method for controlling these pests if the infestation is not too large. Keep the garden clear of weeds and debris, which can harbor these pests, and consider introducing beneficial insects like ladybugs and parasitic wasps, which are natural predators of these pests.

Flea beetles, slugs, and earwigs are other common pests of celery. Flea beetles are small, jumping insects that leave tiny holes in the leaves. Slugs and earwigs can cause more significant damage by chewing large holes in the leaves. Control measures for these pests include trapping, handpicking, and using diatomaceous earth or other organic insecticides.

Lastly, celery leaf mining flies, snails, and parsley worms can also pose problems. Leaf miners create meandering tunnels in the leaves, while snails and parsley worms chew holes in them. Regular monitoring, handpicking, and use of barriers or baits can help manage these pests.

While several pests can attack celery grown in container gardens, there are various methods to protect your plants. Regular monitoring, maintaining good sanitation, and using a combination of physical, cultural, and organic control measures can help keep your celery healthy and productive.

Protecting Container Grown Celery From Diseases

Protecting container-grown celery from diseases in vegetable container gardens is crucial for several reasons. Diseases can significantly impact the health, growth, and productivity of celery plants. They can cause symptoms such as wilting, yellowing, leaf spots, and root rot, which can reduce the quality and yield of the harvest.

Additionally, diseases can spread quickly in a container garden due to the close proximity of the plants, potentially affecting the entire crop. Furthermore, some diseases can persist in the soil or plant debris, making future plantings vulnerable to infection. Therefore, protecting your celery plants from diseases is essential to ensure a healthy, productive garden, and to maintain the continuity of your gardening efforts.

One common disease is Fusarium yellow, which is caused by the fungus Fusarium oxysporum f.sp. apii. This disease results in wilting, yellowing of leaves, and a general decline in the plant's health. Other fungal diseases like early blight, late blight, and Septoria leaf spot can also affect celery plants, leading to leaf spots, wilting, and in severe cases, plant death.

Celery can also be affected by bacterial diseases like bacterial leaf blight and bacterial soft rot. Bacterial leaf blight, caused by Pseudomonas cichorii, leads to water-soaked spots on leaves that eventually turn necrotic. Bacterial soft rot, caused by Pectobacterium carotovorum subsp. carotovorum, results in a wet, slimy rot of petioles and even entire plants.

To organically protect your container-grown celery from these diseases, several strategies can be employed. Firstly, ensure good air circulation among your plants to prevent the buildup of humidity, which can facilitate fungal and bacterial growth.

Secondly, practice crop rotation to prevent the buildup of disease-causing organisms in the soil. Thirdly, use disease-resistant varieties of celery when possible.

Maintaining a clean garden environment is also essential. Remove diseased plants and debris promptly to reduce sources of infection. Water your plants at the base rather than from above to keep the leaves dry and less susceptible to fungal diseases. For bacterial diseases, consider using organic bactericides. Copper-based sprays can help control bacterial diseases. For fungal diseases, organic fungicides like neem oil or baking soda can be effective.

While several diseases can pose a threat to container-grown celery, with good cultural practices and appropriate organic disease control measures, these threats can be effectively managed, ensuring a healthy and productive crop.

HARVESTING CONTAINER GROWN CELERY

Growing celery in container gardens is a rewarding endeavor that allows you to enjoy this crisp and nutritious vegetable right from your own garden. From the time of planting, celery generally takes around 16 to 18 weeks to mature and be ready for harvest. This timeframe can vary slightly depending on the specific variety of celery you are growing and the growing conditions.

The first sign that your celery is ready for harvest is when the stalks reach about 6 to 8 inches in height. At this point, the stalks should be firm, and the plant should have a robust bunch of stalks. The color of the celery should be a vibrant green, although some varieties may have a tinge of white or yellow. It's best to harvest celery early in the morning when the plant is fully hydrated for the crispest stalks.

To harvest your celery, you have two main options: you can either harvest the entire plant at once, or you can harvest individual stalks as needed. If you choose to harvest the entire plant, use a sharp knife to cut the plant off at the soil level. Be careful not to damage the roots if you plan on leaving the root system in place for a possible second harvest.

If you prefer to harvest individual stalks, simply snap off the outermost stalks at the base, taking care not to damage the rest of the plant. This method allows the plant to continue producing stalks for an extended harvest. Whether you're harvesting the whole plant or just a few stalks, handle the celery carefully to avoid bruising or damaging the crisp stalks.

After harvesting, rinse the celery thoroughly and store it in the refrigerator to maintain its crispness. Freshly harvested celery can typically be stored in the refrigerator for up to two weeks. Remember to keep the soil in your container garden replenished with organic matter and nutrients to support continuous growth and productivity.

CONTAINER GROWN CELERY NOTES

Start: Seeds or Seedlings

Germination: 10 to 21 days, 70 – 75 degrees Fahrenheit (21 degrees Celsius)

Seed Life: 5 Years

Soil Type: Sandy loam soil. Loose and drains well, with some organic matter (compost or well-rotted manure) - pH level between 6.0 to 7.0.

Seed Spacing: 1/4 inch deep (in potting pots).

Seedling Spacing: 8-inch depth and maintaining a spacing of 8-12 inches.

Sunlight: 6hrs full sunlight daily.

Growing Temperatures: Temperatures between 60-70 degrees Fahrenheit (15-21 degrees Celsius).

Days To Harvest: 112 to 126 Days

CHAPTER 8
VEGETABLE CONTAINER GARDENING – PEAS

Peas are a delightful addition to any vegetable container garden. Not only are they delicious and nutritious, but they are also relatively easy to grow, even for gardening novices. These cool-season crops are perfect for container gardening due to their compact growth habit and shallow root system. They require minimal space yet yield a bountiful harvest. Not only do they produce sweet, tender pods that can be enjoyed fresh or cooked, but their vibrant green foliage also adds a touch of beauty to any patio or balcony garden. Growing peas in containers allows you to control the growing conditions more precisely, making it easier to provide the perfect environment for these cool-season crops.

In this chapter, we explore the ins and outs of successfully growing peas in your container garden, from choosing the right variety and container to understanding the best practices for planting, care, and harvest.

Incorporating peas into your vegetable container garden can bring a myriad of benefits. Firstly, peas are known for their ability to enrich the soil with nitrogen through a process called nitrogen fixation. This natural process improves the fertility of the soil, thereby boosting the health and productivity of other plants in your garden. Additionally, growing peas in containers allows for better pest control. You can easily monitor and address any pest issues without them spreading to the rest of your garden.

Peas also have a relatively short growing season, which means you can enjoy a quick harvest and then utilize the same container for another crop. Finally, the vertical growth habit of many pea varieties makes excellent use of space, making them ideal for small gardens or balconies. All these factors combined make peas an excellent addition to any vegetable container garden.

THE RIGHT SOIL TO GROW PEAS IN CONTAINERS

Choosing the right soil conditions for growing peas in container gardens is paramount to ensure a bountiful harvest. Peas thrive in well-draining soil, as they are susceptible to root rot if the soil is too waterlogged. Therefore, it's crucial to select a high-quality potting mix that retains enough moisture for the peas' needs, but also allows excess water to drain away easily. You can enhance drainage by adding coarse sand or perlite to your potting mix.

The soil should also be rich in organic matter to provide the necessary nutrients for the pea plants. Adding compost or well-rotted manure to your soil can significantly improve its fertility. Peas are legumes and have the unique ability to fix nitrogen from the atmosphere with the help of symbiotic bacteria in their root nodules. However, they still benefit from a balanced fertilizer, especially one high in phosphorus and potassium, to support robust growth and prolific pod production.

Peas prefer slightly acidic to neutral pH levels, ideally between 6.0 and 7.0. Most potting soils fall within this range, but if you're unsure, you can test your soil using a pH testing kit. If your soil is too acidic, you can add lime to raise the pH, and if it's too alkaline, you can add sulfur or peat moss to lower the pH.

Lastly, remember that soil in containers tends to dry out faster than soil in the ground, so regular watering is essential. However, avoid overwatering as this can lead to root diseases.

The top inch of soil should be allowed to dry out between waterings. With the right soil conditions, your container-grown peas are likelier to thrive, resulting in a plentiful harvest of fresh, delicious peas.

HOW TO SOW PEAS IN CONTAINERS GARDENS

Correct Season To Sow Peas In Containers Gardens

Peas are versatile plants that can be grown in various climates, but they predominantly prefer cool conditions. They thrive in temperatures between 55°F and 65°F, making them an ideal crop for early spring or fall when these temperatures are most common. For most regions, it's recommended to sow peas in vegetable container gardens as early in the season as possible for a bountiful harvest. This early planting also helps avoid the warmer weather that can hinder pea growth.

In warmer climates where temperatures exceed 60 degrees F (16 C), peas are considered a warm season crop and sowing should begin in the spring. If you're using containers, you have the added benefit of starting your peas indoors as early as February, then moving them outside once the weather allows.

For precise timing, consider planting your peas two to three weeks before the final frost date in your region. Another strategy is to use succession planting techniques to extend the harvest period. Regardless of the specific planting time, always remember that peas are a cool-season crop, so early spring or fall plantings generally yield the best results.

Plant Needs & Requirements

Germinating peas from seeds to seedlings correctly is a crucial step when growing them in vegetable container gardens. The germination process is the first stage of a plant's life, and it determines the overall health, growth, and productivity of the plant. Proper germination ensures that the pea plants have a strong start, which can lead to a more bountiful harvest later on.

When peas are germinated correctly, they are more likely to grow into robust plants with a strong root system, making them more resilient to environmental stressors such as pests, diseases, and fluctuating weather conditions. Moreover, correct germination can also ensure optimal use of the limited space available in container gardens.

Overcrowding can be avoided by properly spacing the seeds during germination, leading to better air circulation, and reducing the risk of fungal diseases. In addition, proper germination ensures that each seed has the best chance of survival, minimizing waste and making your gardening efforts more efficient and productive. Therefore, understanding and implementing correct germination practices is key to successful pea cultivation in vegetable container gardens.

Germinating peas from seeds to seedlings involves a few key steps that are relatively straightforward but require attention to detail. Here's a step-by-step guide to help you through the process:

Step 1: Seed Selection and Pre-treatment - Start by selecting high-quality pea seeds from a reputable source. Pea seeds are typically large and round, making them easy to handle. Some gardeners choose to pre-treat their pea seeds before planting to speed up germination. This involves soaking the seeds in water for 24 hours, which helps to soften the seed coat and encourage faster sprouting.

Step 2: Planting the Seeds - Once your seeds are ready, prepare a seed tray or small pots with a good quality seed compost. Sow the seeds about 1 inch deep and 2 inches apart to give each seed enough space to grow. After sowing, water the soil lightly to ensure it is moist but not waterlogged.

Step 3: Creating Optimal Germination Conditions - Pea seeds germinate best at temperatures between 45°F and 75°F. They will not germinate in soil that is too cold or too hot. Therefore, keep your seed tray or pots in a location that maintains these temperatures. If you're starting your seeds indoors, a sunny windowsill or heated propagation mat can provide the necessary warmth.

Step 4: Monitoring Germination Process - Keep the soil evenly moist (but not soggy) during the germination period. Pea seeds typically germinate within 7 to 14 days, depending on the variety and the temperature. Once the seeds have sprouted, they need plenty of light to grow properly. If you're growing them indoors, consider using grow lights to supplement natural light.

Step 5: Transplanting Seedlings - Once your pea seedlings have developed their first set of true leaves (the leaves that follow the initial sprout leaves), they are ready to be transplanted into larger containers or directly into the garden.

Make sure to handle them gently during this process, as their roots can be quite delicate. If you're transplanting them into containers, ensure the containers are deep enough to accommodate the long roots of the pea plants and that they have adequate drainage to prevent waterlogging.

Remember, peas are cool-season crops and prefer cooler temperatures for germination and growth. However, they are also quite hardy and can tolerate light frosts even after they have been transplanted outdoors.

Spacing & Measurement

Ensuring proper spacing and measurements when transplanting pea seedlings into container gardens is crucial for a few key reasons. First, it allows each plant to have sufficient room to grow and develop without competition for resources such as sunlight, water, and nutrients. This leads to healthier, more robust plants and ultimately a higher yield of peas.

Second, adequate spacing promotes good air circulation around each plant, which is essential in preventing the spread of diseases and pests that can quickly decimate closely planted crops.

Lastly, appropriate spacing aids in easy maintenance. It allows for better access when watering, pruning, or harvesting, reducing the risk of accidentally damaging neighbouring plants.

Peas are a popular vegetable to grow in containers, but it's essential to understand the proper spacing requirements to ensure healthy growth and high yields. Generally, peas require adequate space to grow, as overcrowding can lead to stunted growth and decreased productivity. When planting peas in containers, it's recommended to space the plants about 2-4 inches apart.

The distance between the plants will depend on the size of your container, but it's crucial to ensure that each pea plant has enough space to develop properly. If the container is too small, the plants may compete for nutrients and water, and their overall growth will be negatively impacted.

In addition to spacing, the depth of the container is also important for successful pea growing. Pea roots need to penetrate deeply into the soil to access the necessary nutrients and moisture. It's ideal to use a container that is at least 6-8 inches deep to allow the roots to grow freely. When planting pea seedlings, make sure that the top of the root ball is level with the soil surface. Planting at the correct depth ensures that the roots receive enough oxygen, which is essential for good growth.

Proper spacing and measurements are vital when planting pea seedlings in container gardening. By taking the time to ensure that each plant has enough space and the correct depth, you can create an optimal growing environment for your peas and enjoy a bountiful harvest.

In summary, when planting peas in container gardening, it's recommended to space the plants 2-4 inches apart and use a container that is at least 6-8 inches deep. Additionally, it's crucial to ensure that each plant is planted at the correct depth, with the top of the root ball level with the soil surface.

By following these spacing and measurement guidelines, you can create an ideal growing environment for your pea plants and achieve a successful harvest.

Ideal Temperatures & Sun Requirements

The ideal temperatures and sun requirements play a significant role in the successful growth of peas in container gardens. Peas grow best in cooler temperatures, with an optimal temperature range for germination between 40°F and 85°F (4°C to 30°C).

When growing peas in containers, it's essential to monitor the temperature of the soil regularly. If the soil is too cold, it can lead to poor germination rates or even prevent seedlings from emerging altogether. Conversely, if the soil temperature is too high, it can cause pea plants to bolt prematurely, which negatively impacts their yields.

In addition to temperature requirements, peas need an adequate amount of sunlight to grow and produce quality crops. Pea plants thrive in full sun or partial shade, with at least six hours of sunlight per day being optimal.

If grown in too much shade, the plant may become leggy and weak, leading to reduced yields. Conversely, if grown in too much sun, the plant may dry out too quickly, requiring more water and resulting in poor growth.

In summary, the ideal temperatures and sun requirements are critical factors to consider when growing peas in container gardens. The optimal temperature range for germination is between 40°F and 85°F (4°C to 30°C), and the plants require at least six hours of full sun per day to thrive. By adhering to these temperature and sun requirements, you can create an ideal growing environment for your pea plants and achieve a successful harvest.

MAINTAINING YOUR CONTAINER GROWN PEAS

Maintaining your container-grown peas is critical to ensure their healthy growth and a successful harvest in vegetable container gardening. Regular maintenance activities include watering, fertilizing, providing support for climbing, monitoring for pests, diseases, and ensuring appropriate sunlight. Proper watering is crucial as peas require moist but well-drained soil; overwatering or underwatering can lead to poor plant health.

Fertilizing, preferably with a low-nitrogen fertilizer, provides the necessary nutrients that might not be sufficiently available in the container soil. Providing support, such as a trellis or stakes, helps peas (which are naturally vining plants) grow upwards, maximizing space and improving air circulation around the plants.

Regularly checking for pests and diseases allows for early detection and management, preventing potential damage to your crop. Lastly, ensuring your peas receive the right amount of sunlight contributes to photosynthesis and overall plant health. Therefore, maintaining your container-grown peas is not just important, it's essential for the success of your vegetable container garden.

Pruning & Thinning Your Peas

Pruning and thinning container-grown peas in vegetable container gardens are crucial processes that can significantly impact the health and productivity of your plants. Pruning, which involves removing certain parts of the plant, can help improve air circulation and sunlight penetration, both of which are essential for healthy growth. This practice can also help direct the plant's energy towards producing more pods rather than unnecessary foliage.

Thinning, on the other hand, refers to the removal of some plants to reduce crowding and competition for resources. When peas are initially sown, it's common to plant more seeds than necessary to account for potential germination failures.

However, once the seedlings have sprouted, not all of them can be allowed to mature, as this would lead to overcrowding. By thinning out the weaker seedlings, you allow the stronger ones to have better access to water, nutrients, and sunlight, thereby enhancing their growth and yield.

Additionally, both pruning and thinning can help prevent the spread of diseases and pests. Overcrowded conditions are often conducive to the development and spread of fungal diseases and pest infestations. Therefore, by maintaining proper spacing between your plants, you can keep your pea plants healthier and more productive.

Knowing when and how to prune and thin container grown peas is a key aspect of successful vegetable container gardening. The timing for both these tasks can vary depending on the specific variety of peas you're growing and their growth rate, but there are some general guidelines you can follow.

Pruning usually isn't necessary for peas unless they are bush varieties that become particularly dense. If pruning becomes necessary, it should be done when the plants have reached a good size, typically when they are about 8-10 inches tall.

To prune, use a sharp, clean pair of pruning shears or scissors to cut back some of the foliage. Aim to remove about a third of the plant's overall volume, focusing on areas where the leaves are especially crowded. Be careful not to cut into the main stem or any developing pods. This will help improve air circulation within the plant, reducing the risk of fungal diseases.

Thinning, on the other hand, should be done early in the plant's life, typically when the seedlings are about 2-4 inches tall. At this stage, you can clearly see which plants are strongest and most likely to thrive.

To thin your pea plants, gently pull out the weaker seedlings from the soil, being careful not to disturb the roots of the remaining plants. Alternatively, you can cut the unwanted seedlings at soil level with a pair of scissors. The aim is to leave about 2-3 inches of space between each plant, giving them plenty of room to grow without competition for light, water, and nutrients.

Remember, both pruning and thinning should be done on a cool, overcast day to minimize stress to the plants. These practices, when done correctly, can significantly enhance the health and yield of your container-grown peas.

Watering Your Container Grown Peas

Watering is a crucial aspect of maintaining container grown peas in vegetable container gardens. Peas, like all plants, require water for various physiological processes, including photosynthesis, nutrient transportation, and maintaining cell structure.

In container gardening, the importance of watering is amplified due to the limited soil volume, which can dry out quickly, particularly in hot weather or windy conditions. Proper watering ensures that peas receive adequate moisture for their growth and development. Overwatering can lead to waterlogged soil and root rot, while underwatering can cause wilting and stunt growth. Therefore, maintaining a consistent watering schedule based on the plant's needs, soil type, and environmental conditions is important. It helps to promote healthy root development, maximizes nutrient uptake, and ultimately leads to a more productive harvest.

When growing peas in container gardens, proper watering techniques are essential for their growth and productivity. Peas require moist soil, but not overly saturated or dry soil. The amount of water required by pea plants can vary depending on the weather conditions.

It's generally recommended to water pea plants thoroughly once or twice a week, ensuring that the top inch of soil has become dry between waterings. Overwatering can lead to root rot or other problems, while underwatering can stunt their growth and decrease yields.

Pea plants require more water during flowering to allow their pods to swell. It's also crucial to water the plants early in the morning or late afternoon to avoid evaporation and reduce the risk of sunburn. One inch of water per week is usually sufficient, whether from rain or watering. However, this amount may vary depending on the size of the container, the weather, and other factors.

When watering container-grown peas, it's crucial to ensure that the excess water drains off. Excess water can lead to waterlogging and cause the pea plant to suffer from oxygen deficiency, which negatively impacts its growth. A well-draining soil mix and container with drainage holes can help prevent waterlogging and improve drainage.

In summary, proper watering techniques are crucial when growing peas in container gardens. Watering pea plants once or twice a week, ensuring that the top inch of soil has become dry between waterings, is generally recommended.

More frequent watering may be necessary during hot and dry spells, and additional water is required during flowering. By adhering to these watering guidelines, you can provide your pea plants with optimal growing conditions and achieve a successful harvest.

Organic Fertilization For Container Grown Peas

Organic fertilization is particularly beneficial for container-grown peas in vegetable container gardens. As peas are legumes, they have a unique ability to fix nitrogen from the atmosphere into the soil, which aids their growth. However, they still benefit significantly from organic fertilizers.

Organic fertilizers provide a rich array of nutrients, including phosphorus and potassium, which are essential for pea plants' overall health and productivity. The organic matter in these fertilizers improves soil structure, enhancing its capacity to retain water and nutrients, which is crucial for the confined space of a container.

Furthermore, organic fertilizers release nutrients slowly, providing a steady supply throughout the growing season. They also foster beneficial soil microorganisms that aid in nutrient cycling and disease suppression. Hence, organic fertilization is vital in promoting vigorous growth and high yields in container-grown peas while maintaining the health of the soil ecosystem within the container.

Organic fertilizers are an excellent choice for container-grown peas in vegetable container gardens. They not only provide essential nutrients to the plants but also enhance the soil structure and promote the growth of beneficial microbes. Some of the most effective types of organic fertilizers for peas include compost, bone meal, and fish emulsion.

Compost is a great all-purpose organic fertilizer that can be used to enrich the soil in your container garden. It is rich in a wide range of nutrients that pea plants need for healthy growth, including nitrogen, phosphorus, and potassium.

Compost also improves the soil's water-holding capacity, which is crucial for containers that can dry out quickly. You can add compost to the potting mix before planting your peas and then top-dress the soil surface with more compost midway through the growing season.

Bone meal is another excellent organic fertilizer for peas. It is high in phosphorus, a nutrient that peas need to produce healthy roots and abundant flowers and pods. Sprinkle bone meal into the hole when you plant your peas, and then reapply it once the plants start flowering. Be sure to water thoroughly after each application to help the nutrients soak into the soil.

Fish emulsion is a liquid organic fertilizer that is high in nitrogen, which is essential for the vigorous vegetative growth of pea plants. It also contains smaller amounts of phosphorus and potassium. Fish emulsion can be diluted with water and applied to the soil every two to four weeks during the growing season. Be careful not to over-fertilize, as too much nitrogen can lead to lush foliage at the expense of pod production.

When fertilizing container-grown peas, it's important to remember that less is often more. Over-fertilization can lead to salt buildup in the soil, which can damage the plants. It's also crucial to water thoroughly after each fertilizer application to help the nutrients soak into the soil and reach the plant roots.

Lastly, remember that peas are legumes and can fix their own nitrogen from the air, so they don't need as much nitrogen fertilizer as other plants might.

Using organic fertilizers like compost, bone meal, and fish emulsion can greatly enhance the health and productivity of container-grown peas. Just be sure to apply them in moderation and water thoroughly afterwards.

PROTECTING YOUR CONTAINER GROWN PEAS

Extreme Temperatures

Protecting container-grown peas from extreme temperatures in vegetable container gardens is crucial for their healthy growth and productivity. Peas are cool season crops and typically prefer temperatures between 60-75 degrees Fahrenheit. They can tolerate light frosts but may struggle or even die off in extreme heat or cold. Therefore, implementing strategies to safeguard your peas from temperature extremes is essential.

One of the simplest ways to protect your peas from extreme cold is to move the containers to a sheltered location when frost or a cold snap is predicted. This could be inside a greenhouse, a sunroom, or even indoors if necessary.

You can also wrap the containers in bubble wrap or horticultural fleece to provide extra insulation against the cold. In severe cold, consider using a cloche or a plastic cover over the plants themselves, but remember to remove it during the day to prevent overheating.

During periods of high heat, it's important to ensure your pea plants have adequate water. Containers can dry out quickly in hot weather, so you may need to water daily or even twice a day in extreme cases.

However, avoid watering in the middle of the day when the water can evaporate quickly and even scorch the plants. Early morning or evening is best. You can also move the containers to a shaded location to protect them from the hottest part of the day.

Mulching around the base of your pea plants can also help to regulate soil temperature and retain moisture. Organic mulches like straw, compost, or wood chips are excellent choices. They not only insulate the soil from temperature extremes but also gradually break down and enrich the soil with organic matter.

Temperature control is not just about the survival of your peas; it's also about their productivity. Peas that are stressed by extreme temperatures may produce fewer flowers and pods, leading to a reduced harvest. They may also be more susceptible to diseases and pests. Therefore, taking steps to protect your container-grown peas from temperature extremes can result in a more bountiful and healthier crop.

While peas are a relatively hardy and adaptable crop, they do have their limits when it comes to extreme temperatures. By implementing strategies such as relocation, insulation, proper watering, and mulching, you can help your container-grown peas thrive no matter the weather.

Protecting Container Grown Peas From Pests

Protecting container-grown peas from pests is crucial for maintaining the health and productivity of your vegetable container garden. Pests such as aphids, slugs, and spider mites can cause significant damage to pea plants by feeding on their leaves, stems, and pods, thereby reducing their vigor and yield.

In severe cases, a heavy infestation can even lead to the death of the plants. Furthermore, some pests can transmit diseases that further weaken the plants and can spread to other plants in your garden. Therefore, implementing effective pest management strategies not only ensures the survival of your pea plants but also safeguards the overall health and biodiversity of your container garden. By doing so, you can enjoy a bountiful harvest of peas and also provide a nurturing environment for beneficial insects and other organisms.

Aphids are small insects that feed on the sap of pea plants, causing the leaves to curl and yellow. Over time, heavy infestations can weaken the plant and reduce its productivity.

To control aphids, you can wash them off the plants with a strong jet of water or apply an insecticidal soap. Additionally, attracting beneficial insects like ladybugs and lacewings, which are natural predators of aphids, can help keep their population in check.

Slugs and snails are mollusks that feed on the leaves and stems of pea plants, leaving behind distinctive holes and silvery trails. They are especially active at night and during wet weather.

To deter these pests, you can place copper tape around your containers or use organic slug pellets. It's also helpful to remove any hiding places, such as piles of leaves or debris, from around your containers.

Spider mites are tiny arachnids that suck the sap from the undersides of leaves, causing them to turn yellow and drop off. They thrive in hot, dry conditions and can quickly multiply to cause serious damage. Regularly spraying your pea plants with water can help deter spider mites. For more severe infestations, a miticide may be necessary.

Thrips are minute insects that scrape the surface of leaves and fruits as they feed, resulting in distorted growth and reduced yield. Keeping the garden free of weeds, which can serve as hosts for thrips, is an effective prevention strategy. Insecticidal soaps or neem oil can also be used to control thrips.

While several pests can pose a threat to container-grown peas, there are various methods available to protect your plants. These include regular monitoring, good garden hygiene, the use of organic pesticides, and the encouragement of beneficial insects. By implementing these strategies, you can ensure that your pea plants remain healthy and productive.

Protecting Container Grown Peas From Diseases

Protecting container-grown peas from diseases is essential for several reasons. Firstly, diseases can significantly impact the health of the pea plants, causing symptoms such as yellowing leaves, wilting, and stunted growth. This not only reduces the aesthetic appeal of your garden but also affects the productivity of your pea plants, leading to decreased yields.

Secondly, some diseases can spread rapidly to other plants in your container garden if not promptly and effectively managed, thereby threatening the overall health of your garden.

Finally, certain diseases can persist in the soil or plant debris, making it challenging to grow healthy pea plants or other susceptible crops in the same containers in the future. Therefore, taking steps to prevent and manage diseases is crucial to maintaining a healthy and productive vegetable container garden.

Container-grown peas are susceptible to several diseases, including Fusarium wilt, root rot, powdery mildew, brown spot, and gray mold. These diseases could significantly impact the health and yield of your pea plants.

Fusarium wilt, a fungal disease that infects plant vascular tissues, is one of the significant threats to peas. The disease is often spread by cucumber beetles, which carry the spores. To organically manage Fusarium wilt, consider using disease-resistant pea varieties or practicing crop rotation to prevent the buildup of disease-causing organisms in the soil.

Root rot, caused by overly soggy soil conditions, can result in brown and mushy roots, leading to stunted growth and wilting. Good drainage is crucial to preventing root rot. Ensure your containers have adequate drainage holes and avoid overwatering your plants.

Powdery mildew is another common disease that becomes prevalent in hot weather. This disease causes a whitish mold to appear on the leaves and pods, reducing the plant's photosynthetic ability and thus its productivity. Avoid watering the plants from above, as this creates humid conditions favorable for the fungus. Water at the base of the plant instead.

Brown spot and gray mold are other diseases that affect peas. Brown spot causes water-soaked spots on the leaves, while gray mold, also known as Botrytis, leads to a furry gray mold on the plant. Both can be controlled by ensuring good airflow around the plants and removing any infected plant material promptly to prevent the spread.

Protecting your container-grown peas from diseases is crucial for a healthy and bountiful harvest. Use disease-resistant varieties, ensure good watering and hygiene practices, and if necessary, apply organic fungicides. These strategies will help you maintain a healthy and productive vegetable container garden.

HARVESTING CONTAINER GROWN PEAS

Container-grown peas typically take between 60 to 70 days from planting to harvest, depending on the variety and growing conditions. The time it takes for peas to mature can vary based on factors such as sunlight exposure, temperature, water availability, and the overall health of the plant. Generally, dwarf or bush varieties are faster to mature than climbing or vining types.

When it comes to harvesting, timing is crucial for achieving the best flavor. Peas should be harvested when they are young and tender, as they become starchy and less sweet as they mature. For garden peas, which are shelled, harvest when the pods are full and rounded.

For snap peas, pick them when the pods are plump and you can see the shape of the peas inside. Snow peas, on the other hand, should be harvested when the pods are still flat and the peas inside are small and barely noticeable.

To harvest, simply hold the vine with one hand and pluck the pod off with the other. Be gentle to avoid damaging the plant. It's a good idea to harvest regularly – every day or two – as this encourages the plants to produce more pods. If you leave mature pods on the plants, they will stop producing new ones.

After harvesting, peas should be used as soon as possible for the best flavor and texture. If you can't use them immediately, they can be stored in the refrigerator for a few days. For longer storage, peas can be blanched and frozen.

Growing peas in container gardens can be a rewarding experience. With the right care, you can expect to start harvesting your peas within a couple of months after planting. Harvesting at the right time and frequently picking the pods will ensure you get the best tasting peas from your container garden.

CONTAINER GROWN PEAS NOTES

Start: Seeds or Seedlings

Germination: 4 to 14 days, Temperatures between 45°F and 75°F.

Seed Life: 3 Years

Soil Type: Well-draining soil rich in organic matter (compost or well-rotted manure) - pH level between 6.0 to 7.0

Seed Spacing: 1 inch deep and 2 inches apart (in seed tray or small pots)

Seedling Spacing: 2-4 inches apart, with the top of the root ball level with the soil surface (The distance between the plants will vary depending on the size of your container)

Sunlight: Full sun or partial shade, with at least 6 hours of sunlight

Growing Temperatures: 40°F and 85°F (4°C to 30°C)

Days To Harvest: 60 to 70 days

CHAPTER 9
VEGETABLE RAISED BED GARDENING – CARROTS

C arrots, with their vibrant color and crunchy texture, are a favorite among many gardeners and a staple in vegetable raised bed gardening. These root vegetables, scientifically known as Daucus carota, are not only a delicious and versatile addition to any home-cooked meal but also a powerhouse of nutrition, loaded with vitamin A, K, C, and numerous health-promoting antioxidants.

Cultivating carrots in a raised bed garden has its distinct advantages. The loose, well-drained soil is ideal for their growth, providing room for the roots to expand freely, resulting in healthier, larger carrots.

In addition, raised beds can help control pests and disease while making the task of tending to your carrots more manageable. Whether you are a seasoned gardener or just beginning, growing carrots in your raised bed garden can be a rewarding experience.

Raised bed gardening can greatly enhance the growth and yield of your carrot crop. One of the main advantages is the ability to control the soil composition, enabling you to create the perfect loose, sandy loam that carrots prefer. This type of soil promotes straight growth and prevents the roots from becoming stunted or deformed, which can happen in heavy, compacted soil.

Furthermore, raised beds offer excellent drainage, preventing waterlogged soil which can lead to rotting. Raised beds also reduce the risk of soil-borne diseases and pests that can affect carrots, such as carrot fly. Additionally, the elevated design of a raised bed makes it easier to tend and harvest your carrot crop, reducing strain on your back.

Finally, by growing carrots in a raised bed, you can effectively utilize your garden space, planting in blocks rather than traditional rows, leading to a higher yield per square foot.

THE RIGHT SOIL TO GROW CARROTS IN RAISED BED GARDENS

Carrots are root vegetables that require specific soil conditions to grow properly. The ideal soil for growing carrots in raised bed gardens is loose and sandy loam. This type of soil structure allows the carrot roots to easily penetrate the ground, promoting straight growth and preventing deformities. The soil should be well-draining to avoid waterlogging, as this can lead to rotting.

To create the perfect soil for your carrots, start by removing any rocks or debris from your raised bed. These can obstruct the growth of the carrot roots and cause them to become misshapen.

Next, add plenty of organic matter, such as compost or well-rotted manure. This will improve the soil texture, making it lighter and porous, also providing essential nutrients for the carrots.

The pH level of the soil is another important factor to consider when growing carrots. Carrots prefer slightly acidic to neutral soil, with a pH between 6.0 and 7.0. If your soil is too acidic or too alkaline, it can inhibit the absorption of nutrients, leading to poor growth and yield. You can test the pH of your soil using a soil test kit and adjust it if necessary by adding lime to raise the pH or sulphur to lower it.

Lastly, carrots are heavy feeders and will benefit from a slow-release fertilizer added to the soil at planting time. However, avoid using a fertilizer high in nitrogen, as this can cause the carrots to produce lots of foliage at the expense of root development. Instead, choose a fertilizer with a higher proportion of phosphorus and potassium, which promote root growth and overall plant health.

By creating the right soil conditions in your raised bed garden, you can enjoy a bountiful harvest of crisp, sweet carrots. Remember that, like all vegetables, carrots also need plenty of sunlight and regular watering to thrive. So, choose a sunny spot for your raised bed and keep the soil consistently moist, but not waterlogged for best results.

HOW TO SOW CARROTS IN RAISED BED GARDENS

Correct Season To Sow Carrots In Raised Bed Gardens

The correct season to sow carrots in vegetable raised bed gardens is typically during the cool seasons, namely spring or early fall. Carrots are a cool season crop and thrive best when soil temperatures are between 55 and 75 degrees Fahrenheit. This optimal temperature range promotes the best root formation. In the spring, carrots should ideally be planted 4-6 weeks before your average last frost date or as soon as the soil becomes workable.

This timing allows the carrots ample growth time before the arrival of summer heat. If you're planning a fall planting, aim to sow the seeds about 10-12 weeks before the expected first frost. This will allow the carrots to fully mature before winter arrives. It's important to note that carrots should be sown directly into the soil, not initially raised in individual pots or plugs then transplanted, as this can disrupt the growth of their long taproots.

With careful timing and proper care, you can enjoy a bountiful harvest of this nutritious and versatile vegetable from your raised bed garden.

Plant Needs & Requirements

Germinating carrots from seeds to seedlings correctly is a crucial step when growing them in vegetable raised bed gardens. Carrots are root vegetables, and their growth is directly dependent on the initial establishment of the seed in the soil. Unlike many other vegetables, carrots don't transplant well because any disruption can lead to deformed roots.

They need to be sown directly where they will grow to maturity. When seeds are properly germinated, they produce strong, healthy seedlings that can grow into robust plants. Proper germination also ensures optimal use of garden space, as each germinated seed has the potential to produce a full-sized carrot.

Furthermore, successful germination reduces the likelihood of gaps in the row or bed where seeds failed to sprout. If germination is not done correctly, you risk poor root development, which could result in stunted or misshapen carrots. Therefore, understanding and applying correct germination techniques is vital for a bountiful and healthy carrot harvest from your raised bed garden.

Germination is the first step in growing carrots from seeds. Begin by choosing a high-quality carrot seed from a reputable supplier. The variety you choose will depend on your personal preference and the specific conditions of your garden.

To start the germination process, prepare your soil. Carrots prefer well-draining soil that's loose and free of rocks. A raised bed is ideal because it allows you to control the soil quality more easily. Remove any debris from the soil and break up any clumps to create a smooth surface.

Make shallow rows about 1/4 inches deep, and sprinkle your carrot seeds into the rows. Try to space them out as much as possible, aiming for about 2 inches apart, but don't worry if they're not perfect - you'll thin them out later. Gently cover the seeds with soil, press down lightly to make sure they're in contact with the soil, then water thoroughly.

Carrot seeds require consistent moisture to germinate, so it's crucial to keep the soil evenly moist but not waterlogged. Covering the area with a thin layer of straw or a row cover can help retain moisture during this critical period.

The temperature at which carrot seeds germinate is quite flexible, but they prefer cool to moderate temperatures. The ideal soil temperature for carrot germination is between 50 and 85 degrees

Fahrenheit, with germination typically starting at around 50 degrees. It's worth noting that carrot seeds can take anywhere from one to three weeks to germinate, so patience is required.

Once the carrot seedlings are about 2 inches tall, they're ready to be thinned. Thinning is essential because it prevents overcrowding and ensures each carrot has enough space to grow. To thin your carrots, simply pull out the smallest seedlings, leaving the stronger ones to grow, ensuring there's about 2-3 inches between each remaining seedling.

Transplanting carrot seedlings is not generally recommended because carrots are root vegetables, and any disturbance to their growth can lead to deformed roots. However, if you absolutely must transplant them, do so when they're very young - no more than two weeks after germination - and be extremely careful not to damage the delicate taproot.

Remember that growing carrots from seeds to seedlings requires patience, attention to soil and moisture conditions, and careful handling of the young plants. With these steps, you can look forward to a plentiful harvest of this nutritious and versatile vegetable from your raised bed garden.

Spacing & Measurement

Spacing and measurements play a crucial role when transplanting carrot seedlings into vegetable raised bed gardens. Carrots, being root vegetables, need ample space to expand and grow unimpeded beneath the soil surface. If carrot seedlings are too close together, they will compete for nutrients, water, and space, leading to underdeveloped, stunted, or misshapen carrots.

Proper spacing allows each plant to receive an equal share of sunlight, water, and nutrients, thereby promoting healthy growth and ensuring a bountiful harvest. Ideally, carrot seedlings should be spaced about 2-3 inches apart after thinning.

This gives each plant enough room to develop without competing with its neighbors.

Correct spacing also helps prevent the spread of diseases and pests by allowing air to circulate freely among the plants. It's important to remember that while transplanting isn't typically recommended for carrots due to their sensitive taproot, if it's necessary, it should be done with utmost care to avoid damaging the seedlings. The correct spacing and measurements during this process are vital to the success of your carrot crop in a raised bed garden.

The proper spacing and measurements are crucial when planting carrot seedlings in a vegetable raised bed garden. These factors significantly influence the growth, health, and yield of your carrot plants. Carrots, being root vegetables, need a good amount of space to expand and grow beneath the surface of the soil.

When planting carrot seedlings, you'll first need to thin them out. Thinning is a process where you remove some seedlings to give the remaining ones more room to grow. For carrots, the ideal spacing between each plant after thinning is about 2 to 3 inches apart.

This distance allows each carrot enough room to develop fully without competing with its neighbors for nutrients, water, or space. If carrot seedlings are planted too close together, they can inhibit each other's growth, leading to stunted or misshapen carrots.

Raised beds provide an excellent environment for growing carrots because they allow for better control over the soil conditions and make it easier to care for the plants. When setting up your raised bed, a bed that's at least 12 inches deep is recommended to accommodate the length of the carrots. The width of the bed should be such that it provides enough space to plant rows of carrots with at least 6 to 8 inches between the rows. This spacing allows for easy movement between the rows for maintenance tasks like weeding, watering, and harvesting.

Crop rotation is another important aspect to consider. To prevent the build-up of diseases and pests in the soil, avoid planting carrots in the same spot where they or other root vegetables were grown the previous year.

By following these strategies for spacing and measurements, you can set your carrot plants up for success and look forward to a bountiful harvest from your vegetable raised bed garden.

Ideal Temperatures & Sun Requirements

Ideal temperatures and sun requirements are essential factors in successfully growing carrots in vegetable raised bed gardens. Carrots thrive in cool weather, with the optimal soil temperature for germination being between 50 to 85 degrees Fahrenheit. However, they can tolerate temperatures as low as 40 degrees once established.

Carrots grow best when the air temperature is between 60 and 70 degrees Fahrenheit. It's important to note that high temperatures, particularly above 80 degrees, can cause carrots to become woody and less palatable.

As for sunlight, carrots need plenty of it, at least six hours of full sun each day. The sun aids in photosynthesis, which is the process by which plants convert light energy into chemical energy for growth. Without sufficient sunlight, carrot plants may grow slowly, produce small roots, or become more susceptible to diseases and pests.

Therefore, when planning your vegetable raised bed garden, ensure that your carrot plants will have the right temperatures and enough sunlight to develop properly and yield a bountiful harvest.

MAINTAINING YOUR RAISED BED CARROTS

Maintaining your raised bed grown carrots in vegetable gardening is crucial for a variety of reasons. Firstly, regular maintenance ensures that the soil remains loose and well-drained, which is key for carrot growth as they need a loose soil structure to form straight roots. Compacted soil can lead to misshapen or stunted carrots.

Secondly, raised beds tend to dry out faster than traditional garden beds, so consistent watering is necessary to prevent the soil from drying out, but also to avoid waterlogging, which carrots are particularly sensitive to. Thirdly, maintaining the raised bed involves regular weeding. Carrots do not compete well with weeds, and if left unchecked, weed growth can stunt the development of the carrots.

Lastly, regular inspection for pests like the carrot fly is vital because these can damage the crop significantly if not dealt with promptly. Therefore, diligent maintenance of your raised bed grown carrots is essential for a healthy and bountiful harvest.

Pruning & Thinning Your Carrots

Pruning and thinning raised bed-grown carrots in vegetable gardens are crucial practices that can significantly influence the health and yield of your carrot crops. Thinning is particularly important as carrot seeds are small and tend to be sown more densely than required. When these seeds germinate and grow without adequate space, it leads to overcrowding. Overcrowded plants compete for nutrients, water, and sunlight, which can stunt growth and lead to underdeveloped roots.

Thinning out the carrots ensures each plant has enough room to grow and develop fully. It helps promote better air circulation around the plants, reducing the risk of diseases caused by damp and stagnant air. It also makes it easier for the plants to absorb necessary nutrients from the soil without competition.

On the other hand, pruning is not a common practice with carrots as they are root vegetables, and their tops or foliage are not typically pruned. However, if the carrot tops become excessively tall or bushy, you might consider giving them a light trim. Pruning the tops can help redirect the plant's energy towards root development, which is where you want it to go. This ensures that the plant focuses its resources on growing the part of the carrot we eat - the root.

In summary, both thinning and occasional pruning are essential for optimizing the growth and production of your carrot plants. By ensuring ample space for each plant and directing energy towards root growth, you can look forward to a healthy and bountiful harvest.

Thinning and pruning raised bed-grown carrots is a critical part of their cultivation process, ensuring that each plant has sufficient space to grow and develop. Thinning should ideally begin when the carrot seedlings are small, typically around 2 to 3 weeks after planting when they have developed their first set of true leaves. At this stage, the plants are sturdy enough to handle but not so large that they will interfere with each other's growth.

When thinning, you want to aim for about 1 to 2 inches of space between each plant. This gives each carrot enough room to develop fully. To thin, simply grasp the unwanted seedling at the soil level and gently pull it out.

Be careful not to disturb the roots of the nearby plants. If you're concerned about disturbing the roots of the remaining plants, another option is to cut the unwanted seedlings off at the soil level using a pair of scissors.

Pruning carrot tops is less common but can be done if the foliage becomes too lush and appears to be taking energy away from root development. Pruning should be done conservatively, as the foliage is crucial for photosynthesis. To prune, simply trim back the greenery using a clean, sharp pair of garden shears. Cut off the top third of the plant, making sure not to remove more than a third of the total leaf mass at a time to avoid stressing the plant.

Remember, the goal of both thinning and pruning is to ensure healthy growth and development of your carrots. By giving each plant enough space and ensuring they're not expending unnecessary energy on excessive foliage, you can help ensure a bountiful harvest from your raised bed garden.

Watering Your Raised Bed Carrots

Watering is critical for the healthy growth and development of carrots in raised bed gardens. Carrots, like most vegetables, consist mostly of water - about 88% to be precise. Therefore, consistent and adequate watering is vital to their survival and productivity. Water aids in nutrient transportation within the plant, helping the carrot absorb nutrients from the soil and distribute them throughout the plant.

It also plays a significant role in photosynthesis, a process crucial for the plant's energy production. Additionally, because carrots are root vegetables, adequate water is necessary for the formation and growth of the edible carrot root. Without sufficient water, carrots can become stunted, misshapen, or tough. Inconsistent watering can also lead to splitting, where the carrot cracks open, affecting both its aesthetic appeal and its shelf life. Therefore, regular and deep watering is key to producing juicy, tender, and tasty carrots in your raised bed garden.

Carrots, being root vegetables, require consistent and deep watering to promote strong root growth. Generally, carrots need about 1 inch of water per week, whether from rainfall or manual watering.

The soil in raised beds tends to dry out faster than ground-level soil due to improved drainage and increased exposure to wind and sun. Therefore, you may need to water your raised bed carrots more frequently, especially during hot, dry weather. It's best to water early in the morning or late in the evening to reduce water loss from evaporation.

When watering, it's essential to water deeply to encourage the carrot roots to grow down into the soil. Shallow watering can lead to the development of shallow roots and smaller carrots. A good way to ensure deep watering is to apply water slowly at the base of the plants, allowing it to soak into the soil and reach the deeper root zones.

Keep in mind that while carrots need consistent moisture, overly saturated soil can lead to disease and root rot. The soil should be moist but not waterlogged. If you can squeeze water out of a handful of soil, it's too wet.

During the germination phase, the soil surface needs to stay consistently moist. Covering the sown seeds with a thin layer of straw can help retain soil moisture without drowning the seeds.

As the carrots grow, you can gradually reduce the frequency of watering, but increase the amount of water given each time. This encourages the roots to grow deeper into the soil in search of moisture. Remember, the key is to keep the soil evenly moist, not soggy.

Proper watering is a delicate balance, but by observing your plants and the soil condition, you can adjust your watering routine to provide your carrots with the optimal conditions for growth.

Organic Fertilization For Raised Bed Grown Carrots

Organic fertilization plays a pivotal role in the successful cultivation of raised bed-grown carrots in vegetable gardens. Carrots, like all plants, require specific nutrients for optimal growth and production.

These nutrients include nitrogen, phosphorus, and potassium, along with several micronutrients. Organic fertilizers, derived from natural sources such as compost, manure, or bone meal, provide these nutrients in a form that's readily available for plant uptake. They also improve the soil structure and increase its capacity to retain water and nutrients, which is particularly beneficial in the well-draining environment of a raised bed.

Additionally, organic fertilizers contribute to the health of the soil's ecosystem by supporting beneficial microorganisms that aid in nutrient cycling and disease suppression. Unlike synthetic fertilizers, they release their nutrients slowly over time, reducing the risk of nutrient burn and providing a sustained nutrient supply for the plants.

By enhancing soil health and providing essential nutrients, organic fertilization is key to growing robust and productive carrot plants in your raised bed garden.

Organic fertilizers are an excellent choice for feeding your raised bed-grown carrots. They not only provide essential nutrients but also improve soil structure, boost beneficial microbial activity, and promote sustainable gardening practices. There are several types of organic fertilizers that you can use in your carrot garden.

Compost is one of the most popular and readily available types of organic fertilizers. It is rich in a variety of essential nutrients, and its organic matter content helps to improve soil structure and moisture retention.

Compost can be made at home from kitchen scraps and yard waste, making it a cost-effective and eco-friendly option. Before planting, mix compost into the top 6-12 inches of your raised bed soil to provide a slow-release source of nutrients to your carrots throughout the growing season.

Another great organic fertilizer for carrots is well-rotted manure. Manure from animals like cows, horses, or chickens is rich in nitrogen, which promotes lush, healthy foliage growth. However, it's vital to ensure the manure is well-rotted before using it, as fresh manure can burn plants and may contain harmful pathogens. As with compost, incorporate the manure into your soil before planting.

Bone meal is another organic fertilizer that can benefit your carrots. It's high in phosphorus, a nutrient that promotes strong root development in carrots. Sprinkle bone meal onto your soil surface and lightly till it in before planting your carrots.

Seaweed or kelp meal is a nutrient-dense organic fertilizer that provides a wide range of essential nutrients and trace elements. It can be mixed into the soil or used as a foliar spray to give your carrots a nutritional boost during the growing season.

When it comes to application, it's generally best to fertilize your soil before planting your carrots. This allows the nutrients to fully integrate into the soil and become available to the plants as they establish. However, you can also side-dress your carrots with a light application of compost or manure during the growing season to provide an additional nutrient boost. Always remember to water thoroughly after applying any fertilizer to help distribute the nutrients into the soil.

Organic fertilizers offer a multitude of benefits for your raised bed-grown carrots. By understanding the different types and their applications, you can tailor your fertilization strategy to provide the best possible nutrients for your carrot crop.

PROTECTING YOUR RAISED BED GROWN CARROTS

Extreme Temperatures

Protecting your raised bed-grown carrots from extreme temperatures is crucial for their healthy growth and development. Both excessively high and low temperatures can stress the plants, hinder their growth, and affect the quality of the harvest. Let's delve into some strategies to shield your carrots from temperature extremes and why it's important.

During hot weather, high temperatures can cause the soil in raised beds to dry out quickly, leading to water stress in your carrots. Prolonged exposure to heat can also lead to wilting and can make the carrots taste bitter. To protect your carrots from heat, consider using mulch on the surface of the soil. Organic mulches like straw or wood chips help to keep the soil cool and retain moisture. You can also install a shade cloth over your raised beds during the hottest part of the day to protect your plants from intense sunlight and reduce evaporation.

In contrast, cold temperatures can slow down or stop the growth of your carrots. If the temperature drops below freezing, it can damage or kill the plants. To protect your carrots from cold, you can cover your raised beds with a row cover or frost blanket. These covers trap heat from the soil, creating a warmer microclimate for your plants. For prolonged cold periods, consider using a cold frame or mini greenhouse over your raised beds for extra protection.

It's important to protect your carrots from extreme temperatures because these conditions can severely affect their growth and yield. Carrots are biennial plants that prefer cool weather, but they need a stable environment to develop properly. Sudden temperature changes can stress the plants, making them more susceptible to pests and diseases. Moreover, extreme temperatures can directly impact the quality of your carrot crop. High temperatures can make the carrots taste woody and bitter, while freezing temperatures can damage the carrot roots.

Temperature control in raised bed gardens can be more challenging because the soil in raised beds is exposed to air on all sides, making it more susceptible to temperature fluctuations. However, with careful monitoring and the use of protective measures like mulching, shading, and covering, you can create a favourable growing environment for your carrots.

Remember, the key to successful carrot gardening is to provide consistent care and to react promptly to any signs of stress or disease in your plants.

Protecting Raised Bed Grown Carrots From Pests

Protecting your raised bed-grown carrots from pests is crucial for maintaining a healthy and productive garden. Pests can cause significant damage to your carrot crops, affecting both quality and yield.

Common pests that afflict carrot plants include carrot flies, aphids, and nematodes, which can cause deformities in the roots, stunt growth, or even kill the plants. If left unchecked, an infestation can quickly spread and devastate an entire crop. Moreover, some pests can carry diseases, introducing harmful pathogens into your garden that can persist in the soil and affect future plantings. Therefore, implementing pest control measures not only preserves the health of your current crop but also helps to maintain the long-term viability of your raised bed garden.

It's essential to monitor your garden regularly for signs of pests and to take prompt action when necessary, ensuring that your carrots can grow and thrive in a safe and healthy environment.

Raised bed grown carrots can be susceptible to a number of pests that can cause significant damage if not properly managed. Some of the common pests include carrot flies, aphids, wireworms, and nematodes.

Carrot flies are one of the most damaging pests for carrots. They lay their eggs at the base of the carrot plants, and the hatching larvae burrow into the roots, causing tunnels and deformities. To protect your carrots from carrot flies, consider using physical barriers such as insect netting or fleece.

These can be installed over the raised bed to prevent the flies from reaching the plants. Another strategy is crop rotation, which involves changing the location of your carrot crops each year to disrupt the life cycle of the pests.

Aphids are small insects that suck the sap from carrot plants, which can stunt their growth and potentially transmit diseases. They can be controlled by introducing beneficial insects, like ladybugs and lacewings, which are natural predators of aphids. Regularly spraying your plants with a strong jet of water can also dislodge aphids.

Wireworms and nematodes are soil-dwelling pests that target the roots of carrot plants. Wireworms are the larvae of click beetles and can cause serious damage to the roots. Crop rotation and hand-picking are effective methods for controlling these pests.

Nematodes, on the other hand, are microscopic worms that can cause knots or galls on the roots. Again, crop rotation can help, as can adding organic matter to the soil to encourage beneficial microorganisms that can suppress nematodes.

It's also important to maintain the overall health of your garden, as healthy plants are less likely to succumb to pest attacks. This includes proper watering, fertilizing, and weeding practices. Regular monitoring of your garden can also help you detect any pest problems early and take appropriate action.

While pests can pose a significant threat to raised bed-grown carrots, they can be effectively managed through a combination of preventive measures and targeted control strategies. By keeping your garden healthy and being vigilant about potential pest problems, you can ensure a successful carrot harvest from your raised beds.

Protecting Raised Bed Carrots From Diseases

Protecting raised bed-grown carrots from diseases in vegetable gardens is of utmost importance for the overall health and productivity of your garden. Diseases can significantly reduce yield, affect the quality of the harvest, and may even result in total crop failure if not promptly and properly managed.

GREEN ROOTS

These diseases not only affect the current crop but can also persist in the soil, posing a threat to future plantings. Therefore, implementing disease prevention and control measures is critical to ensuring a successful carrot harvest. By doing so, you can maintain the health of your garden, maximize your yield, and enjoy the fruits of your labor in the form of healthy, delicious homegrown carrots.

Carrots grown in raised beds can be susceptible to a range of diseases, including Alternaria Leaf Blight, Black Rot, Cercospora Leaf Blight, Cottony Rot, Crown and Root Rots, and Scab. Each of these diseases can significantly impact the health and yield of your carrot crop.

Alternaria Leaf Blight, caused by the fungus Alternaria dauci, is a common disease that affects the leaves of carrot plants. Symptoms often include yellow-brown spots on the leaves, which can merge and cause the leaf to die. This disease can be managed by using resistant varieties, practicing crop rotation, and removing plant debris promptly after harvest.

Black Rot, caused by the fungus Alternaria radicina, is another disease that can affect carrots. It causes dark, sunken lesions on the root of the carrot. To prevent Black Rot, it's recommended to use disease-free seeds, practice crop rotation, and ensure good soil drainage.

Cercospora Leaf Blight, caused by the fungus Cercospora carotae, creates small, circular, tan spots on the leaves. The best organic defense against this disease is to maintain a clean garden, remove infected plants immediately, and rotate crops regularly.

Cottony Rot, also known as Sclerotinia rot, is a fungal disease that causes water-soaked lesions on the carrot root, which can then develop into a fluffy white mold. This disease can be prevented by ensuring proper soil drainage and removing infected plants promptly.

Crown and Root Rots, caused by Rhizoctonia and Pythium spp. pathogens can cause the tops of carrot roots to become mushy. These diseases can be controlled by ensuring good soil drainage and practicing crop rotation.

Scab, caused by Streptomyces spp., can create both raised and sunken, dry, corky lesions on the carrot root. While rarely severe enough to cause major problems, it can be prevented by maintaining a healthy pH level in your soil.

In summary, keeping your raised bed-grown carrots healthy and free from diseases is crucial for a successful harvest. Regular monitoring, practicing good garden hygiene, crop rotation, and using disease-resistant varieties can go a long way in preventing these diseases.

HARVESTING RAISED BED GROWN CARROTS

Carrots grown in raised bed gardens typically take between 50 to 80 days to be ready for harvest, depending on the variety and growing conditions. Early varieties, such as 'Nantes' or 'Amsterdam Forcing', can be ready in as little as 50 to 60 days, while maincrop varieties like 'Autumn King' might take up to 75 to 80 days. However, it's essential to remember that these are just estimates, and actual harvesting times can vary based on factors like soil quality, sunlight exposure, and weather conditions.

One of the key indicators that carrots are ready for harvest is their size. Generally, carrots are ready to harvest when the diameter of the root at the soil surface is about half an inch to one inch. However, some gardeners prefer to harvest their carrots when they're smaller for a more tender and sweeter flavor.

Another indicator is the color of the carrot. Most carrot varieties turn bright orange when they're ready to harvest, though there are also purple, yellow, and red varieties.

To harvest your carrots, it's best to do so in the morning when the temperatures are cooler. Begin by watering the raised bed thoroughly. This will make the soil softer and easier to work with, reducing the risk of damaging the carrots during the harvest.

Next, gently loosen the soil around the carrot with a hand fork or trowel, being careful not to pierce the carrot. Once the soil is loosened, grasp the carrot greens close to the base and pull upwards with a gentle, twisting motion. If the carrots are resistant, try loosening the soil further to avoid breaking the carrot.

After harvesting, remove the tops immediately to prevent moisture loss from the carrot root. Wash the carrots gently to remove any soil, but avoid scrubbing too hard as this can damage the skin. Carrots can be stored in a cool, dark place for several weeks, or they can be blanched and frozen for longer-term storage.

Raised bed grown carrots provides a rewarding gardening experience with a delicious payoff. By understanding when and how to harvest your carrots, you can ensure the best flavor and quality from your homegrown produce.

RAISED BEDS GROWN CARROTS NOTES

Start: Seeds or Seedlings

Germination: 7 to 21 days, temperatures between 50 and 85 degrees Fahrenheit.

Seed Life: 3 Years

Soil Type: Well-draining loose and sandy loam soil, rich in organic matter (compost or well-rotted manure) - pH level between 6.0 to 7.0

Seed Spacing: 1/4 inches deep , 2 inches apart (ideally in permanent and final location)

Seedling Spacing: 2-4 inches apart. Transplanting carrot seedlings is not generally recommended because carrots are root vegetables, and any disturbance to their growth can lead to deformed roots. However, if you absolutely must transplant them, do so when they're very young - no more than two weeks after germination - and be extremely careful not to damage the delicate taproot.

Sunlight: 6 hours full sunlight

Growing Temperatures: between 60 and 70 degrees Fahrenheit

Days To Harvest: 50 to 80 days

CHAPTER 10
VEGETABLE RAISED BED GARDENING – BUSH BEANS

B ush beans are an excellent choice for vegetable raised bed gardening, offering a bounty of benefits to both novice and experienced gardeners alike. Known for their compact growth habit, bush beans, unlike their pole bean counterparts, do not require trellising, making them a perfect fit for the spatial constraints of raised beds.

They are a prolific producer of tender, flavorful pods and can be grown successfully in most climates. With a shorter growing season than many other vegetables, bush beans are a rewarding crop that can offer multiple harvests throughout the growing season. Whether you're interested in fresh green beans for summer salads, dried beans for hearty winter stews, or simply enhancing the health of your garden soil through their nitrogen-fixing capabilities, bush beans are a versatile and valuable addition to any raised bed garden.

Planting bush beans in a raised vegetable garden bed offers a multitude of benefits that can significantly enhance the health and productivity of your garden.

Firstly, bush beans are known for their nitrogen-fixing abilities, which means they can take nitrogen from the air and convert it into a form that plants can use. This enriches the soil, making it more fertile for future crops.

Secondly, the compact growth habit of bush beans makes them ideal for raised bed gardening, allowing for efficient use of space and easier maintenance. They don't require trellising or staking, reducing the labor and materials needed for successful growth. Additionally, the raised bed environment promotes better drainage, which is beneficial for preventing diseases that bush beans can often be susceptible to, like root rot.

Finally, bush beans have a relatively short growing season and produce an abundant harvest, providing a quick and satisfying yield for gardeners. All these factors make bush beans not just a valuable crop in themselves, but also a great contributor to the overall health and productivity of your raised bed garden.

THE RIGHT SOIL TO GROW BUSH BEANS IN RAISED BEDS

When it comes to growing bush beans in vegetable raised bed gardens, the right soil conditions play a pivotal role in ensuring a healthy and bountiful harvest. Bush beans prefer a well-draining soil, which is one of the major advantages of using raised beds for gardening. Raised beds typically provide superior drainage compared to traditional garden beds, reducing the risk of waterlogged soil that can lead to root diseases.

The ideal soil for bush beans is loamy, rich in organic matter, and has a neutral pH level. Loam, a balanced mix of sand, silt, and clay, provides good drainage while also retaining enough moisture for the bean plants' needs.

A neutral pH level, around 6.0 to 7.0, is optimal for bush beans as it allows for the best nutrient uptake. If your soil is too acidic or alkaline, it can hinder the plant's ability to absorb necessary nutrients, leading to less vigorous growth and lower yields.

Adding organic matter, such as compost or well-rotted manure, can greatly enhance the fertility of your soil. Organic matter not only adds essential nutrients but also improves soil structure, enhancing its ability to retain moisture and nutrients while still draining well. Incorporating organic matter into your raised bed before planting will create a fertile, well-drained environment that bush beans thrive in.

Lastly, bush beans are legumes and have the unique ability to fix nitrogen from the atmosphere with the help of Rhizobium bacteria in their root nodules. This means they can enrich the soil with nitrogen, an essential nutrient for plant growth. However, for this process to occur efficiently, the specific Rhizobium bacteria need to be present in the soil.

If your soil has never been planted with beans or other legumes before, it may be beneficial to inoculate your bush bean seeds with a Rhizobium bacteria inoculant before planting.

By ensuring the right soil conditions - well-draining, rich in organic matter, neutral pH, and possibly inoculated with Rhizobium bacteria - you can create an optimal growing environment for bush beans in your vegetable raised bed garden.

HOW TO SOW BUSH BEANS IN RAISED BEDS

Correct Season To Sow Bush Beans In Raised Beds

Bush beans, being a warm-season crop, thrive best when sown in late spring to early summer once the danger of frost has passed and the soil temperature has reached at least 60 degrees Fahrenheit. They require a long, warm growing season of at least 55-60 days of frost-free weather. To determine the correct timing, check your local last frost date and plan to sow the seeds directly into your raised bed about 1-2 weeks after this date.

Bush beans do not transplant well, so direct sowing is recommended. The soil in raised beds tends to warm up faster than in-ground gardens, which can allow for slightly earlier planting. However, be cautious not to plant too early, as cold, wet soil can lead to poor germination and seed rot.

If you live in an area with a long growing season, you can do successive plantings every 2-3 weeks until mid-summer for a continuous harvest. Remember, bush beans love the sun, so ensure your raised bed is positioned in a spot that gets at least six hours of sunlight each day for optimal growth.

Plant Needs & Requirements

Germinating bush beans from seeds to seedlings correctly is a crucial first step in growing these plants in a raised bed gardens. This process sets the foundation for the plant's overall health, growth, and productivity. Proper germination ensures that the plants have a strong start, which can significantly influence their ability to resist pests, diseases, and adverse environmental conditions. It also affects the quality and quantity of the yield.

When bush bean seeds are correctly germinated, they sprout into robust seedlings with a good root system and vigorous growth. This vigor translates into more robust plants that can produce plentiful harvest.

Additionally, successful germination can help optimize the spacing of your plants, as you won't need to sow extra seeds to compensate for ones that didn't sprout. This can save resources and make maintenance easier by preventing overcrowding. In short, proper germination is a key factor in maximizing the success and efficiency of growing bush beans in a vegetable raised bed garden.

Germinating bush beans from seeds to seedlings requires careful attention to a few key steps. The first step is to prepare your planting site. If you're starting your seeds indoors, choose a seed tray or small pots filled with a good quality seed starting mix. This mix should be well-draining, yet capable of retaining moisture to support the young seedling's growth.

Next, plant your bush bean seeds. Each seed needs to be sown about 1 inch deep into the soil. This depth provides the seed with enough soil coverage to maintain the necessary moisture and heat levels for germination without being so deep that the emerging seedling struggles to reach the surface. After planting, water the soil thoroughly but gently, ensuring it's moist but not waterlogged.

Bush beans typically germinate best at soil temperatures between 70 and 80 degrees Fahrenheit. They can germinate at lower temperatures, around 60 degrees Fahrenheit, but this will usually slow the process. A seedling heat mat can help maintain consistent soil temperature if you're starting your seeds indoors and your home is cooler than this range.

Monitor the pots or trays daily, ensuring the soil remains moist but not soggy. The seeds should start to germinate within 6-12 days. Once the seedlings emerge, they need plenty of light - either from a sunny window or grow lights - to prevent them from becoming leggy and weak.

When it comes to transplanting your bush bean seedlings into your raised bed garden, timing is crucial. Bush beans are generally sensitive to transplanting, so it's often recommended to direct sow them in the garden. However, if you've started them indoors, wait until the risk of frost has passed and the seedlings have at least two sets of true leaves before transplanting.

Harden off the seedlings over a week by gradually exposing them to outdoor conditions to reduce transplant shock. When you're ready to transplant, carefully dig a hole in your prepared garden bed that's large enough for the seedling's root system. Place the seedling in the hole, gently backfill with soil, and water thoroughly. Remember to space the plants about 3-4 inches apart for optimal growth.

The process of germinating bush beans from seeds to seedlings involves careful planting, maintaining optimal temperature and moisture levels, providing ample light, and timing the transplantation correctly. By following these steps, you can increase your chances of growing a successful crop of bush beans in your vegetable raised bed garden.

Spacing & Measurement

Proper spacing and measurements when transplanting bush bean seedlings into vegetable raised bed gardens are crucial for several reasons. Firstly, adequate space allows each plant to receive sufficient sunlight, which is essential for photosynthesis and healthy growth. If plants are too close together, they may shade each other out, leading to weak, leggy growth as they stretch for light.

Secondly, correct spacing helps ensure good air circulation around the plants, which can help prevent the spread of diseases and pests that thrive in stagnant, humid conditions. Additionally, each plant needs enough room to develop its root system. When plants are spaced too closely, they compete for water and nutrients in the soil, potentially leading to stunted growth and lower yields.

Planting bush beans in a raised bed garden requires careful attention to spacing and measurements to ensure healthy growth and a productive harvest. Each bush bean plant needs ample space to grow, develop its root system, and spread its leaves. This not only allows the plant to receive adequate sunlight and air circulation but also prevents overcrowding, which can lead to competition for nutrients and water.

The general guideline for planting bush beans is to space them about 4 to 6 inches apart. This distance allows each plant to have enough room to grow without encroaching on the space of its neighbors. It's crucial to maintain this spacing as it reduces the chance of disease transmission between plants. Diseases can easily spread from one plant to another when they are too close together, especially in damp conditions.

In addition to spacing between individual plants, the rows of bush beans should also be spaced appropriately. The recommended distance between rows is typically 18 to 24 inches. This wider spacing between rows allows for easier access to the plants for care and harvest and promotes better air circulation, which can help prevent diseases caused by excess moisture, such as fungal infections.

When planting in a raised bed, it's essential to take measurements of the bed itself to plan your planting layout accurately.

Depending on the size of your raised bed, you may need to adjust the number of plants or rows you can accommodate. It's always better to err on the side of caution and not overcrowd your bed. Overcrowding can lead to stunted growth and lower yields, as well as increase the likelihood of pest infestations and disease outbreaks.

Proper spacing and measurements are fundamental to successful bush bean cultivation in raised bed gardens. By giving each plant the room, it needs to grow and thrive, you can look forward to a healthy, bountiful harvest.

Ideal Temperatures & Sun Requirements

Proper temperature and sun exposure are crucial factors in successfully growing bush beans in raised bed gardens. Bush beans prefer warm temperatures and require a good amount of sunlight for optimal growth. The ideal soil temperature for bush beans is between 60 and 85 degrees Fahrenheit. At these temperatures, seeds can germinate within 8 to 10 days, and the plants can grow robustly.

Temperatures below this range can slow down germination and growth, while those above can cause stress to the plants. It's also important to note that bush beans are sensitive to frost, so planting should be done after the last expected frost date.

Aside from temperature, bush beans also need plenty of sunlight. They require at least 6 to 8 hours of full sun each day. Sunlight plays a significant role in photosynthesis, the process by which plants convert light energy into chemical energy for growth.

Without adequate sunlight, bush beans may become leggy, produce fewer flowers, and yield less. Therefore, when choosing a location for your raised bed garden, ensure it's a spot that receives ample sun throughout the day.

In summary, achieving the right balance of temperature and sun exposure is essential for the healthy growth and productivity of bush beans. By creating conditions that meet these requirements, you can ensure a bountiful harvest from your raised bed garden.

MAINTAINING YOUR RAISED BED BUSH BEANS

Maintaining your raised bed grown bush beans in vegetable gardening is crucial for several reasons. First, it ensures that the plants have adequate nutrients. As plants in raised beds can exhaust the nutrient supply more quickly than those in the ground, it's essential to replenish these nutrients regularly with organic matter or slow-release fertilizers.

Second, watering needs to be consistent, as raised beds tend to dry out faster. However, overwatering should also be avoided as it can lead to root diseases. Third, raised beds should be checked regularly for pests and diseases. Early detection can prevent significant damage to your Bed Bush plants.

Finally, proper maintenance includes pruning and staking (if necessary) to promote healthy growth and air circulation. Thus, diligent maintenance of your raised bed-grown bush beans is key to a successful and bountiful harvest.

CHAPTER 10

Pruning & Thinning Your Bush Beans

Pruning and thinning your raised bed grown bush beans in vegetable gardens are crucial tasks that can greatly influence the health and productivity of your plants. Initially, pruning involves cutting back specific parts of the plant, such as dead or diseased branches, which not only keeps the plant's shape but also prevents the spread of diseases. It further encourages better air circulation, thus reducing the chances of fungal infections.

In addition, pruning can stimulate the growth of new branches, thereby increasing the potential for more bean pods. On the other hand, thinning is the process of removing some plants to alleviate crowding.

This is vital because overcrowded plants compete for light, water, and nutrients, potentially leading to stunted growth and lower yields. By thinning out your bush beans, each plant has ample resources to grow vigorously and produce a healthy crop. Therefore, regular pruning and thinning are essential maintenance practices for raising successful bush beans in your raised bed garden.

Pruning and thinning bush beans in raised bed gardens are key practices that should be performed at specific stages of the plant's growth cycle and in a particular manner to ensure optimal health and productivity of the plants.

The process of thinning bush beans should ideally begin when the plants are still young, typically when they've grown their first set of true leaves, which usually happens about 2-3 weeks after germination.

At this stage, closely examine the plants and identify any that are weaker or smaller than the rest. These are the plants you'll want to thin out. To do so, gently pull them out from the soil, being careful not to disturb the roots of the surrounding plants. The goal is to leave about 4-6 inches of space between each remaining plant to ensure they have enough room to grow and access essential resources.

As for pruning, it's best to start when the bush beans are about a foot tall, which is typically a few weeks after the thinning process. Pruning at this stage helps to control the size of the plants and encourages more productive growth. Use a sharp, clean pair of garden shears to make clean cuts.

Start by removing any yellow or brown leaves at the bottom of the plant, as these could be signs of disease or pest infestation. Then, prune the plant to maintain its shape and size. Cut back any overly long branches to help balance the plant's growth. This also improves air circulation around the plant, reducing the risk of fungal diseases.

After pruning, ensure to clean up the debris from the garden bed to prevent any diseases or pests from spreading. Additionally, after both pruning and thinning, it's beneficial to provide the plants with a dose of balanced, slow-release fertilizer to support their continued growth and development.

Proper timing and technique in pruning and thinning bush beans are crucial in ensuring a healthy and productive crop. These practices not only help in disease and pest management but also promote a more robust growth, leading to a high yield.

Watering Your Raised Bed Bush Beans

Watering is a crucial aspect of maintaining the health and productivity of your raised bed grown bush beans. Bush beans, like most plants, are predominantly made up of water. They require consistent moisture for various vital processes such as photosynthesis, nutrient transportation, and growth.

Water is integral to the germination process, enabling seeds to swell and break their coatings to allow the embryo plant to emerge and grow. Furthermore, during the flowering and pod development stages, consistent watering is especially important as inadequate water can lead to flower drops and poorly developed pods, thereby affecting yield.

Additionally, regular watering helps to maintain the soil's structure and nutrient content, providing a conducive environment for root development. However, it's also essential to avoid overwatering as it can lead to waterlogged soil and root rot. Therefore, proper watering, which strikes a balance between keeping the soil moist and preventing waterlogging, is critical for raising successful bush beans in your raised bed garden.

Understanding the right watering practices for bush beans in raised bed gardens is key to a healthy and bountiful harvest. Most garden vegetables, including bush beans, require about 1 to 2 inches of water per week, which can fluctuate depending on soil and weather conditions. This amount of moisture ensures the plants have enough hydration for their growth processes and fosters the development of strong root systems.

The initial watering should occur immediately after planting the seeds. Once you've covered the seeds with loose soil, water them until the top couple of inches of soil are damp. This encourages the germination process, which usually takes place within ten days.

As the bush beans grow and mature, maintaining consistent watering becomes even more critical, especially during the flowering and pod development stages. Inconsistent watering can lead to flower drops and poorly developed pods, thereby affecting your overall yield.

However, it's important to remember that while bush beans need consistent watering, overwatering can lead to waterlogged soil and root rot. Therefore, you must strike a balance between keeping the soil moist and avoiding waterlogging. This may involve adjusting the watering frequency based on weather conditions and the soil's moisture levels. For instance, during hot and dry periods, more frequent watering might be necessary.

Knowing how much and when to water your bush beans is crucial for successful growth in your raised bed garden. Regular and correct watering not only fosters healthy growth but also maximizes bean production.

Organic Fertilization For Raised Bed Bush Beans

Organic fertilization plays a pivotal role in the successful growth of bush beans in raised bed gardens. Bush beans, like other legumes, are known for their ability to fix nitrogen from the atmosphere, reducing the need for high-nitrogen fertilizers. However, they still require a balanced supply of other essential nutrients, including phosphorus and potassium, which can be effectively provided through organic fertilization.

Organic fertilizers, derived from plant, animal, or mineral resources, not only supply these necessary nutrients but also contribute to improving the soil structure and its capacity to hold water and nutrients. They enhance the biological activity in the soil, fostering a healthy, vibrant ecosystem that promotes plant health and resilience against diseases.

Unlike synthetic fertilizers, organic fertilizers release nutrients slowly, providing a steady supply of nutrition to the plants over an extended period. This slow-release property reduces the risk of nutrient leaching, making organic fertilizers an environmentally friendly choice. Therefore, using organic fertilizers in raised bed gardens can significantly improve the yield and quality of bush beans while also contributing to sustainable gardening practices.

Choosing the right type of organic fertilizer for bush beans in raised bed gardens is crucial for their growth and productivity. While bush beans, like other legumes, have the ability to fix nitrogen from the air, they still require other essential nutrients that can be supplied through organic fertilizers.

Compost is one of the best organic fertilizers you can use for bush beans. It's rich in essential nutrients and helps improve the soil structure, promoting better root development. Before planting, mix compost into the top few inches of soil in your raised bed. This will provide a slow release of nutrients throughout the growing season.

Another excellent organic fertilizer option for bush beans is aged manure. Chicken, cow, or horse manure that has been well-rotted or composted is high in nutrients and can be particularly beneficial. However, it's important to ensure that the manure is fully composted before using it to avoid burning the plants or introducing harmful pathogens into the garden.

Bone meal is also a beneficial organic fertilizer for bush beans, as it provides phosphorus, which is essential for plant growth and flower production. Bone meal can be mixed into the soil at planting time to provide a steady supply of phosphorus throughout the growing season.

In terms of timing, apply organic fertilizers to your raised bed garden just before or at planting time. This allows the nutrients to start breaking down and become available to your plants just as they are starting to grow. During the growing season, additional side dressings of compost or aged manure can be applied to replenish nutrients and boost growth.

It's also worth noting that proper application is key when using organic fertilizers. Avoid applying them directly onto the plants; instead, work them into the soil around the base of the plants to ensure the nutrients are accessible to the roots.

Using organic fertilizers in your raised bed garden can significantly enhance the growth and yield of your bush beans. By supplying a steady source of essential nutrients, these fertilizers not only support plant health but also contribute to a sustainable and eco-friendly gardening practice.

PROTECTING YOUR RAISED BED BUSH BEANS

Extreme Temperatures

Protecting your bush beans from extreme temperatures in raised bed gardens is crucial for their successful growth and development. Bush beans, like many other vegetables, thrive best in moderate temperatures. They can be sensitive to both excessive heat and cold, which can stunt growth, cause flower drop, or even kill the plants.

When dealing with high temperatures, providing adequate shade can help protect your bush beans. You can use a garden shade cloth or a shade net to shield your plants during the hottest part of the day.

This reduces heat stress and prevents the soil from drying out too quickly. Additionally, mulching around the base of the plants can help retain soil moisture and keep the roots cool. Using organic mulch like straw or wood chips not only helps control temperature but also adds nutrients to the soil as it decomposes.

On the other hand, cold temperatures can be just as detrimental. If a late frost is expected after planting, you should cover your bush beans with a row cover or a frost blanket. This will trap heat from the ground and protect the young plants from the cold. In colder climates, consider starting your beans indoors or wait until all danger of frost has passed before planting them outside.

Consistent watering is also essential in protecting your bush beans from extreme temperatures. Watering in the early morning or late evening can reduce evaporation and ensure that your plants receive enough water during hot weather. In cold weather, avoid overwatering as this can lead to root rot, especially if the soil is cold.

The importance of protecting your bush beans from extreme temperatures cannot be overstated. Extreme heat can cause the plants to wilt, drop flowers, and produce poor-quality pods. Cold temperatures can delay germination, stunt growth, and, in severe cases, kill the plants.

By taking measures to regulate the temperature, you can ensure that your bush beans remain healthy and productive, leading to a bountiful harvest. Remember, the key to successful gardening is to understand the needs of your plants and to create an environment that best supports their growth.

Protecting Raised Bed Bush Beans From Pests

Protecting bush beans from pests in raised bed gardens is essential for maintaining a healthy and productive crop. Pests can cause significant damage to your plants, reducing their vitality and yield.

Certain pests, such as aphids, spider mites, and beetles, are known to target bush beans, feeding on the leaves, stems, and pods. This not only weakens the plant, but can also lead to the spread of diseases. If left unchecked, a pest infestation can devastate your entire crop, turning what could have been a bountiful harvest into a disappointing loss.

Furthermore, some pests can overwinter in garden debris and soil, causing recurring problems year after year. Therefore, regular monitoring, early detection, and prompt control measures are crucial in managing pests and ensuring the well-being of your bush beans.

The use of organic pest control methods is highly recommended as they are environmentally friendly and safe for beneficial insects, promoting a balanced ecosystem in your garden.

Raised bed grown bush beans can be susceptible to a range of pests including aphids, spider mites, and beetles. Each of these pests presents a unique challenge, and understanding their behaviors is vital to effective pest management.

Aphids are small, soft-bodied insects that feed on plant sap, typically congregating on the undersides of leaves. They can cause the leaves to curl, yellow, or distort. Aphids also produce a sticky substance known as honeydew, which can attract other pests like ants and lead to the growth of sooty mold.

Spider mites are another common pest; these tiny arachnids also feed on plant sap, causing the leaves to develop yellow spots, lose their color, and potentially drop off the plant.

Beetles, such as the Mexican bean beetle and bean leaf beetle, can be particularly destructive, chewing holes in leaves, flowers, and bean pods.

To protect your bush beans from these pests, it's crucial to implement an integrated pest management strategy. Regularly inspect your plants for signs of these pests. Aphids can often be knocked off plants with a strong stream of water from a garden hose.

Introducing beneficial insects, like ladybugs, lacewings, and parasitic wasps, can also help control aphid populations as they are natural predators of aphids.

Spider mites can be more challenging to manage due to their small size and rapid reproduction rate. However, they do have natural enemies, such as ladybugs, thrips, and predatory mites, which can help keep their populations in check. Maintaining a humid environment can also deter spider mites, as they prefer dry conditions. If infestations become severe, consider using a miticide.

Beetle management can involve hand-picking and dropping them into soapy water, especially if the population is relatively small. Crop rotation can also help, as beetles tend to lay their eggs in the soil where beans were previously planted.

For larger beetle populations, consider using organic insecticides such as neem-oil or introducing beneficial insects like parasitic wasps that prey on beetle eggs and larvae.

In addition to these strategies, maintaining a clean garden can help prevent overwintering pests, and using floating row covers can provide a physical barrier against pests. While these pests can pose significant challenges, with vigilance and proactive management, it's entirely possible to grow healthy, productive bush beans in your raised bed garden.

Protecting Raised Bed Bush Beans From Diseases

Protecting raised bed grown bush beans from diseases is crucial for several reasons. Firstly, diseases can significantly reduce the yield and quality of your beans, impacting not only the quantity of your harvest but also the taste and nutritional value of the produce. Diseases can cause a variety of symptoms, such as spots or discoloration on the leaves, wilting, stunted growth, or even death of the plant.

Secondly, some diseases can persist in the soil or plant debris, causing problems for future crops. This can limit the success of your gardening efforts year after year. Lastly, managing diseases often requires time, effort, and resources. For example, you might need to apply natural fungicides, remove and dispose of infected plants, or even replace the entire soil in your raised bed.

By taking steps to prevent diseases in the first place, you can save yourself these troubles and ensure a bountiful, healthy crop of bush beans.

Raised bed grown bush beans can be susceptible to various diseases. The Bean Common Mosaic Virus (BCMV) is one such disease, causing symptoms of black root necrosis on the pods of common beans. This virus can severely affect the overall health of the plant, impacting its productivity and growth.

Another disease that can attack bush beans is Fusarium root rot, caused by the fungus Fusarium solani. This fungus can attack older seedlings, leading to yellowing, wilting, and stunting of plants. The Sclerotinia fungus also poses a threat, causing the pods to become soft, leaves to form watery spots, and stems to rot under cool, moist conditions.

Powdery mildew, caused by an Oidium species, can seriously affect all above-ground parts of the bean plant. This disease is primarily found on older plants, causing a white, powdery film on the leaves, stems, and pods.

Alternaria Leaf and Pod Spot, caused by Alternaria species, generally affects older leaves. Two widespread bacterial blights also affect most types of beans, common blight (Xanthomonas campestris pathovar phaseoli) and halo blight.

To organically protect bush beans from these diseases, prevention is key. Choose disease-resistant varieties of bush beans when possible. Practice crop rotation, as many diseases can persist in the soil from year to year. Regularly remove plant debris from your garden, as this can harbor disease-causing organisms.

For diseases like BCMV, once a plant is infected, there's no treatment available, so it's crucial to use disease-free seed and remove any infected plants immediately. For fungal diseases like Fusarium root rot and Sclerotinia, consider using organic fungicides. These can be based on copper or sulfur, or biological agents like Bacillus subtilis.

Powdery mildew can be managed by improving air circulation around your plants, as the fungus thrives in humid, stagnant air conditions. Regular applications of organic fungicides, such as those containing sulfur, can also help.

Bacterial blights can be controlled by avoiding working in the garden when it's wet, as this can spread the bacteria. Copper-based sprays can also be used to manage these diseases.

HARVESTING RAISED BED BUSH BEANS

Bush beans grown in raised beds typically take between 50 to 60 days from planting to reach maturity and be ready for harvest. This timeline can slightly vary depending on the specific variety of bush bean you're growing and the environmental conditions. Warmer temperatures tend to accelerate the growth process, while cooler conditions may extend the duration.

The best indication that your bush beans are ready to be harvested is the size of the pods. Ideally, you should aim to pick the beans when the pods are firm and have reached their full length, but before the beans inside have begun to bulge significantly.

This is usually when the beans are at their most tender and flavorful. If left too long on the plant, the pods can become tough and stringy, and the beans inside may be hard and starchy.

To harvest the beans, gently hold the top of the bean pod and pull downwards with a smooth motion. Be careful not to tug too hard, as this can damage the plant and possibly uproot it.

Alternatively, you can use a pair of sharp scissors or pruning shears to cut the bean pod from the plant, which can minimize any potential harm to the plant.

Bush beans often come into production all at once, so regular harvesting is essential to encourage further flowering and bean production. Ideally, check your plants every couple of days during the harvesting period, as beans can grow rapidly and can quickly become over-mature. Regular harvesting also keeps the plants healthier and reduces the likelihood of disease.

After harvesting, it's best to consume the beans as soon as possible for the best taste and nutritional value. However, they can also be stored in a refrigerator for about a week, or they can be blanched and frozen for longer storage.

Growing bush beans in raised bed gardens is a rewarding endeavor, yielding fresh, tasty beans in just a couple of months. By understanding the growth cycle of these plants and the proper harvesting techniques, you can enjoy a plentiful and ongoing harvest throughout the growing season.

RAISED BEDS GROWN BUSH BEANS NOTES

Start: Seeds

Germination: 6 to 12 days, temperatures between 70 and 80 degrees Fahrenheit.

Seed Life: 5 Years

Soil Type: Well drained loamy soil, rich in organic matter (compost or well-rotted manure) - pH level between 6.0 to 7.0

Seed Spacing: 1 inch deep

Seedling Spacing: 4 to 6 inches apart

Sunlight: 6 -8 hours full sunlight

Growing Temperatures: Between 60 and 85 degrees

Days To Harvest: 50 to 60 days

CHAPTER 11
VEGETABLE RAISED BED GARDENING – EGGPLANT

E ggplant is a popular and versatile vegetable for raised bed gardening. A member of the nightshade family, eggplant thrives in the warmth of summer and produces bountiful yields when grown in rich garden soil. This heat-loving plant has been cultivated for centuries and prized for its unique flavor and texture. When properly cared for, eggplants grown in raised beds will reward home gardeners with an abundant harvest ideal for a multitude of culinary creations.

With their glossy purple skin and oval shape, eggplants add beauty and color to the vegetable garden. While typically purple, eggplant varieties can range from white to green to striped. The egg-shaped vegetables also come in a range of sizes, from small and round to large and oblong.

This diversity allows gardeners to choose the eggplant that best suits their culinary needs and garden design. When planted in a raised bed, eggplant's sprawling bushes can be neatly contained while providing the root space needed for vigorous growth. For gardeners seeking a taste of summer with minimal effort, eggplant is the quintessential choice for raised bed vegetable gardening.

Growing eggplants in raised beds offers numerous benefits for any vegetable garden. The rich, loose soil in a raised bed provides ideal conditions for eggplants to thrive. The beds can be filled with a nutritious potting mix amended with compost, which retains moisture and nutrients that eggplants need.

Raised beds also improve drainage, which is crucial since eggplants are susceptible to root rot in soggy conditions. Additionally, the warmer soil temperatures in raised beds stimulate growth and yield.

Containing eggplants within a raised bed prevents their sprawling growth from invading other parts of the garden. Growers can space plants appropriately to maximize productivity in a compact area.

Raised beds elevate the plants for easier access and prevent soil from splashing onto the foliage during rain or watering. This helps reduce the risk of disease. The beds can be covered with fabric row covers to protect eggplants from insect pests, wind damage, and temperature fluctuations.

Overall, raised beds create an optimal microclimate and growing environment for eggplants to thrive. Gardeners are rewarded with robust plants and bountiful yields of beautiful glossy eggplants when this heat-loving crop is grown in raised beds.

THE RIGHT SOIL TO GROW EGGPLANTS IN RAISED BEDS

Eggplants thrive in nutrient-rich, well-drained soil. When growing eggplants in raised beds, pay close attention to soil quality and composition.

Eggplants grow best in soil with a pH between 5.5 and 6.5. Test your garden soil and amend as needed to reach the ideal acidic range. Mix in aluminum sulfate or sulfur to lower pH or lime to increase pH. The proper pH helps eggplants effectively take up nutrients from the soil.

Incorporate 2-3 inches of organic compost into your raised bed before planting. Compost supplies a slow-release of nitrogen, phosphorus, and potassium. It also promotes soil microbial activity and improves texture. Well-rotted manure, grass clippings, humus and peat moss make excellent compost amendments for raised beds.

Good drainage is crucial for healthy eggplants. Raised beds allow you to fill the frame with an ideal potting mix instead of compacted native soil. Aim for a lightweight mix made up of 1/3 compost, 1/3 peat moss or coco coir and 1/3 vermiculite or perlite. The peat retains moisture, while the vermiculite improves drainage and aeration.

By tailoring the soil composition in your raised beds, you can create the ideal growing environment for your eggplants to thrive and bear abundant fruit.

CHAPTER 11

HOW TO SOW EGGPLANTS IN RAISED BEDS

Correct Season To Sow Eggplants In Raised Beds

When it comes to sowing eggplant in raised bed gardens, timing is everything. Eggplants are extremely sensitive to cold temperatures and require a long, warm growing season to reach maturity and produce fruit. Most experts recommend starting eggplant seeds indoors 6-8 weeks before the anticipated last spring frost. This gives the seedlings time to develop strong roots and leaves before being transplanted outside.

The soil temperature should be at least 60-65°F before transplanting eggplant starts into the garden. Rushing to plant them too early when nights are still cool will stress the plants and make them prone to disease. Be patient and wait until daytime highs are reliably in the 70s and nighttime lows stay above 50°F before moving eggplants into the raised beds. With their love of heat, mid to late spring is the perfect window to transplant eggplants for a successful crop in raised bed gardens.

Plant Needs & Requirements

Germinating eggplant seeds correctly is vital for growing healthy, productive plants in raised bed gardens. Eggplants require very warm conditions of 80-90°F to sprout from seed. Starting the seeds indoors allows gardeners to provide the consistent heat needed for proper germination.

Maintaining the right moisture levels prevents seeds from drying out or rotting during this vulnerable stage. Gradually moving seedlings into stronger light prevents leggy, weak growth. Giving seedlings adequate time, warmth, light, and care to develop strong roots and leaves before hardening off and transplanting reduces shock and results in vigorous plants better equipped to thrive in the garden environment.

Putting effort into nurturing eggplant seedlings by carefully meeting their germination and growth needs leads to robust vegetable plants that yield abundant, high-quality fruits throughout the season in raised bed gardens. Proper seed starting is the foundation for eggplant success.

Germinating eggplant seeds to seedlings involves a few crucial steps. The process begins with selecting high-quality seeds from a reputable source. Eggplants come in various shapes, sizes, and colors, so choose a variety that suits your climate, soil, and personal preference. Once you have your seeds, prepare a seed-starting mix or use a good quality potting soil. Sow the seeds about 1/4 inch deep in small containers or seed trays.

Eggplant seeds require warm temperatures for germination. The ideal temperature range is between 80-90°F. To maintain this temperature, consider using a heat mat under your seed trays, especially if you're starting your seeds in a cooler environment.

Covering the trays with a plastic dome or wrap can also help retain heat and moisture. Make sure the soil remains consistently moist but not waterlogged. Too much water can cause the seeds to rot, while too little can prevent germination.

Most eggplant seeds will germinate within 10-14 days at the correct temperature. Once they sprout, move them to a sunny window sill or under grow lights. They need plenty of light to grow strong and healthy. Rotate the seedlings regularly to ensure even growth and prevent them from leaning towards the light source.

As the seedlings grow, keep an eye out for their first true leaves. These are the second set of leaves that appear after the initial seed leaves (cotyledons). Once these true leaves appear, it's time to transplant the seedlings into larger individual pots. This gives them more room to grow and develop a robust root system.

Eggplant seedlings are ready to be transplanted into your vegetable raised bed garden when they are about 6-9 weeks old and at least 3-4 inches tall. However, timing also depends on outdoor conditions. Eggplants are warm-season crops and sensitive to cold. So, wait until the danger of frost has passed and soil temperatures have warmed to at least 60°F before transplanting your seedlings outdoors.

Also, gradually acclimate the seedlings to outdoor conditions over a week or two (a process known as hardening off) before planting them in the garden. This helps prevent transplant shock and ensures a smooth transition for your seedlings from indoors to outdoors.

Spacing & Measurement

Proper spacing and measurement when transplanting eggplant seedlings into raised bed gardens is vital for several reasons. Eggplants, like many plants, need sufficient space to grow and spread out their leaves and roots. This space allows them to effectively absorb sunlight, water, and nutrients from the soil, which are essential for their growth and productivity. If the plants are too close together, they may compete with each other for these resources, leading to stunted growth and reduced yields.

Proper spacing also promotes good airflow around the plants, which can help prevent the spread of diseases and pests that thrive in damp, crowded conditions. Moreover, orderly arrangement and accurate measurements enable easier maintenance and harvesting. Therefore, ensuring correct spacing and measurements during transplantation is a key step towards a successful eggplant harvest.

Proper spacing and measurements are crucial when planting eggplant seedlings in a vegetable raised bed garden. The first step is to understand the size of your raised bed. This will determine how many eggplant seedlings you can comfortably accommodate.

Eggplants are medium-sized plants that need sufficient space to grow without competition for resources. Typically, it's recommended to space eggplant seedlings about 18-24 inches apart. This distance ensures each plant has ample room to develop a robust root system and expansive foliage. It also allows for good air circulation around each plant, which is essential for preventing diseases and encouraging pollination.

The rows in which the eggplants are planted should be spaced about 30-36 inches apart. This gives you enough room to move between the rows for watering, weeding, pruning, and harvesting without damaging the plants. It also ensures that each plant gets its fair share of sunlight, which is vital for photosynthesis and fruit production.

When planting in a raised bed, you can generally plant more closely than in a traditional row garden because you don't need to leave room for walking paths within the bed itself. For example, in a 4x8 foot raised bed, you could potentially plant up to 16 eggplants (4 plants across and 4 plants down) using a square foot gardening method.

However, remember that overcrowded plants can compete for nutrients, water, and light, leading to reduced yield and potential disease issues. So, while it's tempting to try and fit as many plants as possible into your space, it's important to give each plant the room it needs to thrive.

Finally, consider companion planting when planning your eggplant bed. Certain plants, like beans, peas, and spinach, can benefit eggplants by fixing nitrogen in the soil or providing shade to keep the soil cool. Just be sure to account for the space these companion plants will need as well.

By carefully considering the spacing and measurements when planting your eggplant seedlings, you can maximize your yield and the health of your plants in your raised bed garden.

Ideal Temperatures & Sun Requirements

Maintaining ideal temperatures and sun exposure is crucial for successfully growing eggplants in a vegetable raised bed garden. Eggplants are warm-weather plants that thrive best when temperatures range between 70°F and 85°F, and they grow very slowly in cooler weather.

Consistent nighttime temperatures above 55 degrees are important for their growth, and even better results can be achieved when overnight temperatures are consistently above 60° Fahrenheit. Eggplants don't fare well in cold conditions, so it's crucial to ensure that the temperature stays reliably above 50 degrees F before transplanting them into the garden.

In addition to temperature, sunlight plays a significant role in eggplant growth. These plants require a sunny spot in your garden that receives a minimum of 6 hours of sunlight per day. The amount of sunlight eggplants receive can influence their growth, as they thrive in environments where they can absorb ample sunlight throughout the day.

Therefore, when planning your raised bed garden, it's essential to consider both the temperature and sun requirements of eggplants to promote healthy growth and a bountiful harvest.

MAINTAINING YOUR RAISED BED EGGPLANTS

Maintaining your eggplants in a vegetable raised bed garden is of paramount importance for ensuring a successful harvest. First, maintenance helps to keep the plants healthy and free from diseases and pests. Regularly checking the leaves, stems, and fruits can help detect early signs of infestations, allowing you to take immediate action.

Second, proper watering and feeding practices are part of maintenance. Eggplants require consistent watering, especially during dry spells, and nutrient-rich soil to grow. By maintaining the moisture levels and providing necessary nutrients, you can ensure the plants have what they need to produce bountiful crops.

Third, maintenance includes tasks like pruning and staking, which are crucial for the plant's growth. Pruning helps to improve air circulation and light exposure, while staking prevents the plants from falling over under the weight of the fruits. Lastly, regular maintenance allows you to spot any potential issues early, such as nutrient deficiency or disease, thus increasing your chances of a successful harvest.

Pruning & Thinning Your Eggplants

Pruning and thinning eggplants in a vegetable raised bed garden are essential practices that contribute significantly to the health and productivity of your plants. Pruning involves removing certain parts of the plant, such as overcrowded leaves and branches, to improve air circulation and sunlight exposure. This helps to prevent the onset and spread of diseases, many of which thrive in damp, poorly ventilated conditions.

By pruning your eggplants, you also direct the plant's energy towards producing larger, healthier fruits rather than unnecessary foliage.

Thinning, on the other hand, is the practice of removing some plants entirely to reduce competition for resources such as space, water, and nutrients.

If eggplants are too crowded, they may compete for these resources, resulting in smaller, less healthy plants and fruit.

Thinning ensures each remaining plant has ample room to grow and access to the necessary resources.

Moreover, both pruning and thinning can help to improve the quality of the fruits. Plants that are not overcrowded or burdened by excessive foliage can focus their energy on developing fewer but larger and tastier fruits. Therefore, regular pruning and thinning are important maintenance tasks that can lead to a more bountiful and high-quality eggplant harvest from your raised bed garden.

Pruning and thinning raised bed-grown eggplants are essential gardening practices that can greatly improve the health and productivity of your plants when done correctly and at the right time.

Pruning is typically done in the early stages of the plant's life, once it has grown to about 2-3 feet tall. At this point, the plant should have a few branches and leaves that can be pruned without harming the overall growth of the plant.

Start by removing any lower leaves that touch the ground or are yellowing, as these can attract pests and diseases. Also, prune any suckers, which are small shoots that emerge from the junction between the stem and a branch.

They drain energy from the plant that could be better used for fruit production. Always use sharp, clean pruning shears to make clean cuts and minimize the risk of disease transmission.

Thinning, on the other hand, should be done shortly after the plants have germinated and have grown a couple of sets of true leaves, usually 2-3 weeks after planting.

To thin out your eggplants, carefully pull out or cut off smaller or weaker seedlings, leaving the strongest ones to continue growing. The remaining plants should be spaced about 18-24 inches apart to ensure they have enough room to grow and access to nutrients and sunlight.

Remember to handle your eggplants gently during both pruning and thinning to avoid causing unnecessary stress or damage. After pruning or thinning, water your plants well to help them recover from the process. By following these practices, you'll encourage a healthier, more productive eggplant crop in your raised bed garden.

Watering Your Raised Bed Eggplants

Watering your eggplants in vegetable raised bed gardens is a vital aspect of their care, impacting both plant health and fruit production.

Eggplants, like most vegetables, are largely made up of water, so they require consistent hydration to grow and thrive. Water is essential for the plant's processes, such as photosynthesis and nutrient uptake, and it helps maintain turgidity, keeping the plant upright and robust.

Additionally, consistent watering helps to ensure that the eggplant fruits develop properly and do not become bitter or stunted. However, it's essential to strike a balance because both overwatering and under watering can lead to plant stress and adverse conditions like root rot or wilting. A regular, balanced watering routine contributes to a healthy root system, which in turn supports vigorous plant growth and a bountiful harvest.

Watering raised bed grown eggplants in your vegetable garden plays a crucial role in their growth and productivity. On average, eggplants require about 1 inch of water per week, a guideline that applies to many vegetable plants. This amount ensures that the soil remains moist but not waterlogged, providing the ideal conditions for these plants to thrive.

Remember, the goal is to keep the soil consistently moist, not drenched. Overwatering can lead to root rot and other diseases, while under-watering can cause the plant to wilt and the fruits to become bitter.

It's essential to water your eggplants deeply and less frequently. Deep watering encourages the development of a robust root system, which helps the plant absorb nutrients more efficiently and withstand periods of drought better.

To achieve this, instead of watering a little every day, it's better to water thoroughly a few times a week, depending on the weather conditions and the soil type. In hotter climates or during dry spells, you may need to water more frequently.

Furthermore, when watering eggplants, it's best to water at the base of the plant rather than from above. This method helps keep the leaves dry, reducing the risk of fungal diseases. Also, watering in the morning gives the plants enough time to absorb the water before the heat of the day, reducing evaporation.

However, these are general guidelines, and the exact watering needs can vary based on factors like the local climate, the soil type, and the specific variety of eggplant. For instance, very sandy soils may drain quickly and thus require more frequent watering. Therefore, it's always a good idea to regularly check the soil moisture levels by feeling the soil a few inches below the surface. If it feels dry, it's time to water.

Organic Fertilization For Raised Bed Eggplants

Organic fertilization plays a significant role in the health and productivity of raised bed grown eggplants. Eggplants, like many other vegetables, are heavy feeders, meaning they require a rich supply of nutrients to grow optimally.

Organic fertilizers provide a wide range of essential nutrients, including nitrogen, phosphorus, and potassium, as well as several trace minerals. Unlike synthetic fertilizers, organic fertilizers release these nutrients slowly over time, providing a steady supply that supports sustained growth and reduces the risk of nutrient burn.

Furthermore, organic fertilizers contribute to the overall fertility and structure of the soil. They increase the soil's capacity to retain water and nutrients, promote the activity of beneficial soil microorganisms, and improve soil structure, all of which are particularly important in raised bed gardens where soil conditions can be more challenging to manage.

Therefore, using organic fertilizers can not only boost your eggplant yield but also contribute to a healthier, more sustainable garden ecosystem.

Using organic fertilizers for eggplants in raised bed gardens can significantly enhance their growth and productivity. These fertilizers not only provide essential nutrients to the plants but also improve the soil's overall health, fostering a more conducive environment for plant growth.

One of the most common types of organic fertilizers is compost. Rich in a variety of nutrients, compost is often referred to as "black gold" by gardeners. It is made from decomposed organic matter like vegetable scraps, grass clippings, leaves, and manure. When added to the garden, compost slowly releases nutrients into the soil, improving its fertility and structure. It enhances the soil's ability to hold water and facilitates the proliferation of beneficial microorganisms.

Another excellent organic fertilizer option is well-rotted manure. Manure from herbivores such as cows, horses, or chickens is rich in nitrogen, making it an excellent choice for nitrogen-loving plants like eggplants. However, it's crucial to use well-rotted or composted manure, as fresh manure can burn plants and contain harmful pathogens.

Bone meal is another beneficial organic fertilizer, particularly rich in phosphorous, which is vital for root development and fruiting. Similarly, fish emulsion or fish meal can be an excellent source of nitrogen and other nutrients.

When it comes to applying organic fertilizers, timing is crucial. Generally, it's best to add compost or manure to the soil a few weeks before planting your eggplants, giving it time to break down and enrich the soil. For other organic fertilizers like bone meal or fish emulsion, follow the manufacturer's instructions regarding application rates and frequency.

Application method is also important. When preparing the bed, mix the compost or manure thoroughly with the top layer of soil. For fertilizers like bone meal or fish emulsion, you can either mix them into the soil at planting time or add them as a side dressing, sprinkling them around the base of established plants and then watering thoroughly.

Using organic fertilizers not only nourishes your eggplants but also contributes to a healthier, more sustainable garden ecosystem. Always remember to consider the specific nutritional requirements of your plants and adjust your fertilization practices accordingly.

PROTECTING YOUR RAISED BED EGGPLANTS

Extreme Temperatures

Protecting raised bed grown eggplants from extreme tempera-tures is crucial for their overall growth and productivity. Eggplants are warm-season crops, which means they thrive in temperatures between 70 and 85 degrees Fahrenheit. Exposure to temperatures outside this range can lead to reduced growth, poor fruit set, and, in extreme cases, plant death. Therefore, taking steps to shield your eggplants from temperature extremes is key to a successful harvest.

When dealing with high temperatures, providing shade can be an effective strategy. During heatwaves or in particularly hot climates, use shade cloths or garden fabric to protect your eggplants from the intense midday sun. These materials allow some light through while reducing the heat intensity, helping to keep the plants cooler.

Additionally, mulching around the base of the plants can help retain soil moisture and keep the roots cool, which is especially beneficial in a raised bed garden where the soil tends to dry out faster.

Conversely, in cooler weather or at the start of the growing season when the risk of frost is still present, row covers or cloches can be used to protect the eggplants. These coverings trap heat from the sun during the day, creating a warmer micro-climate around the plants. They can be easily removed during the day when temperatures rise and replaced in the evening when it gets cooler.

Also, consider planting eggplants in black or dark-colored containers. These will naturally absorb more heat from the sun and can provide some protection against cool nights. Just be careful in hot climates as they can also overheat the plants.

Watering practices can also impact how well your eggplants cope with temperature extremes. Watering in the morning allows the plants to take up moisture before the heat of the day, reducing heat stress. On cold nights, watering can also help raise the temperature slightly as water releases heat as it cools.

In summary, protecting your eggplants from extreme tempera-tures involves a combination of shade provision, mulching, use of row covers or cloches, careful watering practices, and some-times the use of heat-absorbing containers. By taking these steps, you can ensure that your eggplants have the optimal tempera-ture conditions they need to grow and produce a plentiful harvest.

Protecting Raised Bed Eggplants From Pests

Protecting raised bed-grown eggplants from pests is crucial for maintaining the health, productivity, and overall success of your vegetable garden. Eggplants, like many other crops, are suscep-tible to a variety of pests, including aphids, flea beetles, cutworms, and Colorado potato beetles.

These pests can cause significant damage to your plants, ranging from cosmetic issues to severe infestations that can stunt growth, reduce yield, and even kill your eggplants. Moreover, some pests can facilitate the spread of diseases, further threatening the vitality of your garden.

By implementing effective pest management strategies, you not only safeguard your eggplants but also help maintain the balance and health of your entire garden ecosystem. This includes regular monitoring, using natural predators, and applying organic pesticides when necessary.

Keeping pest populations under control ensures that your plants can thrive and produce bountiful harvests, making your gardening efforts rewarding and sustainable.

Aphids are small, sap-sucking insects that congregate on the undersides of leaves or on new growth. They suck the plant's juices, causing leaves to curl, yellow, or distort. Moreover, they excrete a sticky substance known as honeydew, which can lead to the growth of sooty mold and attract other pests. Additionally, aphids can transmit harmful plant viruses, further compromising the health of your eggplants.

Flea beetles are another major pest for eggplants. These tiny beetles chew numerous small holes in the leaves, giving them a shot-hole appearance. They are particularly damaging to young plants, which may not survive severe infestations.

Cutworms, the larvae of several species of night-flying moths, are notorious for cutting down young plants at the soil level. They feed at night and hide in the soil during the day, making them a bit more difficult to spot.

The Colorado potato beetle is a significant pest for eggplants. Both the adults and larvae feed on the foliage, and in large numbers, they can defoliate plants, reducing their vigor and yield.

Protecting your eggplants from these pests involves a combination of prevention, monitoring, and control strategies. Regular inspection of your plants can help you spot early signs of infestation and take immediate action.

For aphids, introducing beneficial insects like ladybugs and lacewings, which are natural predators of aphids, can help control their population. If the infestation is severe, you can use insecticidal soaps or neem oil, which are safe for most beneficial insects.

To protect your eggplants from flea beetles, consider using floating row covers early in the season. These covers prevent the beetles from reaching your plants and laying eggs. Diatomaceous earth sprinkled around the base of the plants can also deter these pests.

For cutworm control, handpicking is an effective method if the infestation is not too severe. You can also use plant collars made from cardboard or aluminum foil at the base of the plants to prevent cutworms from reaching the stems. Beneficial nematodes introduced into the soil can also help control cutworms.

To manage Colorado potato beetles, handpicking and destroying the beetles and their eggs can be effective. Crop rotation can also help break their lifecycle and reduce their populations. If these methods are not sufficient, you may consider using organic pesticides like spinosad or Bacillus thuringiensis var. tenebrionis (Bt).

Protecting your raised bed-grown eggplants from pests involves vigilance, knowledge about the pests, and timely intervention. With these strategies, you can ensure the health of your eggplants and enjoy a bountiful harvest.

Protecting Raised Bed Eggplants From Diseases

Protecting raised bed grown eggplants from diseases is vital for a successful harvest. Diseases can dramatically reduce the yield and quality of the eggplants, leading to significant losses.

Diseases such as Cercospora leaf spot, Colletotrichum fruit rot, Damping-off disease, Bacterial Wilt/Southern Wilt, and early blight can cause wilting and yellowing of leaves, stunted growth, and even plant death.

Moreover, diseases often weaken the plant's defense system, making them more susceptible to pest attacks and adverse weather conditions. In addition, disease pathogens can persist in the soil for several years, posing a continuous threat to future crops. Therefore, implementing disease control measures in your raised bed garden is crucial to maintaining the health of your eggplants and ensuring a productive yield.

Raised bed grown eggplants can be susceptible to a number of diseases that can significantly impact their health and productivity. Some common diseases include Cercospora leaf spot, Colletotrichum fruit rot, Damping-off disease, Bacterial Wilt/Southern Wilt, and early blight.

Cercospora leaf spot is a fungal disease that causes small, dark spots on the leaves of the plant. If left untreated, it can lead to significant leaf loss and reduced yield.

Colletotrichum fruit rot, also known as anthracnose, is another fungal disease that can cause dark, sunken spots on the fruit, making it unmarketable.

Damping-off disease is caused by several different fungi and can cause seedlings to collapse and die.

Bacterial Wilt/Southern Wilt is a serious bacterial disease that can cause wilting and death of the plant.

Early blight is a common fungal disease that causes dark, concentric spots on the leaves and can lead to defoliation and reduced yield.

To protect your eggplants from these diseases organically, a combination of good cultural practices and organic treatments can be used. Firstly, practice crop rotation. This involves changing the location of your eggplants each year to disrupt the life cycle of disease-causing organisms.

Secondly, maintain good sanitation in your garden. Remove any infected plant material promptly to prevent the spread of disease. Also, avoid working in your garden when the plants are wet, as this can spread disease spores.

For fungal diseases like Cercospora leaf spot and early blight, consider using organic fungicides like copper or sulfur sprays. These can help control the disease if applied at the first sign of infection.

For bacterial wilt, unfortunately, there is no effective organic treatment once the plant is infected. The best strategy is prevention, which includes using disease-resistant varieties and practicing good sanitation.

Colletotrichum fruit rot can be managed by avoiding overhead irrigation, which can spread the disease, and by applying organic fungicides. Damping-off disease can be prevented by using sterile seed-starting mix and by avoiding overwatering.

While diseases can pose a significant threat to your eggplants, with diligent monitoring and appropriate management strategies, you can maintain the health of your plants and enjoy a successful harvest.

HARVESTING RAISED BED EGGPLANTS

Growing eggplants in a raised bed garden is a rewarding experience, but it does require some patience as they are not the quickest crop to mature. The time from planting to harvest can vary depending on the variety of eggplant and the growing conditions, but generally, it takes between 100 to 150 days for eggplants to be ready for harvest.

After sowing the seeds or transplanting young seedlings into your raised bed, the plants will need several weeks to establish themselves and begin to grow.

Once the plants start flowering, it's usually another 50 to 60 days before the fruits are ready to harvest. However, some varieties may take longer, especially if the weather is cooler. It's also important to note that eggplants are heat-loving plants, so they will grow more slowly in cooler climates and may not produce as much fruit.

Harvesting eggplants at the right time is crucial for the best flavor and texture. Eggplants should be harvested when they are still young and tender, as they can become bitter and tough if left on the plant for too long.

The skin should be glossy and the color should be vibrant, whether it's the traditional dark purple, white, green, or striped. A simple test to determine if an eggplant is ready to harvest is to press the skin with your thumb. If it springs back, it's ready; if the indentation remains, it's overripe.

To harvest the eggplant, use a sharp pair of gardening shears or a knife. Cut the stem about an inch above the top of the fruit to avoid damaging the fruit itself.

Be careful not to pull or twist the fruit off the plant, as this can damage the plant and reduce future yield. After harvesting, handle the eggplants gently to avoid bruising them, as this can lead to spoilage.

While growing eggplants in a raised bed garden requires patience, the reward of fresh, homegrown eggplants is well worth the wait. With careful monitoring and timely harvesting, you can enjoy a bountiful harvest of this versatile vegetable.

RAISED BEDS GROWN EGGPLANTS NOTES

Start: Seeds or Seedlings

Germination: 10 to 14 days, temperatures between 80-90°F.

Seed Life: 4 Years

Soil Type: Nutrient-rich, well-drained soil with organic matter (compost or well-rotted manure) - pH level between 5.5 and 6.5.

Seed Spacing: 1/4 inch deep (in small containers or seed trays).

Seedling Spacing: 18-24 inches apart.

Sunlight: 6hours full sunlight

Growing Temperatures: Between 70°F and 85°F

Days To Harvest: 100 to 150 days

CHAPTER 12
VEGETABLE RAISED BED GARDENING – POTATO'S

otatoes, one of the world's most versatile and beloved vegetables, are an excellent choice for raised bed gardening. They thrive in the rich, loose soil that a raised bed provides, and their robust nature makes them a satisfying crop for both novice and experienced gardeners. Growing potatoes in raised bed not only optimizes space but also simplifies the cultivation process, reducing common problems like pest infestations and diseases.

Moreover, the unique growing habits of potatoes make them a fun and rewarding vegetable to cultivate, providing the tangible thrill of unearthing your own homegrown spuds. Whether you're interested in traditional varieties or wish to explore heirloom and specialty types, potato gardening in raised beds offers an opportunity to deepen your connection with the food you eat, right in your backyard.

Planting potatoes using vegetable raised bed gardening can bring numerous benefits to your garden. Firstly, raised beds provide better drainage, which is essential for potatoes as they are prone to rotting in overly wet soil. The loose, well-aerated soil in a raised bed also makes it easier for the tubers to grow and expand, leading to a healthier and more abundant crop.

Raised beds allow for better control over soil quality, letting you tailor the soil composition to suit the nutrient needs of your potatoes. This method also reduces the risk of soil-borne diseases and certain pests, contributing to a more successful yield.

Furthermore, when it's time to harvest, raised beds make the process less labor-intensive – you can simply pull out the plants or gently dig around them to collect your potatoes. Lastly, potatoes are excellent for crop rotation in raised beds. They help break disease cycles, and their dense foliage can help suppress weed growth, improving the overall health and productivity of your garden.

THE RIGHT SOIL TO GROW POTATO'S IN RAISED BEDS

Potatoes, as hearty as they can be require specific soil conditions to truly thrive, especially when grown in raised bed gardens. The ideal soil for potatoes is a well-draining, loose, and sandy loam. This type of soil provides the perfect environment for the tubers to expand and grow without any obstruction. Any compactness or hardness in the soil can lead to misshapen potatoes or even inhibit their growth altogether.

The pH level of the soil also plays a significant role in potato cultivation. Potatoes prefer slightly acidic conditions, with a pH range of 5.0 to 6.0 being optimal. This acidity level helps to prevent the occurrence of potato scab, a common disease that affects the skin of the tubers. If your soil is naturally alkaline, you can amend it with sulfur or an acidifying fertilizer to achieve the desired pH range.

Soil fertility is equally crucial for successful potato growth. While potatoes are relatively undemanding plants, they do need a fair amount of nutrients to produce a good crop.

A balanced organic fertilizer or well-rotted compost can be mixed into the soil prior to planting to enrich it with the necessary nutrients. However, avoid using fresh manure or high-nitrogen fertilizers, as these can promote leafy growth at the expense of the tubers.

It's also worth noting that potatoes, like all plants, benefit from a diverse soil microbiome. Incorporating organic matter into the soil not only feeds the potatoes but also supports the beneficial bacteria, fungi, and other microorganisms that contribute to plant health and help ward off diseases.

Preparing the right soil conditions for your potatoes can mean the difference between a mediocre harvest and a bountiful one. By ensuring well-draining, slightly acidic, nutrient-rich, and biologically active soil, you set the stage for your potatoes to flourish in your raised bed garden.

HOW TO SOW POTATO'S IN RAISED BEDS

Correct Season To Sow Potato's In Raised Beds

The proper time to sow potatoes in vegetable raised bed gardens can vary depending on your location and the local climate. In cooler climates or northern regions, you should aim to plant potatoes from late March to early May. This timing aligns with when the soil has warmed to at least 45 degrees Fahrenheit and is dry enough to not clump together, allowing the plants to establish before the onset of warmer summer temperatures that could stress the plants and affect tuber formation.

If you're located in a warmer, southern region, you may have the flexibility to plant potatoes a bit earlier, sometimes as soon as February, or you can even plant in late autumn for a winter crop. The goal in these regions is to avoid the hottest part of the year, as potatoes prefer cooler growing conditions.

Raised beds can provide some flexibility with these timelines because they tend to warm up faster than ground soil in the spring, meaning you might be able to plant your potatoes slightly earlier if you're using a raised bed. However, it's still essential to ensure that the danger of frost has passed, as potatoes are sensitive to frost damage.

Additionally, different potato varieties have their own preferred growing seasons - some mature in the summer, while others are better suited to fall harvesting. Therefore, it's also important to consider the specific needs of the variety you're planting.

Plant Needs & Requirements

Germinating potato plants from seeds to seedlings correctly is a critical step in ensuring a successful harvest when growing in vegetable raised bed gardens. This process, also known as "chitting," involves encouraging the potato seeds (or "seed potatoes") to sprout before planting. Doing so can significantly increase your chances of a robust crop.

The importance of this process lies in its ability to give the plants a head start, which can be especially beneficial in regions with shorter growing seasons. By allowing the seed potatoes to develop strong, healthy sprouts before they are planted, you ensure that they can start growing as soon as they are placed in the soil, rather than having to wait for sprouts to form. This not only speeds up the growing process but also reduces the risk of the seed potatoes rotting before they have a chance to sprout.

Furthermore, correctly chitted potatoes tend to produce larger and more numerous tubers, leading to a more bountiful harvest. Taking the time to correctly germinate your potato plants from seeds to seedlings can significantly enhance the success of your potato crop in a raised bed garden.

Germinating potato plants from seeds to seedlings is an essential step in the cultivation process, and understanding how to do it correctly can greatly increase your chances of a successful harvest. To begin, you'll need to acquire certified disease-free seed potatoes from a reputable nursery or garden center. It's important to note that potatoes don't grow from traditional seeds but from tubers or small pieces of larger potatoes.

Before planting, these seed potatoes should be allowed to 'chit' or pre-sprout. This involves placing the seed potatoes in a single layer in a well-lit, cool, but frost-free area. The ideal temperature range for this process is between 50 to 70 degrees Fahrenheit (10 to 21 degrees Celsius). The seed potatoes will develop short, green sprouts after a few weeks. This process gives your potatoes a head start and can lead to earlier and increased yields.

When the sprouts are about 1/2 inch to 1 inch long, which usually takes about 4 to 6 weeks, the seed potatoes are ready to be planted. Plant them in a trench in your raised bed garden, about 2 to 3 inches deep, with the sprouts pointing upwards. The seed potatoes should be spaced about 12 inches apart to allow adequate room for growth.

The ideal soil temperature for potato germination is between 60 and 70 degrees Fahrenheit (15 to 21 degrees Celsius). Cooler temperatures can slow germination, while warmer temperatures can inhibit it altogether. After planting, water the seed potatoes thoroughly, but avoid overwatering, as this can cause the tubers to rot.

The seedlings are ready to be transplanted into their final positions in the raised bed garden when they have developed three to four true leaves, which is typically around 6 weeks after planting. At this point, they should be sturdy enough to handle the transplanting process. When transplanting, be careful not to damage the roots or leaves, and water the seedlings thoroughly after transplanting to help them establish in their new location.

The process of germinating potato plants from seeds to seedlings involves several key steps and requires specific temperature conditions. By understanding these steps and providing the right conditions, you can ensure that your potatoes germinate successfully and are ready for transplanting in your vegetable raised bed garden.

Spacing & Measurement

Proper spacing and measurements when transplanting potato seedlings into vegetable raised bed gardens are crucial for several reasons. Firstly, each potato plant needs ample space to grow and expand, both above and below the ground. Overcrowding can lead to stunted growth and smaller tubers as the plants compete for vital nutrients and water in the soil. Proper spacing ensures that each plant has sufficient access to these resources, leading to healthier plants and a more abundant harvest.

Secondly, adequate spacing helps prevent the spread of diseases and pests. Many common potato diseases, such as late blight, can quickly spread from plant to plant when they are too close together. By keeping an appropriate distance between your plants, you can help minimize the potential for disease transmission.

Lastly, correct planting depth is also important. Planting your seed potatoes too shallow can lead to exposure to sunlight, which can turn your potatoes green and toxic. On the other hand, planting them too deep can make it difficult for the plant to break through the soil surface, hindering its growth. Therefore, a balance must be struck.

The desired spacing and measurements when planting potato seedlings in vegetable raised bed gardens are critical factors that can significantly influence the health and yield of your potato crop. Understanding and applying these guidelines can help ensure a successful harvest.

To start, it's important to know that potatoes, unlike many other vegetables, grow underground from the stem of the plant. Therefore, they need enough space not just for their roots, but also for the tubers (the part we eat) to develop and expand.

When planting potato seedlings, each plant should be spaced about 12 inches apart. This distance allows each plant ample room to grow and spread out. It also helps facilitate better air circulation around the plants, reducing the likelihood of fungal diseases that thrive in damp, poorly ventilated conditions.

The rows of potatoes, on the other hand, should be spaced approximately 30 to 36 inches apart. This allows you easy access to the plants for care and harvesting, and also ensures that each plant gets plenty of sunlight.

The depth at which the seedlings are planted is another crucial measurement. Typically, potato seedlings should be planted about

4 inches deep. This depth is sufficient to protect the developing tubers from exposure to sunlight, which can cause them to turn green and become potentially harmful to consume. After planting, be sure to cover the seedlings with a good amount of soil and mound additional soil around the base of the plants as they grow.

Lastly, raised bed gardens offer an advantage in that they allow for more intensive planting. The loose, well-drained soil typically used in raised beds is ideal for potatoes. However, even in a raised bed, maintaining the recommended spacing is crucial for ensuring that each plant has access to the necessary nutrients and water.

The desired spacing and measurements when planting potato seedlings in raised bed gardens are critical for the health and productivity of your plants. By providing sufficient space for each plant and planting at the correct depth, you can maximize your potato yield and enjoy a bountiful harvest.

Ideal Temperatures & Sun Requirements

Understanding the ideal temperatures and sun requirements for growing potatoes in vegetable raised bed gardens is crucial to achieving a successful harvest. Potatoes are cool-season crops, which means they prefer cooler temperatures for optimal growth. The ideal soil temperature for potato germination is between 60 and 70 degrees Fahrenheit (15 to 21 degrees Celsius). However, once they have sprouted, potatoes can tolerate slightly cooler conditions, with soil temperatures as low as 40 degrees Fahrenheit (4 degrees Celsius).

In terms of sunlight, potatoes require full sun, which means they need at least six hours of direct sunlight each day. Sunlight is crucial for photosynthesis, the process by which plants convert sunlight into energy for growth. Without sufficient sunlight, potato plants may not produce as many tubers, and those that do form may be smaller.

Moreover, the color and flavor of potatoes can be affected by temperature and sunlight. Exposure to sunlight can cause potatoes to turn green and develop solanine, a naturally occurring toxicant. Therefore, it's essential to ensure that the developing tubers are well-covered with soil or mulch to protect them from sunlight.

In summary, maintaining the ideal temperatures and ensuring adequate sunlight are key factors in growing healthy, productive potato plants. By providing these optimal conditions, you can maximize your potato yield and enjoy a bountiful harvest.

MAINTAINING YOUR RAISED BED POTATO'S

Maintaining your potato plants in vegetable raised bed gardening is of utmost importance for a successful yield. Proper maintenance involves practices such as regular watering, hilling, weeding, and monitoring for pests and diseases. Regular watering keeps the soil moist and promotes healthy growth, but overwatering can lead to rot and disease, so balance is key.

Hilling, or mounding soil around the base of the plants, encourages the development of more tubers and prevents them from being exposed to sunlight, which can cause them to turn green and toxic. Regular weeding is also essential as weeds compete with your plants for nutrients and water.

Lastly, keeping an eye out for pests and diseases allows you to catch any potential issues early and treat them before they can significantly damage your crop. Without proper maintenance, your potato plants may not thrive, and your harvest could be significantly reduced. Therefore, consistent care and attention to your raised bed garden are integral for growing healthy, productive potato plants.

Pruning & Thinning Your Potato's

Pruning and thinning potato plants in raised bed gardens are essential practices that can significantly influence the health and yield of your crop. While potatoes don't typically require as much pruning as some other vegetables, removing diseased or damaged foliage can help prevent the spread of diseases and pests. This also allows the plant to direct more energy into growing tubers rather than sustaining unnecessary foliage.

Thinning, on the other hand, refers to the removal of some plants to reduce crowding. While this isn't always necessary with potatoes, particularly if you've followed the recommended spacing guidelines, it can be beneficial in certain situations. If you find that your potatoes are too crowded because they were planted too close together, thinning them out can improve air circulation around the remaining plants, reducing the risk of fungal diseases.

Additionally, overcrowded plants have to compete for resources, which can lead to smaller, less healthy tubers. By thinning out the plants, you ensure that each remaining plant has ample access to water, nutrients, and sunlight, which can result in larger, healthier potatoes.

Pruning and thinning potato plants in raised bed gardens should be timed correctly and done with care to ensure the health and productivity of the crop. While potatoes typically don't require regular pruning like some other vegetables, there are instances where it is beneficial.

Pruning is most often necessary when the foliage of the potato plants becomes diseased. Signs of disease can include yellowing leaves, brown spots, or a powdery mildew-like substance on the leaves. If you notice these signs, prune away the affected leaves immediately to prevent the disease from spreading to the rest of the plant or to neighboring plants. Use sharp, clean shears to cut back the foliage, making sure to dispose of the diseased material far away from your garden to avoid contamination.

Thinning, on the other hand, should be done early in the potato plant's life cycle. After planting your seed potatoes, they will begin to sprout and produce plants. If you notice that the plants are growing too close together, it's time to thin them out. Ideally, each plant should have about 12 inches of space on all sides to allow for proper growth and tuber development.

To thin your plants, simply pull up the smallest and weakest-looking plants until the remaining ones have sufficient space. Be gentle when pulling up the plants to avoid disturbing the roots of the remaining ones.

While pruning and thinning aren't daily tasks in the care of potato plants, they are important steps to take when necessary. Properly pruned and thinned potatoes are more likely to stay healthy and produce a bountiful harvest in your raised bed garden.

Watering Your Raised Bed Potato's

Watering your potatoes in raised bed gardens is a critical step in ensuring a healthy and abundant harvest. Potatoes, like all plants, need water for photosynthesis, nutrient uptake, and overall growth. However, the importance of watering extends beyond simply providing moisture.

In raised bed gardens, the soil tends to dry out faster due to increased exposure to the sun and wind, which means potatoes may require more frequent watering compared to those grown in-ground.

Proper watering also helps to maintain consistent soil moisture levels, which is crucial for the development of tubers. Too much water can lead to problems like rot and disease, while too little can cause the tubers to become deformed or stop growing.

Therefore, maintaining a balance is key - the soil should be kept evenly moist, but not waterlogged. Regular watering, done correctly, can also help to prevent common issues like potato scab, which tends to develop in drier conditions. Ultimately, proper watering practices contribute significantly to the health and yield of your raised bed-grown potatoes.

Watering potatoes in raised bed gardens requires a delicate balance. Too much or too little water can both be detrimental to the growth and development of your potatoes. The key is to maintain evenly moist soil without overwatering, which can lead to rot and disease.

Newly planted potatoes require consistent moisture to encourage sprouting and establishment. After planting, water thoroughly and then aim to water once a week, or whenever the top 1-2 inches of soil feels dry to the touch. This usually means applying about 1-2 inches of water per week, but this can vary depending on the weather and the specific conditions in your garden.

As the plants grow and tubers start to form, it's especially important to provide consistent water. Uneven watering during tuber formation can lead to problems like hollow heart or cracked tubers. Continue with the practice of watering when the top 1-2 inches of soil is dry, but be mindful not to let the soil dry out completely.

When the potato plants begin to flower, this generally signals the start of tuber formation. At this stage, the plants will need more water, so you may need to increase the frequency of watering. However, remember to always check the soil moisture levels before watering to avoid overwatering.

Once the foliage begins to die back, reduce watering significantly. This allows the tubers to mature and the skins to harden, preparing them for harvest. Overwatering at this stage can cause the tubers to rot.

While the exact amount and frequency of watering can depend on various factors such as weather conditions and soil type, a general rule of thumb is to keep the soil evenly moist and adjust watering practices according to the growth stage of the potato plants. By understanding when and how much to water, you can ensure the health and productivity of your raised bed-grown potatoes.

Organic Fertilization For Raised Bed Potato's

Organic fertilization plays a pivotal role in the growth and productivity of potatoes in raised bed gardens. It contributes to the overall health of the soil, improves its structure, and enhances its ability to retain water and nutrients. Organic fertilizers, such as compost or aged manure, provide a slow release of nutrients that are essential for potato growth, including nitrogen, phosphorus, and potassium. These nutrients help promote leafy growth, support root development, and contribute to the size and quality of the tubers.

Furthermore, organic fertilizers also improve the biodiversity of the soil by encouraging the growth of beneficial microorganisms. These microbes aid in nutrient uptake, enhance disease resistance, and improve soil structure by breaking down organic matter into humus.

Thus, organic fertilization is not just about feeding the plants, but also about nurturing the soil ecosystem, leading to healthier, more robust potato plants and a better harvest in your raised bed garden.

In cultivating potatoes in raised bed gardens, the use of organic fertilizers is beneficial for both the plants and the soil ecosystem. There are several types of organic fertilizers that can be used, each with their own unique nutrient profiles and benefits.

Compost is one of the most commonly used organic fertilizers. It's rich in nutrients and helps improve soil structure and moisture retention. Compost can be made from kitchen scraps, yard waste, and other organic materials, making it a cost-effective and environmentally friendly choice. It should be mixed into the soil before planting and can also be added as a top dressing throughout the growing season to provide a slow, steady release of nutrients.

Aged manure is another excellent choice for potatoes. It's especially high in nitrogen, which promotes leafy growth. However, it's important to ensure that the manure is well-aged or composted to avoid burning the plants or introducing pathogens. Like compost, aged manure can be worked into the soil prior to planting and added as a top dressing during the growing season.

Bone meal is a great source of phosphorus, which is essential for root development and tuber formation in potatoes. It can be mixed into the soil at planting time to provide a long-lasting source of this critical nutrient.

Green manures or cover crops, such as clover or alfalfa, can also be used to enrich the soil. These plants are grown and then plowed into the soil, where they decompose and release their nutrients. This method not only adds nutrients but also improves soil structure and suppresses weeds.

When it comes to application, it's generally best to add organic fertilizers to the soil before planting your potatoes. This gives the fertilizer time to break down and start releasing its nutrients before the potatoes begin active growth. Additional side dressings of compost or aged manure can be applied throughout the growing season, especially during periods of rapid growth or just before tuber formation.

Using organic fertilizers in your raised bed potato garden can provide a wealth of benefits. From promoting healthy plant growth and improving soil health to reducing the environmental impact of gardening, it's a choice that yields bountiful rewards.

PROTECTING YOUR RAISED BED POTATO'S

Extreme Temperatures

Protecting your raised bed-grown potatoes from extreme temperatures is crucial for their healthy growth and development. Potatoes are cool-season crops, preferring temperatures between 60 and 70 degrees Fahrenheit. Both excessively hot and cold temperatures can negatively affect the growth of your potatoes, leading to reduced yields or even plant death.

In regions with hot summers, it's important to protect your potatoes from excessive heat. High temperatures can cause stress to the plants, hinder tuber formation, and lead to sunscald of exposed tubers. One effective way to protect your potatoes from heat is by mulching.

Applying a layer of organic mulch, such as straw or shredded leaves, around your potato plants can help to keep the soil cool, conserve moisture, and prevent the sun from directly hitting the tubers. Providing shade can also be beneficial during the hottest part of the day. This can be achieved by using shade cloth or by planting taller crops on the western side of your potatoes to provide afternoon shade.

Cold temperatures, especially frost, can also be harmful to potatoes. While mature potato plants can tolerate light frosts, heavy frosts and freezes can kill the plants. To protect your potatoes from cold, consider using row covers or frost blankets. These can be draped over the plants when frost is expected and removed once the temperature rises. Another method is to mound soil around the base of the plants, which can provide some protection against short periods of cold.

Moreover, knowing when to plant your potatoes can help in avoiding extreme temperatures. Typically, potatoes are planted in early spring, as soon as the soil can be worked. However, in areas with hot summers, consider planting in late summer for a fall harvest, when temperatures are cooler.

Protecting your potatoes from extreme temperatures is vital because these conditions can significantly impact the health of your plants and the quality of your harvest. By taking steps to shield your potatoes from heat and cold, you can ensure a successful, bountiful harvest. It's not just about the immediate growing season either; taking care of your plants and growing them under optimal conditions can improve the soil health and productivity of your raised bed garden for future seasons as well.

Protecting Raised Bed Potato's From Pests

Protecting raised bed grown potatoes from pests is crucial to ensure a healthy and plentiful harvest. Pests, such as Colorado potato beetles, aphids, slugs, and wireworms, can cause significant damage to both the foliage and the tubers of potato plants. This can lead to decreased yields, inferior quality tubers, or even total crop failure in severe infestations.

Beyond the immediate impact on the current crop, some pests can also carry diseases that can affect future plantings. Furthermore, certain pests can overwinter in the soil, becoming an ongoing problem in your raised bed garden if not properly managed. Therefore, implementing effective pest management strategies not only protects your current crop of potatoes but also contributes to the overall health and productivity of your raised bed garden.

Colorado potato beetles are one of the most common and destructive pests of potatoes. These beetles feed on the leaves of the plants, reducing their ability to photosynthesize and grow. Adult beetles lay their eggs on the underside of the leaves, and the larvae, which are humpbacked and striped, also feed on the foliage. To manage these pests, regular inspection of plants and hand-picking of beetles and larvae can be effective. Additionally, crop rotation can help disrupt the beetle's life cycle. Some gardeners also use floating row covers to physically prevent the beetles from reaching the plants.

Aphids are small, soft-bodied insects that suck the sap from potato plants, weakening them and potentially transmitting diseases. They often congregate on the undersides of leaves, making them somewhat difficult to spot.

In addition to causing direct damage, aphids can also produce a sticky substance known as honeydew, which can lead to the growth of sooty mold. Insecticidal soaps or neem oil can be effective against aphids, and introducing beneficial insects like ladybugs and lacewings can also help control aphid populations.

Slugs are another common pest of potatoes. They feed on both the leaves and the tubers, and their feeding can leave unsightly holes and trails on the plants. Slugs prefer moist, shady conditions, so proper watering and removal of unnecessary debris can help reduce slug populations. Traps, such as shallow dishes of beer, can also be used to attract and drown slugs.

Wireworms, the larval stage of the click beetle, are soil-dwelling pests that feed on the roots and tubers of potatoes. They can cause significant damage and reduce the marketability of the tubers. Crop rotation and good sanitation practices, such as removal of plant debris that could harbor pests, can help manage wireworm populations.

Protecting raised bed-grown potatoes from pests involves a combination of regular monitoring, use of appropriate pest control methods, and good cultural practices. By understanding the pests that can affect potatoes and how to manage them, gardeners can ensure a healthy and productive harvest.

Protecting Raised Bed Potato's From Diseases

Protecting raised bed-grown potatoes from diseases is of utmost importance to ensure a healthy and productive harvest. Diseases can affect every part of the potato plant, from the leaves and stems down to the tubers themselves. They can cause a variety of symptoms, including wilting, discoloration, stunted growth, and rotting of the tubers. Some diseases, like late blight, early blight, and scab can wipe out an entire crop if left unchecked. Moreover, many diseases can persist in the soil for several years, posing a threat to future crops as well.

Controlling these diseases not only safeguards the current season's yield but also maintains the viability of your garden for growing potatoes and other crops in the future. Therefore, implementing disease management strategies, such as crop rotation, use of disease-resistant varieties, proper watering and fertilization, and good sanitation practices, is vital for the successful cultivation of potatoes in raised bed gardens.

Late blight is caused by the fungus-like organism Phytophthora infestans and is infamous for its role in the Irish potato famine. It causes water-soaked spots on leaves that quickly turn brown and lead to rapid plant death. The disease thrives in cool, wet conditions and can spread rapidly, potentially wiping out an entire crop.

Organic methods of prevention include planting resistant varieties, practicing good sanitation, and avoiding overhead watering which can create the moist conditions the pathogen loves. Copper-based fungicides can also be used as a last resort.

Early blight, caused by the fungus Alternaria solani, leads to dark brown spots on leaves, often surrounded by a yellow halo. The disease can cause defoliation and reduce yield, particularly if it strikes early in the season.

Organic control measures for early blight are similar to those for late blight: resistant varieties, good sanitation, and avoiding overhead watering. Regular applications of organic fungicides, such as ones containing Bacillus subtilis or copper, can also help keep early blight in check.

Scab, caused by the bacterium Streptomyces scabies, affects the tubers more than the foliage. It leads to rough, scaly patches on the potato skin which, while not harmful, can reduce marketability. Scab is more prevalent in alkaline soils, so maintaining a slightly acidic soil pH can help prevent the disease. Additionally, there are potato varieties that are resistant to scab, and practicing crop rotation can also help reduce the risk.

Protecting raised bed-grown potatoes from diseases involves a combination of selecting resistant varieties, practicing good garden sanitation, and using organic fungicides when necessary. Regular monitoring of the plants for signs of disease can also help catch any potential problems early before they can do significant damage. By understanding the diseases that can affect potatoes and how to manage them, gardeners can ensure a healthy and productive harvest while maintaining the organic integrity of their garden.

HARVESTING RAISED BED POTATO'S

Growing potatoes in raised beds can be a rewarding endeavor, but patience is key as the process from planting to harvest can take several months. The exact timing depends on the variety of potato you're growing and the specific growing conditions in your garden.

Generally, early potato varieties like 'Swift' or 'Rocket' are the quickest to mature, often ready for harvesting approximately 10-12 weeks after planting. These varieties are excellent if you're looking for "new" potatoes — small, tender tubers that are great for salads or boiling.

Maincrop varieties such as 'Russet' or 'Yukon Gold' take longer to mature, usually around 15-20 weeks. These potatoes are larger and ideal for baking, mashing, or storing for use throughout the winter.

Regardless of the variety, a good sign that your potatoes are nearing harvest time is when the plants begin to flower. This indicates that tubers are starting to form. However, for the potatoes to bulk up and skins to harden, you should wait until the foliage has died back completely.

When it's time to harvest, choose a dry day to prevent the tubers from getting wet, which can lead to rot. Begin by gently loosening the soil around the plants with a fork or your hands, being careful not to pierce the tubers. Pull the plant out of the ground and remove the potatoes. Leave them on the soil surface for a few hours to dry and cure, which helps to toughen up the skin and extend storage life.

After harvesting, store your potatoes in a cool, dark, well-ventilated place. Avoid washing them until you're ready to use them, as moisture can promote rot. Properly stored, your homegrown potatoes can provide you with a taste of summer well into the winter months.

Remember, patience and care are key to a successful potato harvest. By knowing what signs to look for and how to properly harvest and store your potatoes, you can enjoy the fruits of your labor for months to come.

RAISED BEDS GROWN POTATO'S NOTES

Start: Seedlings

Germination: 28 to 42 days, between 60 and 70 degrees Fahrenheit (15 to 21 degrees Celsius).

Seed Life: 4 Years

Soil Type: Well-draining, loose, and sandy loam with organic matter (compost or well-rotted manure) - pH level between 5.0 and 6.0.

Potato Chitting Process: Before planting, these seed potatoes should be allowed to 'chit' or pre-sprout. This involves placing the seed potatoes in a single layer in a well-lit, cool, but frost-free area. The ideal temperature range for this process is between 50 to 70 degrees Fahrenheit (10 to 21 degrees Celsius). The seed potatoes will develop short, green sprouts after a few weeks.

Seed Spacing: 2 to 3 inches deep with the sprouts pointing upwards (In permanent raised bed garden after 'chit' or pre-sprout process has been completed)

Seedling Spacing: 12 inches apart, with rows approximately 30 to 36 inches apart.

Sunlight: 6hours full sunlight

Growing Temperatures: 60 and 70 degrees Fahrenheit (15 to 21 degrees Celsius).

Days To Harvest: 105 to 140 days

CHAPTER 13
VEGETABLE RAISED BED GARDENING - PARSNIPS

arsnips, a root vegetable often overshadowed by their more popular cousin, the carrot, are an excellent addition to any vegetable raised bed garden. These versatile vegetables are known for their sweet, nutty flavor and high nutritional value, offering a good source of fiber, vitamin C, and folate. Parsnips are characterized by their long, tapered shape and creamy white color. They thrive in cooler climates and can be surprisingly easy to grow, making them a great choice for gardeners of all skill levels.

Their ability to withstand frost and even improve in flavor after a frost sets them apart from many other garden vegetables. Whether roasted, boiled, or used in soups and stews, parsnips bring a unique flavor profile to the table, making them a worthwhile addition to your raised bed garden.

Planting parsnips in a vegetable raised bed garden offers numerous benefits. Firstly, the loose, well-draining soil of raised beds is perfect for root vegetables like parsnips, allowing them to expand freely and grow to their full size without obstruction. This can lead to larger, more uniform parsnips compared to those grown in traditional garden beds.

Secondly, raised beds provide better control over soil conditions, which is beneficial as parsnips prefer slightly acidic to neutral pH levels. You can easily amend the soil in a raised bed to create the ideal growing environment. Furthermore, raised beds tend to warm up faster in the spring, providing a head start for your parsnip seeds. They also make it easier to manage weeds, reducing competition for nutrients and water.

Finally, the elevated nature of raised beds makes tending to and harvesting your parsnip crop much easier on the back and knees, making gardening more accessible for people of all ages and abilities.

THE RIGHT SOIL TO GROW PARSNIPS IN RAISED BEDS

Growing parsnips in vegetable raised bed gardens requires a keen understanding of the right soil conditions to ensure a bountiful harvest. Parsnips, like other root vegetables, thrive in loose, deep, and well-draining soil that allows their roots to expand freely without encountering obstructions such as rocks or compacted earth.

The ideal soil for parsnips is rich in organic matter, which helps to improve both the soil structure and nutrient content. Incorporating compost or well-rotted manure into your raised bed can significantly enhance the fertility of the soil, providing the necessary nutrients for parsnip growth.

Additionally, organic matter improves the water-holding capacity of the soil, ensuring that parsnips have a consistent supply of moisture, which is crucial for their development.

Parsnips also prefer slightly acidic to neutral pH levels, ranging from 6.0 to 7.0. Soil pH affects the availability of nutrients to plants so staying within this range ensures that parsnips can effectively take up the nutrients they need to grow. If your soil is too acidic or alkaline, it's possible to adjust the pH by adding lime (to raise pH) or sulfur (to lower pH).

Drainage is another important factor to consider. While parsnips need consistent moisture, waterlogged soil can lead to root rot and other diseases. Raised beds naturally offer good drainage, but if your soil is heavy clay, you might want to add some sand or perlite to improve its draining properties.

Lastly, because parsnips are slow growers, they benefit from a weed-free environment. Mulching your raised beds with organic material like straw or wood chips can help suppress weeds, retain soil moisture, and add nutrients back into the soil as they decompose.

In summary, the right soil conditions for growing parsnips in raised bed gardens include loose, deep, well-draining soil rich in organic matter with a slightly acidic to neutral pH. By providing these conditions, you can optimize the growth of your parsnips and look forward to a successful harvest.

HOW TO SOW PARSNIPS IN RAISED BEDS

Correct Season To Sow Parsnips In Raised Beds

Parsnips, a hardy and cool-season crop, are ideally sown in the early spring or late summer when temperatures are cooler. They thrive best in daytime temperatures ranging from 40 to 50 degrees. A unique characteristic of parsnips is that they are best harvested after a hard frost, which aids in converting their starches into sugars, enhancing their sweet flavor.

To ensure that the growing season will be long enough to yield a good crop of roots, it is recommended to sow early-ripening parsnip varieties in May. Understanding your local climate and selecting the right variety can help you determine the best time to sow parsnips in your raised bed garden.

Plant Needs & Requirements

Proper germination of parsnip seeds is a fundamental step in ensuring a successful harvest when growing them in raised bed vegetable gardens. Parsnips are notorious for their somewhat capricious germination habits, making correct initial sowing essential for a productive yield. These seeds should be sown directly into the garden as they don't transplant well. Moreover, parsnip seeds have a relatively short viability period, so using fresh seeds each year can significantly improve germination rates.

Correctly spacing the seeds (about 2 inch apart) will give the plants enough room to grow without competing for nutrients. Because of their inconsistent germination, it's advisable to sow more seeds than you think you'll need and thin out the weaker seedlings later, ensuring that the strongest plants have sufficient space to thrive.

Successful germination is the foundation for the rest of the growing season, influencing both the quantity and quality of your parsnip crop. Therefore, understanding and executing this process correctly is vital for effective parsnip cultivation in your raised bed garden.

Germinating parsnip seeds correctly is a critical first step in their cultivation, and the process begins with the selection of high-quality, fresh seeds. Due to the relatively short viability of parsnip seeds, it's recommended to use new seeds each year. Before sowing, prepare your raised bed by ensuring it's well-drained and enriched with organic matter.

Start the germination process by sowing the parsnip seeds directly into your garden, as they are sensitive to transplanting. Plant them about 1/2 inch deep in the soil and space them approximately 2 inches apart to allow adequate room for growth. Cover the seeds lightly with soil, and water the area thoroughly without causing soil erosion.

Parsnips are cool-season crops and germinate best at temperatures between 50 and 85 degrees Fahrenheit. During this stage, maintain consistent moisture in the soil but avoid oversaturation, which can lead to seed rot. Patience is key when growing parsnips, as the seeds can take anywhere from 14 to 21 days to germinate.

Once the seedlings have emerged and grown to about 2 inches tall, they should be thinned to stand 3 to 6 inches apart. This thinning process ensures that each plant has ample space to grow and access to necessary nutrients. Remember, parsnips do not transplant well, so it's crucial to sow them where they are to grow.

The whole process requires careful attention and patience. Correctly germinating and growing parsnip seedlings can lead to a bountiful harvest of sweet, flavorful roots that are worth the wait.

Spacing & Measurement

Implementing proper spacing and measurements when trans-planting parsnip seedlings into raised bed vegetable gardens is crucial to ensure the healthy growth and development of the plants. Each parsnip plant needs enough room to expand its root system and foliage without competing with its neighbors for nutrients, water, and sunlight.

Overcrowded plants can lead to stunted growth, smaller roots, and they can also become more susceptible to diseases and pests due to the lack of air circulation. Therefore, it's recommended to thin parsnip seedlings to about 3 to 6 inches apart once they're around 2 inches tall.

Ensuring the right spacing not only allows each plant to thrive but also helps gardeners make efficient use of their garden space. Hence, proper spacing and measurements are key to achieving a successful and bountiful parsnip harvest.

When planting parsnip seedlings in a raised bed garden, careful consideration should be given to the spacing and measurements of each plant. As root vegetables, parsnips need enough room underground to develop their long, carrot-like shape without any obstruction. Moreover, the green leafy tops of the parsnip also require sufficient space to grow without crowding each other out.

Following the recommended guidelines, parsnip seedlings should be sown about 1/2 inch deep and approximately 3 - 4 inches apart. This initial spacing allows each seedling to grow without competition for nutrients and water.

Once the seedlings have grown to about 2 inches tall, they should be thinned so that they stand 3 to 6 inches apart. This ensures that each plant has enough space to expand its root system and foliage.

The rows in which you plant your parsnip seedlings should also be spaced correctly. Aim for rows that are about 10 to 12 inches apart. This distance provides ample room for you to move between and tend to your plants without causing damage to them. It also promotes better air circulation, reducing the risk of fungal diseases that can thrive in damp, stagnant conditions.

In the context of raised bed gardening, these measurements help you maximize your available space. Raised beds typically offer improved soil conditions and easier maintenance, but space is often at a premium.

By following these recommended spacing guidelines, you can ensure a healthy crop of parsnips while making efficient use of your garden space.

Remember, parsnips are slow growers and don't transplant well, so it's essential to sow them directly where they will grow and mature. With patience and proper care, you'll be rewarded with a bountiful harvest of sweet, tender parsnips.

Ideal Temperatures & Sun Requirements

Understanding and maintaining the ideal temperatures and sun requirements when growing parsnips in raised bed gardens is crucial for their successful cultivation. Parsnips are biennial plants that grow best in cooler climates, typically preferring temperatures between 40°F and 75°F. They can tolerate frost and actually become sweeter after a few frosts, which convert the starches in the root into sugars.

Therefore, they're often planted in early spring or late summer for a fall harvest. As for sunlight, parsnips require a minimum of six hours of full sun each day for optimal growth, although they can tolerate partial shade. However, too much heat or direct sunlight can cause the roots to become woody and less flavorful, so it's important to monitor the sun exposure in your garden. By providing the right temperature and sunlight conditions, you'll encourage the healthy growth of your parsnip plants and increase your chances of a bountiful and flavorful harvest.

MAINTAINING YOUR RAISED BED PARSNIPS

Maintaining your raised bed grown parsnips is essential for a variety of reasons. First and foremost, regular maintenance helps ensure the plants are growing in optimal conditions, which translates into a healthier, more productive crop.

This includes tasks such as weeding, which prevents unwanted plants from competing with your parsnips for resources, and pest management, which involves regularly inspecting your plants and acting promptly if you spot any signs of damage or disease.

Regular watering is also important, as consistent moisture levels help parsnips form deep, straight roots. Furthermore, mulching can help conserve soil moisture, regulate soil temperature, and suppress weeds. Finally, rotating your crops each year is a key aspect of maintenance that helps prevent the build-up of pests and diseases in the soil.

In essence, maintaining your parsnips in vegetable raised bed gardening not only maximizes your yield but also keeps your garden healthy and sustainable in the long run.

Pruning & Thinning Your Parsnips

Pruning and thinning parsnips in raised bed gardens is an essential part of their care and can significantly impact the success of your crop. Thinning, which involves removing some seedlings to give others more room to grow, is particularly crucial for parsnips.

Due to their size and growth habit, parsnips need plenty of space both above and below the ground to develop properly. If plants are too close together, they can compete for nutrients, water, and sunlight, leading to smaller, less healthy roots. Thinning ensures each plant has enough space to expand its root system and foliage, ultimately yielding a larger and healthier crop.

Pruning, on the other hand, usually refers to the removal of certain parts of a plant to improve its overall health or productivity. While this isn't typically a central aspect of parsnip care, it can be beneficial in some circumstances. For example, if a parsnip plant becomes diseased or infested with pests, pruning away the affected areas can help prevent the issue from spreading to the rest of the plant or neighboring plants.

Both thinning and pruning play key roles in managing a successful parsnip garden. These practices help ensure that each plant has the resources it needs to thrive and can help protect your plants from disease and pest issues.

The process of thinning and pruning parsnips in raised bed gardens begins soon after planting. Thinning is an essential task to perform when the seedlings are approximately 1 inch tall, typically occurring about 2-3 weeks after sowing. This practice ensures that each parsnip has enough space to develop a healthy and robust root system.

Overcrowding can stunt growth and result in misshapen parsnips. To thin effectively, use a pair of clean, sharp scissors and cut the excess seedlings at soil level, maintaining a distance of about 2-3 inches between each plant. Cutting is recommended over pulling out the seedlings to avoid disturbing the roots of the remaining plants.

Parsnips require minimal pruning compared to other vegetables. However, it's essential to regularly inspect your plants for any signs of disease or damage. Dead or yellowing leaves should be removed using a pair of sterilized garden shears, which can help prevent the spread of diseases.

This practice not only aids in maintaining the overall health of the plant but also directs the plant's energy towards root growth, which is beneficial as the root is the edible portion of the parsnip.

Another aspect to consider is the removal of flower stalks if the parsnip plant starts to bolt or flower. Bolting indicates that the plant is focusing on reproduction rather than root development. By promptly pruning the flower stalks, you can redirect the plant's energy back to root growth, thereby enhancing the yield.

In summary, while thinning and pruning parsnips in raised bed gardens may require a bit of effort and careful attention, these practices are crucial for ensuring the health and productivity of your crop.

Watering Your Raised Bed Parsnips

Watering is a vital part of nurturing parsnips in raised bed gardens, as it directly influences the plant's health, growth, and productivity. As root vegetables, parsnips need consistent moisture levels for their roots to develop properly. Inadequate water can lead to stunted growth, resulting in smaller and less flavorful produce.

Additionally, inconsistent watering or prolonged dry periods can cause the roots to become hard and woody. On the other hand, overwatering should be avoided as it can lead to waterlogged soil, which can potentially cause root rot.

In the context of raised bed gardens, the importance of watering is further emphasized because these beds tend to dry out faster than traditional in-ground gardens. Hence, maintaining a regular and appropriate watering schedule is crucial to ensure that your parsnips flourish into healthy, tasty vegetables.

Watering is a crucial part of cultivating healthy parsnips in raised bed gardens. The general rule of thumb for watering vegetables is about one inch of water per week, including rainfall. However, specific plants like parsnips can have different requirements.

For seedlings such as parsnips, it's recommended to keep the soil consistently moist but not waterlogged. Raised beds typically drain faster than traditional in-ground gardens, therefore, it's particularly important to monitor the soil's moisture levels to ensure your parsnips are getting enough water.

Raised bed gardens often require more frequent watering, especially during dry weather. This is because the soil in raised beds tends to warm up faster and lose moisture quicker than ground soil. Therefore, it's essential to keep a close eye on your raised bed garden, particularly during hot, dry periods.

The timing of watering also plays a significant role in maintaining the health of your parsnips. Early morning is often considered the best time to water as it allows the water to soak into the soil before the heat of the day evaporates it. Evening watering should be avoided as it can lead to the growth of mold or other diseases due to the moisture sitting on the leaves overnight.

Proper watering is key to growing healthy parsnips in a raised bed garden. It involves not only the right amount of water but also watering at the correct time. By ensuring your parsnips receive adequate and timely watering, you can significantly improve the quality of your harvest and the overall health of your plants.

Organic Fertilization For Raised Bed Parsnips

Organic fertilization plays a crucial role in the healthy growth of parsnips in raised bed gardens. As parsnips are deep-rooted vegetables, they require nutrient-rich soil to thrive. Organic fertilizers, sourced from plant, animal, or mineral resources, are ideal for this purpose as they slowly release nutrients into the soil, promoting long-term soil health.

Unlike synthetic fertilizers that can cause nutrient imbalances and harm beneficial soil organisms, organic fertilizers maintain a balanced ecosystem within the soil. They improve the soil structure, enhance its water-holding capacity, and encourage the growth of beneficial microorganisms. These microorganisms break down organic matter into plant-available nutrients, creating a sustainable nutrient cycle.

Furthermore, organic fertilizers are environmentally friendly, reducing the risk of chemical runoff that could contaminate water sources. Therefore, organic fertilization is not only essential for the growth and yield of parsnips in raised bed gardens but also for the overall health of the soil and environment.

Compost is one of the best organic fertilizers for all types of plants, including parsnips. It's rich in a wide range of nutrients and helps improve the soil structure, which is crucial for root vegetables. Before planting your parsnips, mix compost into the top layer of your soil. This will give your parsnips a nutrient-rich environment to start growing in.

Another excellent organic fertilizer for parsnips is well-rotted manure. Like compost, it's rich in nutrients and can enhance the soil's structure. However, it's important to ensure that the manure is well-rotted; fresh manure can be too high in nitrogen and potentially damage your plants. If you're using manure, incorporate it into the soil a few weeks before you plan to sow your parsnip seeds.

Bone meal is another organic fertilizer that can be beneficial for parsnips. It's high in phosphorus, which can promote root development. To use bone meal, sprinkle it on the soil surface and then lightly rake it into the top layer of soil before planting.

As for when and how to fertilize, it's generally recommended to add organic fertilizers to the soil before planting. This gives the nutrients time to break down and become available to the plants.

For parsnips, incorporate your chosen fertilizer into the soil a few weeks before you plan to sow the seeds. Throughout the growing season, you can add more compost or other organic matter to the soil surface as a mulch, which will slowly release additional nutrients into the soil.

Using organic fertilizers like compost, well-rotted manure, and bone meal can provide your parsnips with the nutrients they need to thrive. By incorporating these fertilizers into the soil before planting and adding more as a mulch during the growing season, you can create a nutrient-rich environment for your parsnips and improve the overall health of your raised bed garden.

PROTECTING YOUR RAISED BED PARSNIPS

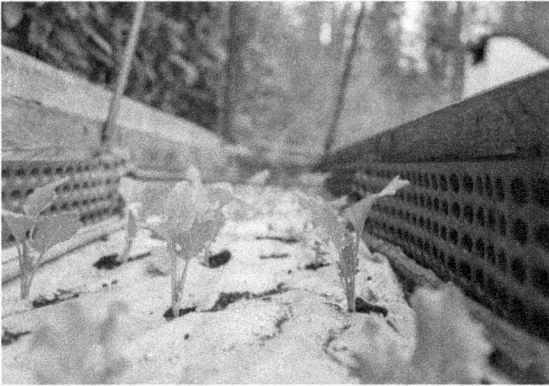

Extreme Temperatures

Protection of raised bed-grown parsnips from extreme temperatures is a crucial aspect of gardening, as it significantly impacts the overall health and yield of the crop. Parsnips, like any other root vegetable, have specific temperature requirements for optimal growth. They are cool-season vegetables, best suited to temperatures between 40°F and 75°F. While they can tolerate frosts and even improve in flavor after a light freeze, prolonged exposure to extreme cold or heat can be detrimental.

When faced with extreme cold, parsnips may experience stunted growth or damage to the foliage. In contrast, extreme heat can lead to bolting, where the plant prematurely goes to seed, resulting in a woody and unpalatable root. Therefore, implementing strategies to moderate soil temperature is key to ensuring a successful harvest.

One effective way to protect parsnips from extreme temperatures is through mulching. Mulch serves as an insulating layer, helping to keep the soil cool during hot weather and warm during cold spells. Organic mulches such as straw, shredded leaves, or wood chips are ideal, as they also contribute to soil fertility as they decompose.

Using row covers or garden fabric can also help shield parsnips from harsh weather conditions. These materials create a microclimate that can raise the temperature by several degrees, protecting plants from frost damage. In hot weather, shade cloth can be used to reduce the intensity of the sun and keep the bed cooler.

Water management is another important factor in temperature regulation. Regular watering helps keep the soil cool and prevents it from drying out in high heat. However, it's essential to avoid waterlogged conditions, particularly in cold weather, as this can lead to root rot.

Investing time and effort in protecting parsnips from extreme temperatures is crucial because these conditions can directly affect the quality and quantity of your yield. The texture and flavor of parsnips can be negatively impacted by temperature extremes, resulting in a less satisfying harvest. Moreover, plants under stress from temperature fluctuations are more susceptible to pest and disease issues, further jeopardizing your crop.

By taking steps to manage temperature extremes in your raised bed garden, you can ensure the healthy growth of your parsnips and enjoy a bountiful and flavorful harvest.

Protecting Raised Bed Parsnips From Pests

Protecting your parsnips from pests in raised bed gardens is fundamentally important for a variety of reasons. Parsnips, like any other crop, can be significantly damaged or even destroyed by a variety of pests, including aphids, carrot fly, and root-knot nematodes.

This damage not only reduces the yield and quality of your harvest, but it can also weaken the plants, making them more susceptible to diseases and less able to withstand environmental stresses. Furthermore, a pest infestation can quickly spread throughout a raised bed and even jump to other beds, potentially threatening the health of your entire garden.

By taking steps to protect your parsnips from pests, you're ensuring the vitality of your plants, the productivity of your garden, and the quality of the food you grow. Ultimately, effective pest management is an integral part of successful gardening and cannot be overlooked.

Parsnips grown in raised bed gardens can fall victim to several pests, including aphids, carrot flies, and root-knot nematodes. Each of these pests presents unique challenges and requires specific strategies for effective management.

Aphids are small, soft-bodied insects that feed on plant sap, causing leaves to curl, yellow, or become distorted. They can also transmit plant diseases. To control aphids, you can introduce beneficial insects like ladybugs and lacewings into your garden, which are natural predators of aphids.

A strong spray of water from a garden hose can also help dislodge them from the plants. If the infestation is severe, consider using a plant-friendly insecticidal soap.

Carrot flies are another common pest that can cause significant damage to parsnips. These tiny flies lay their eggs near the base of the plants, and the larvae burrow into the roots when they hatch, causing serious harm.

One effective method to deter carrot flies is crop rotation, as it disrupts the life cycle of the pests. It's also helpful to use fine mesh netting or horticultural fleece to physically prevent the flies from reaching the plants.

Root-knot nematodes are microscopic worms that live in soil and can cause galls or knots to form on plant roots, hindering the plant's ability to absorb water and nutrients. One of the best ways to manage root-knot nematodes is to practice good sanitation by removing and disposing of infected plants and not composting infected plant material. Crop rotation can also be beneficial, as certain crops, such as marigolds and mustard greens, can suppress nematode populations.

In general, maintaining healthy soil and practicing good garden hygiene can go a long way towards preventing pest problems. Regularly inspect your plants for signs of pests, and take action at the first sign of trouble. By staying vigilant and proactive, you can protect your parsnips and enjoy a successful harvest.

Protecting Raised Bed Parsnips From Diseases

Protecting your raised bed grown parsnips from diseases is crucial for maintaining the health and productivity of your garden. Diseases not only reduce the yield and quality of your crop, but they can also spread rapidly, potentially affecting other plants in your raised bed garden.

Some diseases can persist in the soil or on plant debris, posing a threat to future plantings. Moreover, disease-infected plants are often more susceptible to pest infestations and may struggle to absorb the nutrients they need from the soil, further impacting their health and growth.

By implementing preventative measures and promptly addressing any signs of disease, you can help ensure a healthy, bountiful harvest. Ultimately, effective disease management is essential for the long-term success of any vegetable garden.

Raised bed grown parsnips can be affected by several diseases, including bacterial blight, parsnip canker, southern blight, and carrot powdery mildew. Each of these diseases presents unique challenges and requires specific strategies for effective organic management.

Bacterial blight, caused by Pseudomonas marginalis, is a minor disease of parsnip but can occur wherever parsnips are grown. Symptoms include water-soaked spots on leaves that eventually become necrotic.

To organically manage this disease, ensure good air circulation around plants by not overcrowding them and avoid overhead watering which can spread the bacteria.

Parsnip canker, caused by the fungus Itersonilia pastinacae, is another common disease that affects parsnips. The damage is usually only superficial but can lead to secondary infections that cause root rot. Organic control measures include crop rotation, removing and destroying infected plant material.

Southern blight, or white mold is a fungal disease that favors wet conditions. To prevent it organically, keep planting beds well-drained and add aged compost. Avoid overhead watering and maintain good garden hygiene by removing plant debris that could harbor the fungus.

Carrot powdery mildew, although more common in carrots, can also affect parsnips. The disease appears as a white powdery coating on leaves. Organic control methods include using resistant varieties, ensuring good air circulation around plants, and using organic fungicides like sulfur or potassium bicarbonate.

In general, maintaining healthy soil, practicing good garden hygiene, and regular inspections for signs of disease can help prevent many common diseases. By being proactive and vigilant, you can protect your parsnips and enjoy a successful harvest.

HARVESTING RAISED BED PARSNIPS

Growing parsnips in raised bed gardens requires patience, as they are slow to germinate and require a lengthy growing season. After seeding, parsnips typically take around 120 days to mature fully. They are slow to germinate, with seedlings usually emerging in 2 to 3 weeks or longer in soil temperatures below 50°F (10°C). Despite this slow start, parsnips can be grown successfully in most regions, provided they have a long growing season.

The process of harvesting parsnips is fairly straightforward, but timing is key for optimal flavor. Parsnips are a cool-season root vegetable that benefits from exposure to near-freezing temperatures for at least 2 to 4 weeks before harvest. This chilling period helps convert the parsnip's starches into sugars, resulting in a sweeter taste.

Parsnips are ready to harvest from autumn onwards, although delaying harvest until after the first hard frost often results in the sweetest flavor. To harvest, carefully loosen the soil around the parsnip with a garden fork before gently pulling the root from the ground. Be careful not to damage the root during harvest, as this can affect its storage life.

After harvesting, brush off any loose soil and store the parsnips in a cool, dark place. They can also be left in the ground throughout winter and harvested as needed, as they are very hardy and can withstand freezing temperatures. However, it is best to harvest all remaining parsnips before spring, as the onset of warmer weather can cause them to become woody and less palatable.

RAISED BEDS GROWN PARSNIPS NOTES

Start: Seed or Seedlings

Germination: 14 to 21 days, temperatures between 50 and 85 degrees.

Seed Life: 1 Years

Soil Type: Well-draining soil, with organic matter (compost or well-rotted manure) - pH level between 6.0 and 7.0.

Seed Spacing: 2 inches apart (directly into the garden as they don't transplant well).

Seedling Spacing: 3-4 inches apart, with rows approximately 10-12 inches apart.

Sunlight: 6 hours full sunlight

Growing Temperatures: Temperatures between 40°F and 75°F

Days To Harvest: 100 to 120 days.

CHAPTER 14
VEGETABLE RAISED BED GARDENING – CUCUMBERS

C ucumber, a refreshing and versatile vegetable, is an excellent choice for raised bed gardening. Thriving in warm, well-drained soil, cucumbers are known for their rapid growth and high yield, making them a rewarding addition to any vegetable garden. Raised bed gardening offers the perfect environment for cultivating cucumbers, providing improved soil conditions, better drainage, and easier main-tenance.

Whether you're planning on enjoying them fresh in salads, pick-ling for long-term storage, or using in a variety of culinary dishes, growing cucumbers in raised beds can be a fruitful and enjoyable endeavor. This chapter will walk you through the process of successfully growing cucumbers in your raised bed garden, from planting to harvest.

Planting cucumbers using vegetable raised bed gardening can be incredibly beneficial to your garden for several reasons. Firstly, raised beds offer superior drainage compared to traditional in-ground gardens, which is particularly advantageous for cucum-bers as they prefer well-drained soil.

Secondly, the soil in raised beds warms up more quickly in the spring, providing a cozy environment for cucumber seeds to germinate and grow.

Additionally, raised beds allow you to control the soil composi-tion more effectively, enabling you to create the ideal nutrient-rich setting for your cucumber plants. The elevated design of raised beds also makes it easier to maintain the plants, reducing the need for bending and kneeling, and can help to keep pests like slugs and snails at bay.

Lastly, by growing cucumbers vertically in a raised bed, you can save space, increase yield, and improve air circulation around the plants, reducing the risk of disease. All these factors contribute to healthier, more productive cucumber plants, making raised bed gardening an excellent choice for any gardener.

THE RIGHT SOIL TO GROW CUCUMBERS IN RAISED BEDS

When it comes to growing cucumbers in raised bed gardens, the right soil conditions are crucial for healthy growth and bountiful harvests. Cucumbers prefer a well-draining soil that is rich in organic matter. The ideal soil type for cucumbers is loamy soil, which is a balanced mix of sand, silt, and clay. This type of soil provides good drainage while still being able to retain enough moisture and nutrients to support the plants' needs.

Adding organic matter like compost or well-rotted manure to your raised bed can greatly improve its fertility and structure. Organic matter not only adds essential nutrients to the soil but also improves its ability to hold onto water and nutrients, making them more readily available to the cucumber plants. It also aids in aeration, ensuring the roots have access to the oxygen they need for healthy growth.

Cucumbers also prefer a slightly acidic to neutral pH level, ideally between 6.0 and 7.0. This pH range allows for optimal nutrient absorption. If your soil is too acidic or too alkaline, it can inhibit the plants' ability to take up necessary nutrients, leading to poor growth and potential disease problems.

You can test your soil pH with a simple test kit from a garden center and adjust it as necessary using lime (to raise pH) or sulfur (to lower pH).

Lastly, since cucumbers are heavy feeders, they require a soil rich in nutrients. A slow-release organic fertilizer can be mixed into the soil at planting time to provide a steady supply of nutrients throughout the growing season.

Regular side-dressing with compost or a balanced vegetable fertilizer can also help to maintain soil fertility and ensure your cucumbers have all the nutrients they need to produce a plentiful crop.

By paying attention to these soil conditions, you can create an optimal growing environment for your cucumbers in your raised bed garden, setting the stage for a successful growing season.

HOW TO SOW CUCUMBERS IN RAISED BEDS

Correct Season To Sow Cucumbers In Raised Beds

The correct season to sow cucumber seeds in vegetable raised bed gardens is typically in the spring when soil temperatures have sufficiently warmed. As cucumbers are warm-season vegetables, they require soil temperatures to be at least 60°F (15°C) for germination, with ideal temperatures ranging between 70-95°F (21-35°C). Therefore, sowing cucumber seeds directly outdoors should wait until the danger of frost has passed, generally around mid-May in many regions.

However, the beauty of raised bed gardening is that the soil tends to warm up more quickly compared to traditional in-ground gardens, potentially allowing you to sow your cucumber seeds a bit earlier. Raised beds can also retain heat longer into the fall, extending the growing season.

Regardless of when you plant, ensure that your chosen location is sunny, as cucumbers thrive in full sun exposure. Also, keep the soil consistently moist but not waterlogged to promote healthy growth and prevent blossom end rot, a common issue in cucumbers due to uneven watering.

Remember that the exact timing may vary depending on your local climate and weather conditions, so it's always best to check and time in line with your local area's climate for the most accurate planting dates.

Plant Needs & Requirements

Germinating cucumber plants from seeds to seedlings correctly is a critical step when growing in vegetable raised bed gardens. Proper germination lays the foundation for the overall health and productivity of the cucumber plants. When seeds are sowed correctly and at the right depth, they receive the optimal amount of light and heat needed to trigger germination.

Correct planting depth ensures that the emerging seedlings have enough energy to push through the soil surface and start photo-synthesizing. If planted too deep, the seedlings may struggle to reach the surface and could exhaust their energy reserves, leading to weak or failed germination.

Once germinated, properly cared-for seedlings will grow strong root systems, which are essential for nutrient uptake and stability of the plant. Additionally, robust seedlings are better equipped to withstand pest attacks, diseases, and weather fluc-tuations compared to weak ones. Hence, proper germination and seedling care can greatly influence the success of your cucumber crop in raised bed gardens.

Germinating cucumber seeds and caring for the resulting seedlings requires a few key steps to ensure healthy growth. First, you'll want to start by choosing high-quality seeds from a reputable source. This increases your chances of successful germination and strong productive plants.

Begin the germination process by planting the cucumber seeds in small pots or seed trays filled with a good quality seed starting mix. This type of soil is lighter and finer than regular garden soil, which helps the tiny roots of the seedlings to estab-lish more easily. Plant the seeds about 1 inch deep into the soil and lightly cover them. Water the seeds thoroughly but gently, ensuring the soil is evenly moist but not waterlogged.

Cucumber seeds prefer warm conditions for germination, with the optimal soil temperature range being between 70-95°F (21-35°C). At these temperatures, cucumber seeds will usually germinate within 3 to 10 days. To maintain these temperatures, especially in cooler climates or earlier in the season, consider using a heat mat under your seed trays.

Once your seeds have sprouted and grown into seedlings with at least two sets of true leaves (not counting the initial pair of seed leaves), they are generally ready to be transplanted into your raised bed garden. However, before transplanting, it's important to 'harden off' your seedlings. This involves gradually introducing them to outdoor conditions over a period of about a week to help them adjust to the change in environment.

Start by placing them outside in a sheltered spot for a few hours each day, gradually increasing the time they spend outdoors and the intensity of sun exposure.

When it comes to transplanting, carefully remove the seedlings from their pots or trays to avoid damaging the roots. Make a hole in the prepared soil of your raised bed that is deep enough to cover the roots and a little bit of the stem.

Place the seedling in the hole, backfill with soil, and press gently around the base of the plant to firm the soil and remove any air pockets. Water the transplanted seedlings thoroughly and continue to keep the soil evenly moist as they establish in their new location.

By following these steps, you can successfully germinate cucumber seeds and grow them into strong, healthy seedlings ready for transplanting into your raised bed garden.

Spacing & Measurement

Spacing and measurements are critical factors to consider when transplanting cucumber seedlings into raised bed gardens.

Proper spacing allows each plant to receive adequate sunlight, which is essential for photosynthesis and overall growth. It also ensures that plants have enough room to spread their leaves and vines, allowing them to produce a bountiful harvest.

Appropriate spacing helps maintain good air circulation, which can prevent the spread of diseases and pests that often thrive in crowded, humid conditions. As for measurements, accurate depth and distance between each planting hole ensure that the roots are well-established and can access nutrients efficiently.

Furthermore, it aids in efficient water use, preventing both underwatering and waterlogging issues. Ultimately, careful attention to spacing and measurements during transplantation contributes significantly to the health and productivity of your cucumber plants in raised bed gardens.

Planting cucumber seedlings in a vegetable raised bed garden requires strategic spacing and measurements to ensure optimal growth and yield. In terms of spacing, it's important to give cucumbers enough room to grow without crowding each other out.

The desired in-row spacing for cucumber seedlings is typically about 12 to 36 inches apart. This spacing allows each plant to have sufficient access to sunlight, water, and nutrients, which are essential for their growth and development.

For gardeners who wish to maximize their use of space, growing cucumbers vertically on a trellis or garden arch is a viable option. This method allows more plants to be grown in a given area, and it can also help prevent pests like cucumber beetles, which are a common problem for cucumber plants.

However, it's important to note that the ideal spacing can vary depending on the specific variety of cucumber you're growing. For instance, bush varieties, which tend to be more compact, may require less space than vining varieties. It's recommended to always check the seed packet for the most accurate planting instructions for your chosen cucumber variety.

Proper spacing and planting depth are key to successfully growing cucumber seedlings in a vegetable raised bed garden. By following these guidelines, you can look forward to a bountiful harvest of fresh, homegrown cucumbers.

Ideal Temperatures & Sun Requirements

Ideal temperatures and sun requirements are critical factors when growing cucumbers in raised bed gardens. Cucumbers are warm-season vegetables, which means they thrive under warm conditions. The desired temperature for cucumber growth ranges from 60 to 95 degrees Fahrenheit, with optimal growth occurring between 70 to 85 degrees. Temperatures below 50 degrees can hinder growth and potentially damage the plant.

Aside from temperature, cucumbers also have specific sun requirements. They prefer full sun exposure, meaning they need at least 6 to 8 hours of direct sunlight each day. Adequate sunlight is essential for photosynthesis, the process by which plants convert light energy into chemical energy for growth. Lack of sufficient sunlight can lead to poor growth and lower yields.

Understanding and meeting these temperature and sun requirements are fundamental to successful cucumber cultivation. Providing cucumbers with their ideal growing conditions will not only ensure healthy plant growth but also contribute to a bountiful harvest.

MAINTAINING YOUR RAISED BED CUCUMBERS

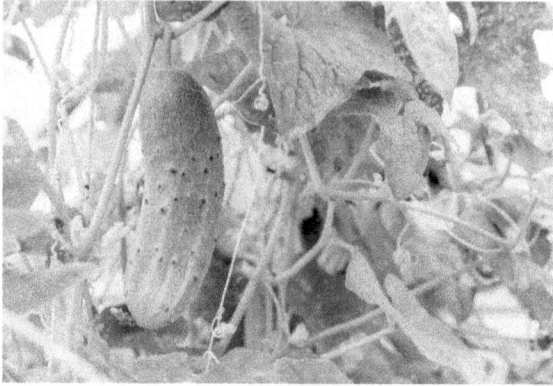

Maintaining your raised bed grown cucumbers is crucial for several reasons. First, regular maintenance helps to ensure plant health and productivity. This includes tasks like watering, weeding, and checking for pests or diseases. Regular watering is vital as cucumbers are made up of about 95% water and require consistent moisture to grow properly.

Weeding is important to prevent competition for nutrients and space. Monitoring for pests and diseases allows for early detection and treatment, thereby preventing potential damage to the plants. Additionally, proper maintenance includes providing support for vining varieties of cucumbers, which not only helps keep the fruit clean and disease-free but also makes harvesting easier.

Lastly, regular maintenance allows you to observe the overall growth and development of your plants, enabling you to make any necessary adjustments to their care. Hence, maintaining your cucumber plants in a raised bed garden is a key factor in ensuring a successful and bountiful harvest.

Pruning & Thinning Your Cucumbers

Pruning and thinning of cucumbers in raised bed gardens are critical practices for optimal plant health and productivity. Firstly, these activities help regulate the growth of the cucumber plants and prevent overcrowding, which can lead to competition for sunlight, nutrients, and water. Overcrowded plants are also more susceptible to diseases and pest infestations due to the lack of air circulation and the creation of a damp, shady environment that pests and diseases thrive in.

Secondly, pruning involves removing excess leaves and non-fruiting branches, which allows more energy to be directed towards the growth of fruits, thereby increasing yield. It also improves sun exposure and air circulation, reducing the likelihood of fungal diseases.

Thinning, on the other hand, involves removing weaker or excess plants to ensure that the remaining ones have adequate space to grow and develop. This practice also helps in managing nutrient distribution among the plants.

Furthermore, both pruning and thinning make it easier to monitor the plants for any signs of stress or disease, allowing for early detection and treatment. Therefore, regular pruning and thinning are essential for maintaining a healthy, productive cucumber crop in raised bed gardens.

Pruning and thinning cucumbers in raised bed gardens should ideally start when the plants have grown several leaves and are starting to form vines. This is usually about three weeks after planting, but it can vary depending on the specific variety of cucumbers and growing conditions.

To prune cucumbers, begin by identifying the main stem, which is typically the longest and thickest. Along this stem, you'll notice smaller side shoots or branches, some of which may already have flowers or fruits. Start pruning by removing any branches that do not have flowers or fruits. These branches are often found at the base of the plant, and their removal helps direct more energy towards fruit production. Use a sharp, clean pruner to make a clean cut close to the main stem without damaging it.

In addition to this, remove any dead, diseased, or yellowing leaves to prevent the spread of disease and improve overall plant health. Always remember to wash or sanitize your tools before moving from one plant to another to avoid spreading diseases.

Thinning, on the other hand, involves removing entire plants to reduce overcrowding. This is best done when the plants are still young and have just started to develop true leaves, usually about two weeks after germination. Carefully pull out the weaker or smaller plants, leaving about 12-18 inches of space between each remaining plant. This ensures that each plant has enough space to grow and access to adequate nutrients, water, and sunlight.

Both pruning and thinning should be done regularly throughout the growing season to maintain optimal plant health and productivity. However, be careful not to over-prune or over-thin, as this can stress the plants and reduce yield.

Proper timing and technique in pruning and thinning your cucumber plants in raised bed gardens are essential for ensuring a healthy and bountiful harvest. These practices help create the ideal growing environment, allowing your cucumbers to thrive and produce to their full potential.

Watering Your Raised Bed Cucumbers

Watering is a fundamental aspect of maintaining cucumbers in raised bed gardens. Cucumbers are made up of about 95% water and require consistent watering to grow properly and produce a healthy crop. Inadequate watering can lead to stress in the plants, causing issues such as stunted growth, yellowing leaves, and reduced yield. Additionally, inconsistent watering can result in bitter-tasting fruits, a common problem in cucumber cultivation.

Cucumbers prefer soil that is consistently moist but not water-logged. Raised beds tend to drain more quickly than traditional garden beds, so they may require more frequent watering, especially during hot, dry periods. Overwatering, on the other hand, can lead to root rot and other diseases.

Therefore, it's crucial to strike a balance, ensuring your cucumbers receive enough water to thrive without becoming water-logged. Regular watering also helps in nutrient uptake, as nutrients dissolve in water and are then absorbed by the plant roots. Thus, providing your cucumbers with the right amount of water is key to their health and productivity in a raised bed garden.

On average, cucumbers in a raised bed garden should receive about 1 inch of water per week. This amount can be adjusted depending on the weather conditions and the stage of growth of the cucumber plants. For instance, during hot, dry weather, cucumbers may need more water, sometimes even daily watering, to maintain soil moisture and prevent the plants from wilting. Conversely, in cooler or rainy weather, less watering may be necessary.

When watering, it's best to do so early in the morning. This allows the water to soak deeply into the soil, reaching the roots, and gives any water that splashes onto the leaves time to evaporate before the heat of the day, reducing the risk of fungal diseases. Avoid watering late in the evening, as this can leave the plants damp overnight, creating an environment conducive to disease development.

It's also important to water cucumbers at the base of the plant, near the soil surface, rather than from above. This helps to ensure that the water goes straight to the roots where it's needed and reduces the chance of leaf diseases caused by wet foliage.

While cucumbers need a good deal of water for healthy growth, it's important to balance their needs with the potential risks of overwatering. Consistent monitoring of soil moisture and adjusting watering practices based on weather conditions and plant needs will help ensure a successful cucumber crop in a raised bed garden.

Organic Fertilization For Raised Bed Cucumbers

Organic fertilization plays a crucial role in the successful cultivation of cucumbers in raised bed gardens. Cucumbers, like all plants, require essential nutrients to grow and produce fruit. These nutrients, including nitrogen, phosphorus, and potassium, are readily available in organic fertilizers.

Organic fertilizers, such as compost or manure, not only provide these vital nutrients but also enhance the structure of the soil, improving its ability to hold water and allowing roots to penetrate more deeply. This leads to healthier, stronger plants that are better able to resist pests and diseases. In addition, organic fertilizers release nutrients slowly over time, ensuring a steady supply of nutrients throughout the growing season.

Besides, using organic fertilizers contributes to environmental sustainability by recycling organic waste and reducing the dependence on synthetic fertilizers, which can contribute to soil degradation and water pollution. Therefore, for the health of your cucumbers, the quality of your soil, and the well-being of the environment, organic fertilization is an important practice in raised bed gardening.

One of the commonly used organic fertilizers for cucumbers is compost. It is rich in nutrients and works wonders in improving the soil texture, promoting better water retention and drainage, crucial for the healthy growth of cucumbers. The compost can be mixed into the topsoil of the raised bed before planting cucumbers, and more can be added every few weeks during the growing season as a side dressing to replenish nutrients.

Another excellent organic fertilizer option is manure, particularly aged or composted manure. Manure is high in nitrogen, which cucumbers need for their leafy growth. Like compost, it can be mixed into the soil before planting and added as a side dressing throughout the growing season.

Bone meal is yet another organic fertilizer that cucumbers love. It's rich in phosphorus, necessary for flowering and fruiting. Gardeners can sprinkle bone meal into the planting hole or mix it into the soil before planting cucumbers and then reapply it every four weeks during the growing season to support continuous fruit production.

When it comes to fertilizing cucumbers, it's generally recommended to do so every 3-4 weeks. However, gardeners should monitor their plants for signs of nutrient deficiency, such as yellowing leaves or stunted growth, and adjust their fertilization practices as necessary. It's also important to water thoroughly after applying fertilizer to help it soak into the soil and reach the plant roots.

Using organic fertilizers for cucumbers in raised bed gardens offers multiple benefits. By choosing the right type of fertilizer and applying it correctly, you can ensure healthy growth and high yields in your cucumber plants.

PROTECTING YOUR RAISED BED CUCUMBERS

Extreme Temperatures

Protecting cucumbers grown in raised bed gardens from extreme temperatures is critical for their healthy growth and productivity. Cucumbers are warm-season crops that thrive in temperatures between 60°F and 90°F. When temperatures fall below or rise above this range, the plants can suffer from cold damage or heat stress, which can affect their growth, flowering, and fruiting.

In areas with cool springs or short growing seasons, gardeners can use several strategies to protect cucumber plants from cold temperatures. One common method is to cover the plants with floating row covers or cloches. These lightweight materials trap heat from the sun, creating a warmer microclimate around the plants.

They can be left on the plants day and night but should be removed or vented during warm days to prevent overheating. Another option is to use wall-o-water protectors or water-filled plastic tubes that absorb heat during the day and release it at night, keeping the plants warm.

To protect cucumber plants from heat, it's essential to provide adequate water. Cucumbers are made up of about 95% water and need consistent moisture, especially during hot weather. Mulching around the plants can help conserve soil moisture and keep the roots cool.

Using shade cloth or plant umbrellas can also be effective in protecting cucumber plants from intense sun and high temperatures. These shading devices can be installed over the plants during the hottest part of the day to reduce heat stress.

Maintaining optimal temperature conditions for cucumbers is crucial for several reasons. Firstly, cucumbers can be sensitive to both cold and heat stress. Cold temperatures can slow down their growth, delay flowering, and make them more susceptible to diseases.

On the other hand, heat stress can cause poor fruit set, misshapen fruits, and bitter taste. Secondly, consistent temperature conditions can promote more vigorous growth and higher yields. Lastly, maintaining a suitable temperature can help ensure the production of high-quality fruits with good taste and texture.

Protecting cucumbers in raised bed gardens from extreme temperatures is key to their success. With the right strategies, gardeners can ensure their cucumber plants thrive in any weather conditions, leading to a bountiful harvest.

Protecting Raised Bed Cucumbers From Pests

Protecting cucumbers grown in raised bed gardens from pests is crucial for maintaining the health and productivity of your plants. Pests, such as aphids, cucumber beetles, and squash bugs, can cause significant damage to cucumbers by feeding on their leaves, stems, and fruits. They can also spread diseases like bacterial wilt and mosaic virus, which can lead to wilting, stunted growth, and reduced fruit production.

A severe pest infestation can wipe out an entire crop, resulting in a disappointing harvest. Therefore, implementing effective pest management strategies is key to ensuring a successful cucumber yield. By keeping pests at bay, you not only protect the individual plants but also contribute to the overall health of your garden ecosystem.

Cucumbers grown in raised bed gardens can be susceptible to a variety of pests, including aphids, cucumber beetles, and squash bugs. Each of these pests can cause considerable damage, affecting both the health of the plant and the quality of the harvest.

Aphids are small, soft-bodied insects that feed on plant sap, extracting it directly from the leaves and stems of cucumber plants. They reproduce rapidly, and heavy infestations can lead to yellowing and curling of leaves, stunted growth, and reduced yield. Aphids also excrete a sticky substance known as honeydew, which can promote the growth of sooty mold fungus, further damaging the plant.

Cucumber beetles come in two main types: striped and spotted. Both types can cause significant harm to cucumbers. They feed on the leaves, flowers, and fruit of the plant, causing direct physical damage. Perhaps more significantly, they can transmit bacterial wilt, a disease that causes wilting and death of the plant.

Squash bugs are another common pest of cucumbers. These insects suck the sap out of the plant, causing leaves to wilt, discolor, and die. Heavy infestations can result in significant plant stress and even death.

To protect cucumbers from these pests, several strategies can be employed. Regular monitoring is crucial - catching an infestation early can make control much easier. Physical removal can be effective for small infestations of all three pests. For aphids, a strong spray of water can knock them off the plant, while cucumber beetles and squash bugs can be handpicked and dropped into soapy water.

Insecticidal soaps and neem oil can also be used to control aphids and cucumber beetles. These treatments work by smothering the insects or disrupting their feeding, but they must be applied directly to the pests to be effective.

For long-term, sustainable control, consider incorporating beneficial insects into your garden. Ladybugs and lacewings are natural predators of aphids, while parasitic nematodes can help control cucumber beetles. Introducing these beneficial organisms can help keep pest populations in check, reducing the need for more aggressive control measures.

Protecting Raised Bed Cucumbers From Diseases

Safeguarding cucumbers in raised bed gardens from diseases is critical for a healthy and abundant harvest. Cucumbers are susceptible to a variety of diseases, including powdery mildew, bacterial wilt, and cucumber mosaic virus. These diseases can severely affect the health of the plants, leading to stunted growth, yellowing leaves, wilting, and reduced fruit production.

In some cases, diseases can even cause total plant death. Moreover, certain diseases like bacterial wilt are transmitted via pests, making them difficult to control once established.

By protecting your cucumbers from diseases, you not only ensure the vitality and productivity of your plants but also prevent the potential spread of diseases to other plants in your garden. Hence, disease prevention and management are vital for maintaining a robust and productive vegetable garden.

Powdery mildew is a common fungal disease that appears as a white or gray powdery substance on the leaves and stems of cucumber plants. This disease can diminish the vigor of the plant, leading to reduced yield and potentially even plant death if left untreated.

Organic control measures for powdery mildew include the use of sulfur or potassium bicarbonate sprays, which can prevent the spread of the disease. Additionally, planting resistant varieties and ensuring good air circulation around your plants can help prevent the onset of powdery mildew.

Bacterial wilt is another disease that can affect cucumbers. This disease is caused by the bacterium Erwinia tracheiphila and is often spread by the cucumber beetle. Infected plants typically exhibit wilting symptoms and eventually die. There are no effective organic treatments for bacterial wilt once a plant is infected. However, organic prevention techniques include controlling the cucumber beetle population using methods such as row covers or organic pesticides like neem oil or pyrethrin.

Cucumber mosaic virus (CMV) is a disease that presents as a mottled or mosaic pattern on the leaves of cucumber plants. It can lead to stunted growth and reduced fruit production. CMV is typically spread by aphids, so controlling the aphid population is crucial for preventing this disease. Organic methods for aphid control include introducing beneficial insects, such as ladybugs and lacewings, which are natural predators of aphids.

While cucumbers in raised bed gardens can be vulnerable to several diseases, there are various organic methods available to protect your plants. These include using disease-resistant varieties, practicing good plant hygiene, ensuring optimal growing conditions, and controlling pest populations. By implementing these strategies, you can help ensure a healthy and productive cucumber crop.

HARVESTING RAISED BED CUCUMBERS

Growing cucumbers in a raised bed garden can be a rewarding endeavor. On average, cucumbers take between 50 to 70 days to mature from the time of planting, depending on the variety and growing conditions. Some quick-maturing varieties can even be ready for harvest in as little as 45 days. It's important to note that these timelines are approximate and can be influenced by factors such as the quality of the soil, the amount of sunlight the plants receive, and the overall care and attention given to the plants.

When it comes to harvesting cucumbers, timing is crucial. Cucumbers should be harvested when they are at their peak size and before they begin to turn yellow. For most varieties, this means when they are about 6 to 8 inches long. However, pickling cucumbers are often harvested when they are smaller, around 2 to 3 inches long. A cucumber is overripe and likely bitter if it has turned yellow.

To harvest cucumbers, use a pair of sharp scissors or a knife to cut the stem above the fruit. It's best not to pull or twist the cucumbers off the vine, as this can damage the plant and potentially reduce future yield. Harvesting should be done regularly, as leaving ripe cucumbers on the vine can signal the plant to stop producing new fruits.

After harvesting, cucumbers can be stored at room temperature for up to a week. However, they're best when consumed fresh. Remember to wash them thoroughly before eating or preserving to remove any residual dirt. By understanding the timeline and proper harvesting techniques, you can maximize your cucumber yield and enjoy fresh, homegrown cucumbers throughout the growing season.

RAISED BEDS GROWN CUCUMBERS NOTES

Start: Seed or Seedlings

Germination: 3 to 10 days, 70-95°F (21-35°C).

Seed Life: 4 Years

Soil Type: Well-drained, loamy soil that is rich in organic matter (compost or well-rotted manure) - pH level between 6.0 and 7.0.

Seed Spacing: 1 inch deep and 2 inches apart in small pots or seed trays filled with a good quality seed starting mix.

Seedling Spacing: 12 to 36 inches apart.

Sunlight: 6 – 8 hours full sunlight.

Growing Temperatures: 70 to 85 degrees.

Days To Harvest: 50 to 70 days.

CHAPTER 15
ACKNOWLEDGEMENTS

I t is with profound appreciation and heartfelt gratitude that we extend our sincerest thanks to the remarkable team at Green Roots. Their vast knowledge, wealth of experience, unwavering commitment, and tireless dedication have been instrumental in bringing this book to fruition. The team's collective endeavor has not only made this project possible but has also infused it with a depth of understanding and practical wisdom that is truly unparalleled.

We owe a special debt of gratitude to Charles Craig, Annie Hayford, Jessica Reid, Adam Spencer, and Nicole Robinson. Each one of them has made invaluable contributions that have significantly shaped the quality and substance of this book. Their expertise, creativity, and diligence have added layers of depth to the content, making it a rich and comprehensive resource for all readers.

The ethos of Green Roots team is exemplified by their strong desire to make a positive impact in people's lives. Their dedication to developing the community through gardening is truly unmatched. Their passion shines through in every page, reflecting their commitment to share their love for gardening with a wider audience.

This book represents the culmination of over 20 years of collective expertise, experience, insight, and passion in the field of gardening. It is a testament to the team's unwavering dedication to creating a comprehensive resource that caters to gardeners of all levels of experience, from novices to seasoned veterans.

We are extremely proud to have created this book, which stands as a beacon of knowledge and a guide for gardeners worldwide. Our hope is that it will inspire, educate, and empower readers, enhancing their gardening journey and enriching their experiences now and for many years to come.

AFTERWORD

As we draw to a close on this comprehensive exploration of container and raised bed gardening, it becomes abundantly clear that these methods offer a plethora of benefits for individuals from all walks of life. Whether you live in a bustling city with limited outdoor space or in a sprawling rural area, the flexibility and adaptability of these gardening techniques can be tailored to suit your unique circumstances.

One of the most salient advantages of container and raised bed gardening is their accessibility. These methods break down barriers that have traditionally made gardening an exclusive hobby for those with spacious backyards. By making efficient use of vertical space and allowing for the cultivation of plants in portable containers, anyone from apartment dwellers to those with physical limitations can engage in the rewarding practice of growing their own food.

Moreover, container and raised bed gardening provide opportunities for year-round cultivation. This is particularly advantageous for individuals living in regions with harsh winters or unpredictable weather patterns. By strategically placing containers indoors or using protective coverings for raised beds, it's possible to maintain a continuous supply of fresh produce throughout the year.

Another significant benefit lies in the control these methods offer over the gardening environment. With traditional ground gardening, gardeners are often at the mercy of soil conditions and local pests. However, with container and raised bed gardening, you can curate the quality of your soil, manage water drainage, and mitigate the risk of pest infestations more effectively.

Beyond personal benefits, these methods also contribute positively to global environmental efforts. By growing your own produce in container and raised bed gardening, you're reducing the carbon footprint associated with transporting store-bought fruits and vegetables.

Container and raised bed gardening are more than just trendy techniques; they represent a shift towards more inclusive, sustainable, and resilient food production systems. They empower individuals to take control of their food sources, encourage a closer connection with nature, and contribute to a greener planet. Regardless of your gardening experience or living situation, embracing these methods can yield not only a bountiful harvest but also a wealth of personal satisfaction and ecological benefits.

Throughout the course of this book, you've embarked on a comprehensive journey, delving into both the theoretical and practical aspects of container and raised bed gardening. We have traversed a wide range of topics, encompassing essential elements such as optimal plant spacing, understanding temperature needs for different plant species, managing pests effectively, and promoting soil health.

You've also acquired knowledge on how to choose the most suitable vegetable plants, considering factors like their growth habits, susceptibility to pests, and specific requirements for optimum cultivation.

We've placed emphasis on understanding the diverse types of containers and raised bed gardens available to you. From the classic charm of clay pots and wooden boxes to the innovative appeal of fabric containers and elevated raised beds, each type brings unique advantages and considerations.

The choice of container or raised bed can profoundly influence the health and productivity of your plants, underlining the importance of carefully considering aspects such as the material of the container, its size, and drainage capabilities.

We dove headfirst into the various preparation techniques integral to successful container and raised bed gardening. A prime example is understanding the watering needs of your plants. Recognizing that overwatering or underwatering can lead to a myriad of issues is critical to maintaining a healthy garden.

As you embark on your cultivation journey, equipped with this wealth of knowledge, remember that gardening is a delicate blend of art and science. It demands patience, keen observation, and an openness to learn from experiences. The ultimate aim is to constantly experiment, observe, and tweak your approach until you discover what works best for your individual garden.

Container and raised bed gardening are strategic methodologies that can significantly enhance the health and yield of your garden. As you put into practice what you've learned, we genuinely hope you experience the joy and satisfaction that comes from nurturing a flourishing vegetable garden.

We invite you to share your gardening journey with us and other gardening enthusiasts at our Facebook community - facebook.-com/groups/greenroots/.

As you're now well-prepared to commence your gardening journey, we kindly request you to provide an honest review of this guide. Your feedback and thoughts are invaluable to us, helping determine how effectively we've assisted you in enhancing your gardening skills. Please feel free to post your comments in the review section of your purchased retailer, and rest assured, we'll be eagerly awaiting them.

"Garden is not just a hobby, but a way of life" - Green Roots

ALSO BY GREEN ROOTS

Fruit and Veggies 101 - Vegetable Companion Planting : Companion Guide On How To Grow Vegetables Using Essential, Organic & Sustainable Gardening Strategies (Perfect For Beginners)

Fruit and Veggies 101 - Salad Vegetables : Gardening Guide On How To Grow The Freshest & Ripest Salad Vegetables (Perfect for Beginners)

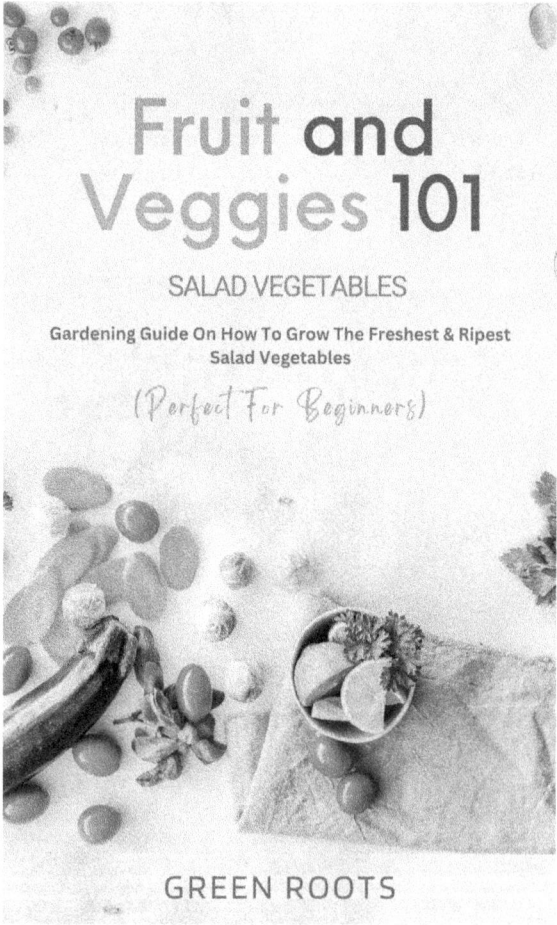

Fruit **and** Veggies **101**

SALAD VEGETABLES

Gardening Guide On How To Grow The Freshest & Ripest Salad Vegetables

(Perfect For Beginners)

GREEN ROOTS

Fruit and Veggies 101 - Summer Fruits: Gardening Guide On How To Grow The Freshest & Ripest Summer Fruits (Perfect For Beginners) Includes - Fruit Salad, Smoothies & Fruit Juices Recipes

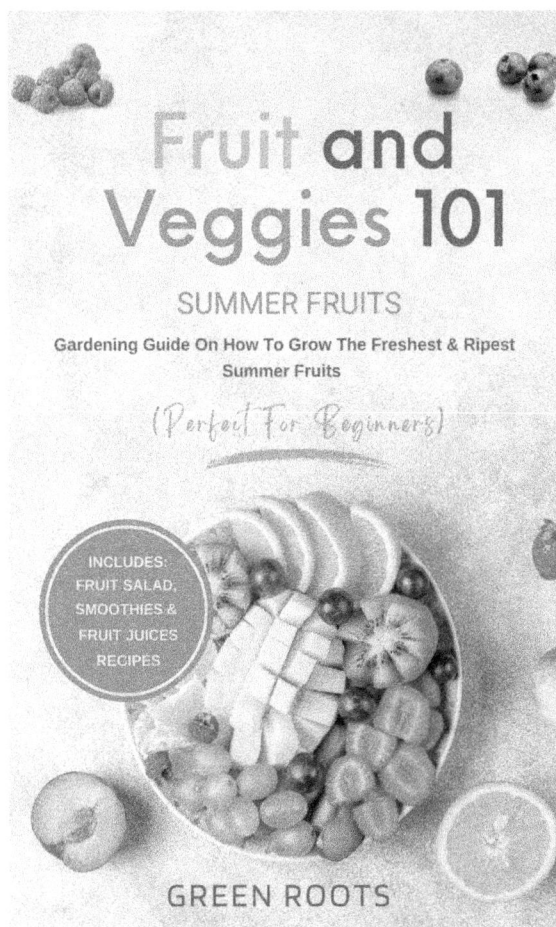

Fruit and Veggies 101

SUMMER FRUITS

Gardening Guide On How To Grow The Freshest & Ripest Summer Fruits

(Perfect For Beginners)

INCLUDES: FRUIT SALAD, SMOOTHIES & FRUIT JUICES RECIPES

GREEN ROOTS

Fruit and Veggies 101 - The Winter Harvest: Gardening Guide On How To Grow The Freshest & Ripest Winter Vegetables (Perfect for Beginners)

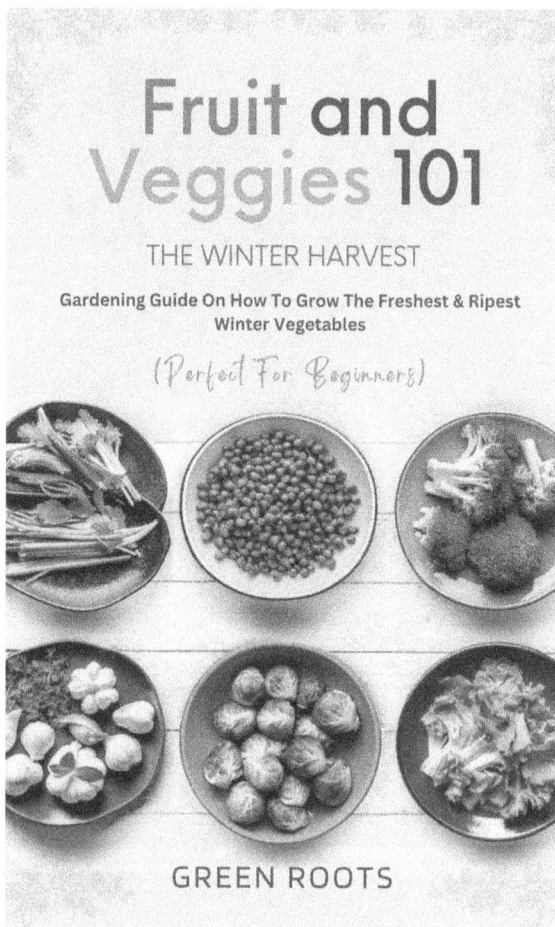

Fruit and Veggies 101

THE WINTER HARVEST

Gardening Guide On How To Grow The Freshest & Ripest Winter Vegetables

(Perfect For Beginners)

GREEN ROOTS

GLOSSARY

Acidic

Something that forms or becomes acid and has a pH of less than 7.

Allelopathic

Refers to the biological phenomenon where one plant inhibits the growth of another by releasing certain biochemicals into the environment.

Aeration

The act of circulating air through a garden, soil, and plants.

Aged manure

Old manure that has matured through a long period by letting it sit in a container.

Alkaline

Something that contains alkali and has a pH above 7.

Aphids

Tiny insects which consume the liquid plants produce, such as sap.

Aerate

The process of introducing air into the soil to improve its structure and promote root growth.

Alliums

A family of plants that includes onions, garlic, leeks, and chives. They are known for their strong scent, which can deter many pests.

Apiaceae

Also known as the carrot or parsley family, this group includes vegetables like carrots, celery, parsley, and fennel. They are often used in companion planting for their ability to attract beneficial insects.

Bacteria

A microorganism that causes disease and, at other times, improves the well-being of an organism.

Buttoning

A condition affecting certain vegetables, especially those in the cabbage family, like broccoli and cauliflower. Buttoning occurs when these plants form small, button-like heads prematurely instead of developing a single large one

Biodegradable

Something that can decompose into the soil and not harm the soil or other living organisms in it.

Bolting

When vegetable crops prematurely run to seed, usually making them unusable

Blunt

Something that is not sharp but softer around its edges and unable to penetrate through something.

Blanch

A method for growing vegetables. A condition in which a plant's young shoots are covered to block light, preventing photosynthesis and the production of chlorophyll, leaving them pale in color.

Bulb

A plant's fruit or organ grows in soil right above its roots and is typically edible when it's a vegetable plant.

Bushy

Something that is overgrown or grows to be dense, big, and has lots of leaves.

Beneficial Insects

Insects that help control pest populations by preying on them or acting as pollinators. Examples include ladybugs, lacewings, and bees.

Brassica

A plant family that includes cabbage, broccoli, kale, and Brussels sprouts. These plants are often companion planted with aromatic herbs or Alliums to deter pests.

Cabbage loopers

An insect or moth tends to be found crawling and laying eggs on cabbages. This insect is a cabbage pest that destroys crops.

Calcium carbonate

Insoluble chalk is natural and white. This is also called ground limestone.

Collar

A round object is used to cuff the base of a plant to protect it from pests such as worms and maggots.

Compaction

The compression of soil particles removes air pockets and hardens the soil. It is considered harmful when gardening and if you want to achieve successful results.

Companion planting

Planting two or more plants next to each other and is protective of each other to avoid disease and pests. It can improve harvest results and improve growth.

Compost

A combination of biodegradable plants, objects, or waste that has been mixed to rot and build up nutrients necessary to soil health and fertility.

Container garden

A garden of plants grown in a pot that holds soil.

Crop rotation

Planting various crops in succession on the same piece of land helps to improve soil health, maximize nutrients, and reduce pest and weed pressure. This practice is known as crop rotation.

Cutworms

A damaging and destructive moth larva is a vegetable pest found in soil and on plants.

Companion Planting

A gardening method that involves growing different types of plants together for mutual benefit, often in terms of pest control, pollination, or nutrient uptake.

Crop Rotation

The practice of growing different types of crops in the same area in sequential seasons to improve soil health and reduce pest and disease problems.

Cucurbitaceae

A plant family that includes squash, cucumber, and melon. These plants often benefit from being planted with corn and beans, a combination known as "Three Sisters."

Debris

Remains or objects in the soil, such as rocks and previously dead crops, need to be removed to maintain the health of your garden.

Drainage

The process by which liquids or water is expelled from something, such as soil.

Drilling tractor

A gardening sowing machine that drills holes into the ground and helps a gardener avoid manual soil drilling to plant his plants.

Ecosystem

Different biological organisms interact with each other to maintain an environment.

Evaporation

Water that turns into vapor.

Fertile soil

Soil that is healthy enough to give plants all nutrients they need to grow successfully until harvest.

Fertilization

Making soil fertile through the use of fertilizers.

Frost

Ice crystals can form on plants when temperatures are freezing or too cold.

Frost Cloth

A covering made of insulation that is positioned over plants, shrubs, trees, and crops to shield them from frost, wind, and chilly weather.

Fungus

Living organisms feed on other living organisms and create mold or discolored plants when present. They can destroy plants and cause disease.

Germinate

When a plant starts to grow out of a shell and form shoots or leaves.

Harvest

A collection of mature and ripe plants and their fruit. It's when your plants have matured, and you collect them from their stems.

Heart rate

How fast or slow are your heartbeats? It's a number or calculation which determines the heart's speed.

Humus

Decomposed organic matter consists of soil and compost.

Hybrid seed

Seeds have been altered and are offspring of two different types of seed varieties of the same plant.

Interplanting

Growing two or more types of plants together in the same space to maximize the use of garden space and enhance productivity.

Leguminosae

Also known as Fabaceae or the legume family, this group includes peas, beans, and lentils. These plants can fix nitrogen from the air into the soil, benefiting other plants grown with them.

Mesh

A material you lace over your garden plants that protects them from insects and pests.

Minerals

Substances are naturally occurring and are needed to produce fertile soil and healthy plants.

Moisture

Dampness is caused by diffused water or liquid.

Mulch

Decayed matter, such as compost, is placed on the soil's surface to lock moisture in or protect the soil from harsh weather conditions.

Nitrogen

A nutrient is needed to give plants their green color and healthy leaves.

Nutrients

Elements that feed plants the necessary food they need to grow.

Organic matter

Decomposed humus is in the soil and is essential in growing healthy vegetables.

Organic produce

Food that has been made or grown without the use of chemical alterations.

Pathogens

Organisms that cause disease in plants. These can include fungi, bacteria, viruses, nematodes (tiny worm-like creatures), and even certain types of insects.

Pesticides

Organic or chemical substances kill or repel insects and other pests from a garden.

Pests

Living organisms are destructive to a garden and need to be repelled or prevented from reaching plants.

pH

A chemistry figure which communicates a scale of alkalinity or acidity. It helps you know how alkaline or acidic soil is.

Phosphate

Phosphoric acid is a salt needed for the soil's health.

Potassium

It is a nutrient that helps plants grow and is essential in their life cycle.

Pruning

Maintain a garden by cutting or trimming dead or potentially unwanted parts of a plant.

Pest Control

Methods used to manage and reduce damage from pests, which can include cultural practices, biological control, and organic or synthetic pesticides.

Raised Bed Gardening

A method of gardening where the soil level is raised above the existing ground level, usually enclosed by a frame.

Roots

The bottom stingy and firm bits of a plant grow and stretch into the soil. They absorb the nutrients and water for a plant's needs.

Seedling

A small and recently germinated plant that is ready to be planted.

Soggy

A mushy, soft, and overly damp area such as soil.

Soilless

Matter which seeds can be grown in and is an alternative to soil.

Sowing

The act of planting, drilling, or scattering a seed onto or into the soil to grow.

Sprout

When a plant produces its first shoots or leaves.

Stem

The structure of a plant that supports all its branches, leaves, and fruit.

Suckers

Plant suckers are vigorous vertical growth originating from a plant's root system or lower main stem.

Solanaceae

A plant family that includes tomatoes, peppers, and eggplants. These plants often benefit from being planted with basil or marigold, which can deter certain pests.

Succession Planting

The practice of planting crops in a staggered manner so that as one crop is harvested, another one is ready to take its place.

Thinning

Separating seedlings clumped together or removing some over-crowded plants from the soil to space out your garden to give others the chance of growing properly.

Transplanting

When you take a plant from one soil, area, or tray into another area or garden, this is also known as replanting it into another space.

Trap Crop

A plant that is used to attract pests away from the main crop. The pests are then easier to control on the trap crop.

Weed Control

Methods used to manage and reduce the growth of weeds, which can compete with crops for light, water, and nutrients. This can include mulching, hand weeding, and using weed-suppressing plants.

BIBLIOGRAPHY

Albert, S. (2023, December 24). *How to grow green onions, spring onions, and scallions.* Harvest to Table. https://harvesttotable.com/how-to-grow-scallions/

Arsenault, R. (2023a, December 3). *How to grow green onions.* Grow a Good Life. https://growagoodlife.com/how-to-grow-green-onions/

Arsenault, R. (2023b, December 3). *How to grow green onions.* Grow a Good Life. https://growagoodlife.com/how-to-grow-green-onions/

Blackwood, M., RN. (2022, February 22). *How to grow green onions.* Healthier Steps. https://healthiersteps.com/how-to-grow-green-onions/

Bloomfield, C., & Grant, B. L. (2023, June 6). *Common Pepper Plant Problems – Pepper Plant Diseases And Pests.* Gardeningknowhow. https://www.gardeningknowhow.com/edible/vegetables/pepper/common-pepper-plant-problems.htm

Chen, M. (2022, August 30). *Peppers.* Home and Garden Education Center. https://homegarden.cahnr.uconn.edu/factsheets/peppers/

Dorn, S. (2023, October 9). *How to grow green onions | Growing green onions in containers year round.* Balcony Garden Web. https://balconygardenweb.com/how-to-grow-green-onions-growing-green-onions-in-containers/

Emily. (2020, October 28). *Insect and Varmint Solutions for your Onions.* Onion Patch. https://www.onionpatch.dixondalefarms.com/insect-and-varmint-solutions-for-your-onions/

Growing onions in home gardens. (n.d.). UMN Extension. https://extension.umn.edu/vegetables/growing-onions

Growing peppers in the home garden. (n.d.). Ohioline. https://ohioline.osu.edu/factsheet/hyg-1618

Home | Home & Garden Information Center. (2024, January 2). Home &Amp; Garden Information Center. https://www.clemson.edu/extension/hgic/pests/plant_pests/veg_fruit/hgic2219.html

Iannotti, M. (2022, October 30). *How to Grow Green Onions: From Seeds & Regrowing.* The Spruce. https://www.thespruce.com/how-to-grow-scallions-4125799

Jabbour, N. (2022a, February 24). *How to grow green onions: The ultimate seed to harvest guide.* Savvy Gardening. https://savvygardening.com/how-to-grow-green-onions/

Jabbour, N. (2022b, February 24). *How to grow green onions: The ultimate seed to harvest guide.* Savvy Gardening. https://savvygardening.com/how-to-grow-green-onions/

BIBLIOGRAPHY

Johnston, C. (2022, May 16). *How to grow green onions.* Growfully. https://grow-fully.com/how-to-grow-green-onions/

Kennedy, L. (2023a, June 10). *How to grow green onions in containers.* Little Yellow Wheelbarrow. https://www.littleyellowwheelbarrow.com/how-to-grow-green-onions/

Kennedy, L. (2023b, June 10). *How to grow green onions in containers.* Little Yellow Wheelbarrow. https://www.littleyellowwheelbarrow.com/how-to-grow-green-onions/

Koehler, K. (2023, July 14). *How to grow green onions: Your complete guide.* A-Z Animals. https://a-z-animals.com/blog/how-to-grow-green-onions-your-complete-guide/

Naomi Stephens, Permaculture Designer. (2023, March 14). How to grow green onions in containers: Planting, care, harvesting, storing and solving pest problem. *Permaculture Apart.* https://www.permacultureapartment.com/post/how-to-grow-green-onions

Oleson, N. (2021a, June 3). *How to spot, treat, and prevent scallion diseases - Food Gardening Network.* Food Gardening Network. https://foodgardening.mequoda.com/articles/how-to-spot-treat-and-prevent-scallion-diseases/

Oleson, N. (2021b, June 3). *What to Do About Pests that Can Harm Your Scallion Plants - Food Gardening Network.* Food Gardening Network. https://foodgardening.mequoda.com/articles/what-to-do-about-pests-that-can-harm-your-scallion-plants/

Peppergeek. (2023, July 20). *Pepper plant diseases and Problems.* Pepper Geek. https://peppergeek.com/pepper-plant-diseases-problems/

Seed, S. T. (2022, August 3). *How to Grow Green Onions | Grow Scallions from Seed.* Sow True Seed. https://sowtrueseed.com/blogs/gardening/how-to-grow-green-onions

Tobacco Streak | Tomato | Agriculture: Pest Management Guidelines | UC Statewide IPM Program (UC IPM). (n.d.). http://ipm.ucanr.edu/PMG/r783102311.html

Tomato | Diseases and Pests, Description, Uses, Propagation. (n.d.). https://plantvillage.psu.edu/topics/tomato/infos/diseases_and_pests_description_uses_propagation

Winter, C. (2022a, January 4). *15 Common scallion plant problems and what to do about them.* Morning Chores. https://morningchores.com/scallion-plant-problems/

Winter, C. (2022b, January 4). *15 Common scallion plant problems and what to do about them.* Morning Chores. https://morningchores.com/scallion-plant-problems/

4 things you need to grow your own lettuce in containers • Gardenary. (n.d.). https://www.gardenary.com/blog/4-things-you-need-to-grow-your-own-lettuce-in-containers

Admin. (n.d.). *Top steps for preventing carrot root fly infestations: a guide.* https://homeupgradeplace.com/steps-for-preventing-carrot-root-fly-infestations/

BIBLIOGRAPHY

Alabama Cooperative Extension System. (2023, October 5). *Common diseases of snap and lima beans - Alabama Cooperative Extension System.* https://www.aces.edu/blog/topics/lawn-garden/common-diseases-of-snap-and-lima-beans/

Albert, S. (2023a, December 23). *Grow carrots any time of the year in five steps.* Harvest to Table. https://harvesttotable.com/grow-carrots-anytime-of-the-year-in-five-steps/

Albert, S. (2023b, December 25). *Carrot and parsnip growing problems and easy solutions.* Harvest to Table. https://harvesttotable.com/carrot_and_parsnip_growing_pro/

Albert, S. (2023c, December 27). *Eggplant Growing Problems and Solutions - Harvest to table.* Harvest to Table. https://harvesttotable.com/eggplant_troubleshooting/

Alina. (2023, January 12). *Cucumbers in raised beds: how to plant & grow - Plantura.* Plantura. https://plantura.garden/uk/vegetables/cucumbers/cucumbers-in-raised-beds

Anderson, T. (2023, October 5). *Quickstart Guide to Container Vegetable Gardening.* Lovely Greens. https://lovelygreens.com/container-vegetable-gardening/

Anonymous. (2020, September 30). *Carrot & Parsnip, Bacterial blight.* Center for Agriculture, Food, and the Environment. https://ag.umass.edu/vegetable/fact-sheets/carrot-parsnip-bacterial-blight

APHIDS Management Guidelines--UC IPM. (n.d.). http://ipm.ucanr.edu/PMG/PESTNOTES/pn7404.html

Azcarraga, L. (2023, December 26). *Growing lettuce in containers: A Beginner's Guide — Meadowlark Journal.* Meadowlark Journal. https://meadowlarkjournal.com/blog/growing-lettuce-in-containers

Ballew, J. (2022, July 21). *Eggplant Insect Pests & Diseases | Home & Garden Information Center.* Home & Garden Information Center | Clemson University, South Carolina. https://hgic.clemson.edu/factsheet/eggplant-insect-pests-diseases/

Battles, R. (2023, February 21). *Vegetable Gardens - Robbyn battles the house agent.* Robbyn Battles the House Agent. https://www.thehouseagent.com/vegetable-gardens/

Beet Armyworm | Peppers | Agriculture: Pest Management Guidelines | UC Statewide IPM Program (UC IPM). (n.d.). http://ipm.ucanr.edu/PMG/r604300211.html

Beetles, weevils, and grubs. (n.d.). http://www.missouribotanicalgarden.org/gardens-gardening/your-garden/help-for-the-home-gardener/advice-tips-resources/pests-and-problems/insects/beetles/colorado-potato-beetle.aspx

Bibi. (2023, August 14). Powdery Mildew on Pea Leaves: Find out How to Revive Your Pea Patch! - LeafyJournal. *LeafyJournal.* https://leafyjournal.com/powdery-mildew-on-pea-leaves/

Biggs, C. (2024, January 5). Eggplant Growth Stages (A Comprehensive Guide). *Backyard Mastery.* https://backyardmastery.com/eggplant-growth-stages/

Buhv. (2021, May 8). *Parsnips | Growing Cool Weather Crops | Nick's Garden Center*

| *Denver CO*. Nick's Garden Center. https://nicksgardencenter.com/gardening-blog/plants/parsnip/

Carrot | Diseases and Pests, Description, Uses, Propagation. (n.d.). https://plantvillage.psu.edu/topics/carrot/infos

Celery Archives - Statyourself. (n.d.). Statyourself. https://statyourself.com/tag/celery/

Christian, E. (2022, April 9). *How to grow peas in containers and pots*. Confessions of an Overworked Mom. https://confessionsofanover-workedmom.com/grow-peas-in-containers/

Cohrs, M. (2023a, October 4). *16 tips for growing eggplant in raised garden beds*. Epic Gardening. https://www.epicgardening.com/eggplant-raised-beds/

Cohrs, M. (2023b, October 4). *17 tips for growing cucumbers in raised garden beds*. Epic Gardening. https://www.epicgardening.com/cucumbers-raised-beds/

Cohrs, M. (2023c, October 4). *17 tips for growing cucumbers in raised garden beds*. Epic Gardening. https://www.epicgardening.com/cucumbers-raised-beds/

Colorado State University Extension. (2023, August 2). *Growing Container salad Greens - 9.378 - extension*. Extension. https://extension.colostate.edu/topic-areas/nutrition-food-safety-health/growing-container-salad-greens-9-378/

Cramer, E. (2021, January 1). *Cucumber spacing in the home garden*. Epic Gardening. https://www.epicgardening.com/cucumber-spacing/

Cucumber beetles in home gardens. (n.d.). UMN Extension. https://extension.umn.edu/yard-and-garden-insects/cucumber-beetles

Dorn, S. (2023a, October 9). *Everything about growing peas in containers and pots*. Balcony Garden Web. https://balconygardenweb.com/growing-peas-in-containers-grow-in-pots/

Dorn, S. (2023b, October 9). *Growing lettuce in containers | How to grow lettuce in pots*. Balcony Garden Web. https://balconygardenweb.com/growing-lettuce-in-containers-how-to-grow-lettuce-in-pots/

Drew. (2023, May 1). *Growing parsnips: when, where & companion plants - Plantura*. Plantura. https://plantura.garden/uk/vegetables/parsnips/growing-parsnips

Dwank. (2022, October 16). *How to Deal with Aphids - Dwank.com*. Dwank.com. https://dwank.com/how-to-deal-with-aphids/

Earth Wild Gardens. (2022, June 30). How deep should your garden soil be? Find the perfect depth for optimal plant growth - Earth Wild Gardens. *Earth Wild Gardens*. https://earthwildgardens.com/how-deep-does-garden-soil-need-to-be/

Ellis, M. E. (2021a, April 26). *Growing eggplants: How to plant eggplant in the garden*. Gardeningknowhow. https://www.gardeningknowhow.com/edible/vegetables/eggplant/growing-eggplant.htm

Ellis, M. E. (2021b, April 26). *How to grow peas: Requirements for growing peas*. Gardeningknowhow. https://www.gardeningknowhow.com/edible/vegetables/peas/how-grow-peas.htm

Fertilizers' Types – FMPAC. (n.d.). https://fmpac.com.pk/about-fertilizers/fertilizers-types/

Gardens, O. (2023, March 16). *5 tips for planting cucumbers on raised garden beds.* Olle Gardens #1 Metal Raised Garden Beds. https://www.ollegardens.com/blogs/news/5-tips-for-planting-cucumbers-on-raised-garden-beds

Ghiggins. (2022, September 6). *Carrots, Identifying diseases.* Center for Agriculture, Food, and the Environment. https://ag.umass.edu/vegetable/factsheets/carrots-identifying-diseases

Grant, A. (2021a, April 22). *Pot grown Garden peas: How to grow peas in a container.* Gardeningknowhow. https://www.gardeningknowhow.com/edible/vegetables/peas/grow-peas-in-containers.htm

Grant, A. (2021b, May 17). *Common lettuce pests: Lettuce pest control information.* Gardeningknowhow. https://www.gardeningknowhow.com/edible/vegetables/lettuce/lettuce-pest-control.htm

Grant, B. L. (2021, June 28). *How to grow lettuce in a container.* Gardeningknowhow. https://www.gardeningknowhow.com/edible/vegetables/lettuce/growing-lettuce-containers.htm

Greenhouse cleaning / RHS Gardening. (n.d.). Royal Horticultural Society. https://www.rhs.org.uk/advice/profile?PID=731

Griffiths, M. (2021, July 25). *How to grow peas – in pots and in the ground.* homesandgardens.com. https://www.homesandgardens.com/advice/how-to-grow-peas

Grow, L. (2022, June 16). *Lettuce Grow Blog - Common garden pests and natural solutions.* https://www.lettucegrow.com/resources/pests-goodbye

Growing eggplant in home gardens. (n.d.). UMN Extension. https://extension.umn.edu/vegetables/growing-eggplant

Growing peas. (n.d.). Extension | West Virginia University. https://extension.wvu.edu/lawn-gardening-pests/gardening/wv-garden-guide/growing-peas-in-west-virginia

Growing Peas at Home in Containers & Pots - Squire's Garden Centres. (2022, July 6). Squire's Garden Centres. https://www.squiresgardencentres.co.uk/garden_advice/growing-peas-at-home-in-containers-pots/

Growing peas in home gardens. (n.d.). UMN Extension. https://extension.umn.edu/vegetables/growing-peas

Growing scallions in home gardens. (n.d.). UMN Extension. https://extension.umn.edu/vegetables/growing-scallions-home-gardens

Hajdu, I. (2023, November 10). *Six soil management practices guaranteed to produce best yields.* AGRIVI. https://www.agrivi.com/blog/five-ways-to-manage-the-soil-for-planting/

Hayes, B. (2022a, April 5). The complete guide to growing peas in containers - Gardening chores. *Gardening Chores.* https://www.gardeningchores.com/growing-peas-in-containers/

Hayes, B. (2022b, April 5). The complete guide to growing peas in containers -

Gardening chores. *Gardening Chores.* https://www.gardeningchores.com/growing-peas-in-containers/

Holt, J. (2023, January 2). *How to Grow Eggplant from Seed — The Seed Sage | Raised Bed Garden & Garden Design Services.* The Seed Sage | Raised Bed Garden & Garden Design Services. https://theseedsage.com/blog/how-to-grow-eggplant-from-seed

Home Vegetable Gardening | Illinois Extension | UIUC. (2024, January 23). https://extension.illinois.edu/veggies/cucumber.cfm

How to Grow Eggplant from Seed in an Organic Kitchen Garden • Gardenary. (n.d.). https://www.gardenary.com/blog/how-to-grow-eggplant-from-seed-in-an-organic-kitchen-garden

How to grow organic carrots in a Raised-Bed Kitchen garden • Gardenary. (n.d.). https://www.gardenary.com/blog/how-to-grow-organic-carrots-in-a-raised-bed-kitchen-garden

How to grow peas. (n.d.). https://www.ufseeds.com/pea-seed-to-harvest.html

How to plant sugar snap peas in your garden in 3 easy steps • Gardenary. (n.d.). https://www.gardenary.com/blog/how-to-plant-sugar-snap-peas-in-your-garden-in-3-easy-steps

Huffstetler, E. (2022, September 26). *How to test soil pH with and without a kit.* The Spruce. https://www.thespruce.com/how-to-prevent-bolting-in-vegetable-crops-1388584

Hunt, R. (2023, September 24). *The best time of year to grow eggplant in your garden.* House Digest. https://www.housedigest.com/1397898/best-time-grow-eggplant-garden/

Iannotti, M. (2022a, August 8). *How to grow parsnips.* The Spruce. https://www.thespruce.com/growing-and-caring-for-parsnips-1403474

Iannotti, M. (2022b, October 30). *How to Grow Green Onions: From Seeds & Regrowing.* The Spruce. https://www.thespruce.com/how-to-grow-scallions-4125799

Jabbour, N. (2022, February 24). *How to grow green onions: The ultimate seed to harvest guide.* Savvy Gardening. https://savvygardening.com/how-to-grow-green-onions/

Jagdish. (2022, November 14). *How to grow eggplants in raised beds: Step-by-Step Guide to planting and care.* Asia Farming. https://www.asiafarming.com/how-to-grow-eggplants-in-raised-beds-step-by-step-guide-to-planting-and-care

Jane. (2021, October 12). Growing cucumbers in raised beds - cottage at the crossroads. *Cottage at the Crossroads.* https://cottageatthecrossroads.com/growing-cucumbers-in-raised-beds/

Jeanne. (2023, October 24). *Easy tips for growing lettuce in containers.* Home Garden Joy. https://homegardenjoy.com/site/2023/04/growing-lettuce-in-containers.html

Johnson, K. (2023, May 19). Sustainable pest control for your urban garden. *Everything Backyard.* https://everythingbackyard.net/sustainable-pest-control-for-your-urban-garden/

BIBLIOGRAPHY

Johnston, C. (2022, July 14). *Growing lettuce in containers: an easy guide*. Growfully. https://growfully.com/growing-lettuce-in-containers/

Jordan. (2023, February 27). *Green Onion Growing Guide*. Limitless Growth. https://limitlessgrowth.co/green-onion-growing-guide/

Kellogggarden. (2021, July 19). Growing eggplant. *Kellogg Garden Organics^{TM}*. https://kellogggarden.com/blog/growing/growing-eggplant/

Kennedy, L. (2023a, May 26). *How to grow onions in containers: expert tips and techniques*. Little Yellow Wheelbarrow. https://www.littleyellowwheelbarrow.com/how-to-grow-onions-in-containers/

Kennedy, L. (2023b, June 10). *Growing peas in Containers 101: (2022)*. Little Yellow Wheelbarrow. https://www.littleyellowwheelbarrow.com/growing-peas-in-containers/

Kris Bordessa, National Geographic author/certified master food preserver. (2022a, April 4). *Growing lettuce in containers to eliminate pest damage*. Attainable Sustainable®. https://www.attainable-sustainable.net/growing-lettuce-in-containers/

Kris Bordessa, National Geographic author/certified master food preserver. (2022b, April 4). *Growing lettuce in containers to eliminate pest damage*. Attainable Sustainable®. https://www.attainable-sustainable.net/growing-lettuce-in-containers/

Kyle. (2023, February 27). *How to grow tomatoes in the UK*. UK GROW SHOP. https://www.ukgrowshop.com/2023/02/how-to-grow-tomatoes-in-the-uk/

Lamp'l, J. (2021a, May 8). *How Do I Grow Eggplant? | Planting, Care & Harvest Guide | joegardener®*. Joe Gardener® | Organic Gardening Like a Pro. https://joegardener.com/how-do-i-grow-eggplant/

Lamp'l, J. (2021b, December 8). *How Do I Grow Parsnips | Planting & Harvesting Guide | joegardener®*. Joe Gardener® | Organic Gardening Like a Pro. https://joegardener.com/how-do-i-grow-parsnips/

Lettuce | Diseases and Pests, Description, Uses, Propagation. (n.d.). https://plantvillage.psu.edu/topics/lettuce/infos

Lettuce | NC State Extension Publications. (n.d.). https://content.ces.ncsu.edu/lettuce

Lugo, J. (2024, January 17). How to grow cucumbers in a raised bed. *Gardeners Basics*. https://www.gardenersbasics.com/tools/blog/how-to-grow-cucumbers-in-a-raised-bed

Marine, M. (2023, October 28). *21 tips for growing cucumbers in raised beds & containers*. Simplify, Live, Love. https://simplifylivelove.com/how-to-grow-cucumbers-in-raised-beds/

Martinez, E. (2023, April 22). *How to prune tomato plants?* AirServer App. https://www.airserverapp.com/how-to-prune-tomato-plants/

Master, W. (1970, January 1). *Why are my green onions turning yellow? Exploring causes and remedies -:)*. Cucurbit Breeding. https://cucurbitbreeding.com/green-onions-turning-yellow/

BIBLIOGRAPHY

Michaels, K. (2023, March 8). *How to grow peas in containers*. The Spruce. https://www.thespruce.com/growing-peas-in-container-gardens-848242

Naomi Stephens, Permaculture Designer. (2023, March 14). How to grow green onions in containers: Planting, care, harvesting, storing and solving pest problem. *Permaculture Apart*. https://www.permacultureapartment.com/post/how-to-grow-green-onions

Parsnip Canker | Gardener's Supply. (n.d.). www.gardeners.com. https://www.gardeners.com/how-to/parsnip-canker/7335.html

Parsnip Grow Guide. (n.d.). GrowVeg. https://www.growveg.com/plants/us-and-canada/how-to-grow-parsnip/

Parsnips. (n.d.-a). Almanac.com. https://www.almanac.com/plant/parsnips

Parsnips. (n.d.-b). Royal Horticultural Society. https://www.rhs.org.uk/vegetables/parsnips/grow-your-own

Parsnips. (n.d.-c). Almanac.com. https://www.almanac.com/plant/parsnips

Patterson, S. (2021, May 18). *Parsnip harvesting - How and when to harvest parsnips*. Gardeningknowhow. https://www.gardeningknowhow.com/edible/vegetables/parsnips/how-to-harvest-parsnips.htm

Pea | Getting started with peas in containers. (n.d.). https://plantvillage.psu.edu/posts/3696-pea-getting-started-with-peas-in-containers

Pepper Weevil | Peppers | Agriculture: Pest Management Guidelines | UC Statewide IPM Program (UC IPM). (n.d.). http://ipm.ucanr.edu/PMG/r604301011.html

Pheron@. (2023, July 12). *Tree Planting/Care Instructions: Watering tips to help your tree thrive*. Pelfrey Company Tree Services. https://www.pelfreytree.com/tree-planting-care-instructions-watering-tips-to-help-your-tree-thrive

Planet Natural. (2023, January 10). *Organic Gardening since 1991 | Planet Natural Garden Supply*. https://www.planetnatural.com/pest-problem-solver/houseplant-pests/aphid-control/

Plants, B. (2011, August 29). *How much water do vegetables need?* Bonnie Plants. https://bonnieplants.com/blogs/garden-fundamentals/how-much-water-do-vegetables-need

Potatoes. (n.d.). Royal Horticultural Society. https://www.rhs.org.uk/advice/grow-your-own/vegetables/potatoes

Powdery Mildew on Vegetables Management Guidelines--UC IPM. (n.d.). http://ipm.ucanr.edu/PMG/PESTNOTES/pn7406.html

Root diseases of carrot. (n.d.). Bayer. https://www.vegetables.bayer.com/ca/en-ca/resources/growing-tips/agronomic-spotlights/root-diseases-of-carrot.html

Rose, S. (2023, March 14). *Growing lettuce in containers for endless leafy greens*. Garden Therapy. https://gardentherapy.ca/growing-lettuce-in-containers/

Sewell, D. (2014, September 27). *Quick tip: Sowing Parsnips*. Greenside Up. https://greensideup.ie/quick-tip-sowing-parsnips/

Shidler, A. (2023, June 22). *How to plant and grow parsnips*. Gardener's Path. https://gardenerspath.com/plants/vegetables/grow-parsnips/

Shuman, S. (2023, December 6). *How to grow Carrots: Beginners Starter guide*. The

Beginner's Garden. https://journeywithjill.net/gardening/2023/03/02/how-to-grow-carrots-beginners-starter-guide/

Simmons, C. (2023, August 4). *How many plants can I put in one container?* Garden Planters. https://gardenplanters.net/how-many-plants-can-i-put-in-one-container/

Spicer, K. (2023a, August 24). *How to identify and prevent common lettuce diseases.* Gardener's Path. https://gardenerspath.com/how-to/disease-and-pests/lettuce-disease/

Spicer, K. (2023b, August 24). *Tips for growing peas in containers.* Gardener's Path. https://gardenerspath.com/plants/vegetables/grow-peas-containers/

Spicer, K. (2023c, November 14). *11 of the Best Fertilizers for Growing Vegetables.* Gardener's Path. https://gardenerspath.com/plants/vegetables/best-vegetable-fertilizers/

Squash bugs in home gardens. (n.d.). UMN Extension. https://extension.umn.edu/yard-and-garden-insects/squash-bugs

Stephan. (2023, May 21). *Celery in Your Garden: Everything you need to know to get started.* live-native.com. https://www.live-native.com/celery-in-your-garden-everything-you-need-to-know-to-get-started/

Strauss, M. (2023a, May 3). *10 tips for growing a bountiful lettuce harvest in containers.* Epic Gardening. https://www.epicgardening.com/lettuce-containers/

Strauss, M. (2023b, May 6). *How to grow peas in pots or containers.* Epic Gardening. https://www.epicgardening.com/peas-containers/

Swainston, D. (2023, April 26). *How to grow lettuce in pots – expert tips for quick and easy tasty leaves in containers.* homesandgardens.com. https://www.homesandgardens.com/gardens/how-to-grow-lettuce-in-pots

T, K. (2022, February 16). *How to use worm castings for tomatoes | 5 easy ways.* Eco Family Life. https://ecofamilylife.com/garden/how-to-use-worm-castings-for-tomatoes/

Team, K. (2023, March 13). *Can You Spray Neem Oil On Palm Trees? An Expert's Guide - Know Your Pantry.* Know Your Pantry. https://www.knowyourpantry.com/oils/can-you-spray-neem-oil-on-palm-trees/

Thomas, J. (2023, August 11). *How to plant carrot seeds (for maximum germination).* Homesteading Family. https://homesteadingfamily.com/how-to-plant-carrot-seeds-for-maximum-germination/

Tilley, N. (2022, January 29). *Eggplant problems: Eggplant pests and diseases.* Gardeningknowhow. https://www.gardeningknowhow.com/edible/vegetables/eggplant/eggplant-problems-eggplant-pests-and-diseases.htm

Tinsman, A. (2023, August 21). *How to grow potatoes indoors – 7 points to note.* How to Houseplant. https://howtohouseplant.com/grow-potatoes-indoors/

Utah State University. (n.d.). *Planting, spacing, & thinning.* USU. https://extension.usu.edu/vegetableguide/cucumber-melon-pumpkin-squash/planting-spacing-thinning

Walliser, J. (2020, November 3). *9 diseases killing your eggplant - Hobby Farms.*

BIBLIOGRAPHY

Hobby Farms. https://www.hobbyfarms.com/9-diseases-killing-your-eggplant-4/

Walliser, J. (2021, August 27). *Cucumber plant spacing for high yields in gardens and pots*. Savvy Gardening. https://savvygardening.com/cucumber-plant-spacing/

Watson, K. (2023, December 16). *How to grow eggplant*. The Rose Table. https://therosetable.com/2021/01/09/how-to-grow-eggplant/

Westerfield, R. R. (n.d.). *Home Garden lettuce*. UGA Cooperative Extension. https://extension.uga.edu/publications/detail.html?number=C1018&title=home-garden-lettuce

WoodBlocX. (2023, April 3). *Growing carrots in WoodBlocX raised beds*. WoodBlocX. https://www.woodblocx.co.uk/blog/how-to-grow-carrots-in-raised-beds/

Cover Design by Freepix

www.ingramcontent.com/pod-product-compliance
Lightning Source LLC
Chambersburg PA
CBHW030155070426
42447CB00031B/285